OUTDOOR LIFE
DEER
HUNTER'S
YEARBOOK
1985

Outdoor Life Books, New York

Stackpole Books, Harrisburg, Pennsylvania

Published by

Outdoor Life Books
Times Mirror Magazines, Inc.
380 Madison Avenue
New York, NY 10017

Distributed to the trade by

Stackpole Books
Cameron and Kelker Streets
P.O. Box 1831
Harrisburg, PA 17105

ISSN 0734-2918

ISBN 0-943822-26-2

Manufactured in the United States of America

Contents

Preface

In my 20 years as an editor of Outdoor Life, I've been in a good position to observe the many changes that have taken place in American deer hunting. It used to be that you hunted deer in the same way your friends and relatives had always hunted them. Many Southerners never thought of anything except hound hunting; Western deer hunters relied on wide scouting, intensive glassing, and long-range shooting; Pennsylvania stand-and-drive hunters never thought of using masking scents to hide their telltale odors when waiting on stand; Midwesterners had never even heard of "rattling up" a buck by clashing antlers together; and so on. If deer could be shot in the traditional way, why experiment?

All this has changed substantially, and many new techniques have appeared. The behavior of deer in many places had changed, so hunting methods had to change, too. Trophy mule deer in the West are so hard pressed in some areas that they are just as wary as any Eastern whitetail. Some Western hunters are now adopting Eastern methods to take the big deer of the West. Formerly, a mule deer hunter who used a tree stand to play the waiting game would have been thought of as slightly balmy. Nowadays, it's a common practice where mule deer are wary of leaving heavy cover in daylight. Many former hound hunters in the South, on the other hand, now find themselves using binoculars and scoped rifles, and shooting at long ranges because land clearing for big-field agriculture has opened up the country. Then there are deer scents used to attract bucks. These scents are now used throughout the East.

An outdoorsman's magazine must keep on top of these changes in order to provide the information hunters want, and Outdoor Life currently publishes more stories on deer hunting than any other national hunting and fishing magazine. Most of the stories presented here appeared recently in the magazine or in its offshoot, the *Deer and Big Game Annual*. A few classic stories from earlier years have also been included because some things do *not* change.

You'll find that the authors do not always agree. For instance, in "Hunt High For Muleys," Brian Kahn recommends hunting remote areas at high altitudes if you want big mule deer. Jack White, in "Muleys In Your Pocket," points out that many mule deer are staying in the lowlands all year and that, therefore, it often pays to hunt them close to home in woodlots and crop fields—much as whitetails are hunted in the East. This simply demonstrates that this is an enormous country and that terrain and deer behavior vary greatly. There's room for considerable divergence in hunting methods. By reading these stories, however, you ought to be able to come up with something that will work quite well, no matter where you hunt.

You'll also find that some of the stories included in the yearbook are not exclusively devoted to providing the reader with useful information. Deer hunting is a great sport, and reading about it is a great pleasure; some stories were selected purely because they are a joy to read.

George H. Haas
Senior Editor
Outdoor Life Magazine

Whitetail Challenge

By Lew Dietz

As I have for more than 40 years, I went into Maine's north woods for a deer hunt last fall. I left my car at Fort Kent on the Maine/Canada border and made the final stage of the trip with my friend Bart in his all-terrain vehicle.

The trek entailed making a loop into Canada and crossing back into Maine, fording a swollen river in the process. The only other access was even more difficult. It required a punishing 35-mile push north from the Allagash over all but impassable, abandoned logging roads.

The reward was more than commensurate with the effort. For a week I saw no tracks save those of game and those of my two-legged friends. The hunters, friends, and friends of friends, ranged in age from 20 to 70. There were fathers and sons, brothers and cousins, and as different as people can be. What they had in common was the love of the hunt and a deep appreciation of the wilds and the privilege of hunting in them.

Arnold Toynbee, in his monumental work, "A Study of History," dismissed Maine and its people as relics of 17th-century New England. After associating with Maine hunters for half a century, I've become reconciled to that judgment.

If we are persuaded by the increasingly common notion today that hunters are dehumanized cretins without redeeming social assets, my Maine gunning friends and trail companions must qualify as anachronisms—characters misplaced in time.

I expect there are hunters here in Maine and elsewhere whom I would not choose as friends. But taken as a breed, I have found hunters to be both gentlemen and gentle men. The Maine men with whom I have shared the chase hunt as their fathers and grandfathers hunted, unabashedly for the love of it. Nor do they feel any need to defend their pleasure or to apologize for bearing arms in the pursuit of this ancestral blood sport.

I much doubt that I have been brutalized by my addiction to hunting or corrupted by my long association with hunting men. I find my interludes in the Big Woods restorative and cleansing. It is a form of escape, perhaps. We live in a neurotic time, beset by exploiters, wasters, and plunderers. A few brief days with men at ease with the wilderness and at peace with themselves is a healing respite.

Perhaps only in northern New England and in certain regions of the South has the lore and love of the hunt been passed on, father to son, for centuries. An understanding of the ethos of the hunt and a respect for its unwritten code is a matter of tradition. The sad truth is that, though a man can learn to use a gun in a few easy lessons, the skills and attitudes that make hunting a rewarding human experience are not so much acquired as instilled.

And, as I hunted that week in November, it was borne in upon me that, should the American tradition of hunting lapse, the last remnants of our wilderness would be doomed for lack of caring.

Jake who, with Bart, owns the camp, had come in the day before with his son Sam and brother Will to open the place. It was Sunday, and the three were out cruising the territory for game sign when we arrived. They wandered in as we were stowing grub and gear.

Jake, a sly leprechaun of a fellow, said the deer were there but that they weren't moving much. However, he had seen a number of buck scrapings that indicated the rut had begun. Then, as an afterthought, he added, "Charlie's still here. Saw his track on the ridge road."

For men who have hunted a territory over the years, there is always a Charlie, a big and wise buck

Everyone talks and talks about "old Charlie"—the trophy buck—in deer camp, but hardly anyone ever shoots him. My own downfall was a grouse that fussed about so much, I turned to watch. The buck came out, and that's when I said, "Goodbye, Charlie." Illustration by Joe Isom.

deer, a patriarch that has proved too smart for mere men. Needless to say, he left moose-size tracks. That, of course, was an exaggeration. Nor was there any way to be certain that the outsize spoor could be assigned to a single antlered behemoth. More friend than quarry, a Charlie is the all-but-obligatory myth savored and perpetuated by hunting men.

Bart smiled. "Hollis tells me he has Charlie figured out," he said. "He'll arrive Wednesday, and we shall see."

Hollis was Bart's brother-in-law and, of all the group, perhaps the purest of hunters. Hollis was a figurer, a theoretician, with the patience and dedication to see his strategies through. For Hollis, though venison was a welcome by-product, hunting was an end in itself.

There would be nine or 10 hunters in the camp in the course of the week. I saw little of any of them in the interim between hunts. But men who share isolation even briefly tend to form lasting friendships. Sharing a hunting camp is much like cruising in a small sailing vessel. The crew is bound by common interest, and each member of the crew contributes to the small community according to his talent. The difference is that a hunting camp is more loosely structured.

There was no need to assign tasks when the hunt began. The division of work long since had been established by custom. Jake, a compulsive neatener, saw to it that the floor was broom-clean, the dish rags hung to dry, the long table rid of crumbs. Bart, a relaxed and visceral fellow whose portly construction betrayed his love of food, was the cook. Each morning he would post his menu. Some of his creations were a bit exotic for common palates, but the crew could always count on steak on Friday and beanhole beans on Saturday. And, of course, deer liver and heart, served with onions and bacon, was an expected treat.

Early in my tenure, I assumed the post of Bart's assistant, a job corresponding roughly to that of a cookee in a logging camp, the difference being that I was given to offering advice, solicited and otherwise—something a cookee would venture to do at the risk of his neck.

And there was the lugger of wood and the stoker of the fires. In our camp, this job fell to George, a great, lumbering hulk of a man addicted to chewing on cold cigars. There is always the mother hen of the crowd, the benign spirit who remains up until the others are bedded down to see to it that the fires are banked, the kettle purring, and the lights extinguished. For us, this was John. He had spent most of his life in the Maine woods as a walking boss for lumber operators, and his knowledge of the wilderness was rich and vast. John served also as our weather prognosticator. Once the lights were out, he would step out into the night in his longjohns to sniff the air and consult the sky, returning to announce to the quiet camp his forecast.

The dishwashing assignment was left open, and for good reason. Invariably, there would be an eager young guest, usually a friend of a son of one of the coterie, who innocently would volunteer for this chore. The custom was to await the initiate's unwary offer. He was never denied the honor, and the job was his for the duration, or until such time as a compassionate regular would decide to spell or assist him.

I awoke the first morning of the hunt to the rich aroma of coffee and bacon in the making. At 4:30, Bart bellowed the logging camp exhortation.

"Roll out, you tigers! It's daylight in the swamp!"

For most men, putting on pants seems the logical way to start a morning. Bart would first put on his hunting hat, a green porkpie. He was making pancakes in his longjohns and slippers. Also, he was singing a snatch from a Puccini opera. Bart had once met Ezio Pinza.

"Today is the day I will meet Charlie," he announced. "I feel it in my Irish bones. Did I tell you Hollis has Charlie figured out?"

"Yes," I said, "you told me."

At the breakfast board, plans were made for the day ahead. To a man, these were stillhunters who prided themselves not so much in their shooting as in the mastery of the arts that bring a hunter face to face with the quarry. Like the woodland Indians, from whom the early settlers learned the skills of the stalk, they preferred to succeed as hunters rather than shooters.

In the predawn, each man let it be known where he proposed to hunt that day. This knowledge could be critical in the event a hunter did not come in by several hours after dark. Jake said he'd try the Green Road; Will opted for the Swing Around Road, designations that would have no meaning beyond the group. Nor would Dodge City, the remains of an old logging camp, or Jackstraws, a bad piece of blowdown, mean anything to a stranger. And then there was Hank's Bend where, some years before, Hank LeBlanc had shot the biggest black bear ever seen in that country.

I chose Deer Boulevard, a whimsy of my own concoction. This was a quaggy, overgrown, old logging haul road at the foot of the ridge, a territory that had been productive for me the year before. Like Hollis, I am a figurer. I need to be. I judge myself to be a good observer, adequate woodsman, fair hunter, but no more than a passable shot beyond a 100-yard range. Further, I tend to woolgather, to permit my mind to wander from the business at hand, a habit that has been the salvation of many a deer.

Typically, a hunting week will break down into three parts. The initial days are devoted to investigation, to ranging over a wide area in an attempt to locate deer concentrations and ascertain patterns of deer movements. Usually, by the third day, each hunter has narrowed his target area, basing his decision on his observations. Ideally, the climax should come on the final days of the hunt; the denouement satisfying the expectancy developed in the early stages of the drama.

All the proper elements were present on my first day as I cruised three miles of that old haul road. Near a cedar swamp, three miles from the camp, I came upon fresh droppings in assorted sizes that suggested a deer-bedding place was nearby. On the trek back, I came upon the pawings of an extremely large buck. Charlie, or a reasonable facsimile, had scraped the soft earth in five or six places. Then, to make my day replete, I had a snatch-vision of a bear as it took off up the ridge.

The rewards of the hunt are many and various for those who relish the simple creature pleasures. There is the joy of coming in out of the cold to a warm fire, the easing out of boots with the prospect of being revivified with good whisky and branch water. And, as the others wander in, there are experiences to exchange.

On this and other nights, the talk continued on into the early evening. Stories of other hunts were told and retold. The best relished were those of misadventures. Big George inexplicably had missed a deer at 30 paces. John had dozed off on a stump and awakened to find the tracks of a deer that had walked by him in the interim. By eight, the talk tapered off to desultory exchanges. One by one, the hunters wandered off to hit the sack. It was nine when I crawled gratefully into my eiderdown womb. The last thing I heard that night was John coming in.

"We'll have rain by morning," he said.

And rain it did that next day, a gentle, soaking rain that filled the brooks and made morasses of the trails.

The first kill was scored by Jake that day. He wandered into camp an hour after dark with liver and heart on a green stick.

After supper, a few of us went out to help him bring in the kill. "It sure ain't Charlie," Will said, as we hoisted it into the game tree.

Hunting maturity is not a matter of years. It comes with the developing of appreciation and understanding of the multitude of things that constitute the totality of nature. Lacking the naturalist's eye, a hunter is no more than an armed interloper in the wild domain. Jake's boy Sam had spent a good hour of that hunting day watching two otters at play. Bart's day was made when he sighted a wolf crossing over the ridge.

Hollis had arrived by the time we got in from the woods that next evening. He'd no more than stowed his gear than he was called upon to resolve an accumulation of troubles. Bart's rig had clutch problems. A lifelong farmer, Hollis was by necessity a good haywire mechanic. He listened to the symptoms and offered his diagnosis.

Then George told him of missing a deer at 30 paces. Hollis asked to see George's ammo clip. He discovered that the clip held rounds of the same bullet weight, but of different manufacture. "You should use the same brand cartridges that you used to sight in your rifle, George," he said. "I've found variance in brands of as much as eight inches at 100 yards."

Later I asked him about the rumor that he had Charlie figured out. Hollis smiled. "Let's say I have one thing figured out," he said. "Charlie rides the thermals."

Hollis proceeded to explain his thesis. "As you know," he said, "the thermal currents in the early morning flow downhill from the ridges to the lake. Along about eight, or almost the instant the sun touches the top of the ridge, he waits for the thermal to reverse so he can travel into it. If he's down in the black growth, he'll be sure to get up the ridge before the thermal switches. But he doesn't travel directly into the wind, he quarters it. This gives him a larger green sector, or that part of the circle in which he's protected by his nose. This gives the hunter a smaller green sector, or that part of the circle in which he has a wind advantage. Of course, all deer are inclined to feed into the wind. But some deer are a bit careless at times. Charlie is never careless."

George rolled a cold cigar in his teeth.

"With you on his trail, Hollis," he said, "Charlie is going to need some advanced education. Let's all chip in and send Charlie to Yale. It's the sporting thing to do."

Hollis didn't see Charlie that next day, or any other deer, but John and Jake's son Sam scored with big bucks, both 10-pointers in the 250 to 270-pound range. Bart, who had decided on the second day out that the deer were feeding and bedding in the mixed growth, had his hunch confirmed on Thursday at high noon. He jumped three deer out of a fir thicket halfway up the ridge and downed the largest, an eight-pointer.

Time was running out for me and for Will, as well. We were going out Saturday morning with Sam. As the first days of a hunt are exploratory and the middle days concerned with site selection and the establishment of a modus operandi, the hunter in the final period tends to exercise his hunches or fall back on his more esoteric strategies.

Thursday night, Will felt his five days' worth of whiskers. "It's all very simple," he said. "Tomorrow, I'll take a walk in the woods. I always see deer when I'm just taking a walk in the woods. The trouble with you, Hollis, is that you think deer when you hunt. If a dog can scent emotions and pick up thought waves, why can't a deer? I'm going to take a quiet walk in the woods and think about strawberry shortcake."

Matter of fact, Will did get his deer that next morning, though he couldn't for the life of him recall what had been on his mind at the moment of truth. I missed my big chance, and I do remember what was on my mind: I was undone by a partridge. I was sitting on a log in the still of the morning when the bird dropped into a spruce thicket behind me. I turned to watch him as he fussed about. When I turned back to the trail I was covering, there, staring at me, was the biggest buck deer I'd ever seen. Before I could swing my body around into postion, he took one great arching leap and it was good-bye Charlie.

I went out with Sam and Will the next morning. The snow we all had been waiting for had begun to fall. We made it across the swollen river, but just barely, and only by employing the expedient of disengaging the jeep's fan belt so it wouldn't throw water over the spark plugs.

A week later, I had a note from Bart. Hollis had shot his buck in the Jackstraws. It was a deer they estimated would go close to 300 pounds woods-dressed. "Hollis wants to assure you that it wasn't Charlie," he wrote.

Though I appreciated Hollis's reassurance, it wasn't necessary. For all of us, Charlie would be there so long as that piece of wilderness we shared with him remained inviolate. To preserve the myth of his immortality was an article of faith, a putting off of the day when the last of wilderness would be civilized off the face of the earth.

PART 1

THE QUARRY

What Is A Whitetail?

By Glenn Helgeland

Mark Paulus operates a food store and butcher shop in Cedarburg, Wisconsin. Each autumn, principally in late November, at the conclusion of Wisconsin's firearms deer season, he and his butcher-shop employees cut and package about 300 whitetails.

A couple of years ago, Paulus remembers, two hunters brought in a buck.

"It was a nice buck," Paulus said. "Maybe around 140 pounds hog-dressed."

When the two hunters brought in the deer for processing, the man who tagged it began discussing with Paulus how the deer should be cut up and packaged.

A few seconds later, the hunter's partner called over his shoulder, "Hey, Joe, when you get done with that, c'mon over here. Got something to show you."

Joe did, and Paulus tagged along.

"See that carcass over there," the guy said while pointing.

"Yeah. What about it?" Joe asked.

"That's about the size of the one I missed two years ago. It was a big one. I must have had buck fever."

"I almost hated to say anything," Paulus told me later, "but I had to."

He let the guys gaze at the carcass in awe a moment, then said, "Sorry to disappoint you my friends, but that's the carcass of a 2,200-pound holstein bull, not a whitetail buck."

"I didn't know what else to say," Paulus went on. "It was kind of embarrassing for him and me."

So what exactly is a whitetail deer? It is a beautiful, thrilling, inspiring, maddening, frustrating animal that inhabits a good share of the United States and a good share of every whitetail hunter's thoughts at various times of the year. Each autumn it drives sev-

eral million hunters crazy as it goes about being a full-time wild animal for part-time hunters.

What is its average weight? How tall is it at the shoulders? Where is the liver located? The questions are endless, fascinating, and necessary.

Hunter safety instructors have plenty of stories of the honest but drastic mistakes students make when asked to locate certain things in or on a deer.

So what's the big deal? Well I, for one, believe it *is* a big deal. The more you know about the whitetail, the richer you are for it. As a hunter, you'll do a more humane job of taking that animal when the moment of truth arrives because you'll do a better job of placing your shot, tracking, trailing, and recovering the animal.

To begin with, simply saying "the whitetail" is misleading. There are 30 subspecies of whitetails in North and Central America with eight more subspecies in northern South America. We have 17 of the subspecies within the United States—the largest being the northern whitetails and the smallest being the Florida Key deer. Generally, the farther North you go, the darker and larger the whitetails will be.

How large are whitetails? Deer are much smaller than we generally believe they are. A good northern whitetail will be about 40 inches or less at the shoulder, 95 inches from end of rump to tip of nose, and will weigh 160 pounds alive. Central American subspecies are rarely more than 24 inches in height and 48 inches in length. An adult Florida Key deer is seldom taller than 28 inches at the shoulder or more than 80 pounds. A good Coues buck in Arizona may be up to 31 inches at the shoulder and about 98 pounds.

How big can they get? In *The Deer of North America*, Leonard Lee Rue III notes that the largest body size known was on a Minnesota whitetail taken in 1926. The monster dressed at 402 pounds and was estimated to have a live weight of 511 pounds. A buck taken in 1924 in northern Wisconsin weighed 386 pounds dressed, with an estimated live weight of 491 pounds. Another Wisconsin buck, taken in Iron County in 1941, dressed at 378 pounds and was estimated to have weighed 481 pounds alive.

A buck taken in New York's Adirondack Mountains in 1890 was really checked over. It weighed 388 pounds before dressing, after bleeding. Live weight was estimated at 400 pounds. The animal was 115 inches from nose tip to tail tip and 51 inches at the shoulder with a 37-inch neck circumference behind the ears. The rack had nine tines on one beam, 10 on the other. The longest tine was 13 inches!

A whitetail's frame—its skeletal size—continues to increase, but obviously in much less dramatic fashion than in its early days, until it is 5½ to 6½ years old. Bucks will sometimes continue to add a little weight until the age of 8½, but does usually stay at a mature weight or lose a bit after 4½ or 5½ years. Mature, northern whitetail bucks generally weigh 200 to 300 pounds. Mature does weigh 25 to 40 percent less.

Why, then, does a 200-pound buck generate such attention? Because most deer are taken considerably before they reach maturity. Here are some average live weights for whitetails at various ages, according to a Nebraska study:

Age	Male	Female
6 months	87	81
1½ years	156	128
2½ years	192	137
3½ years	217	144
4½ years	238	151

Pennsylvania averages, which are a compilation of data from several studies, showed the following:

Age	Male	Female
6 months	54	54
1½ years	102	92
2½ years	117	100
3½ years	127	100

Here are some interesting numbers from a New Jersey study that show how food quality affects deer weight:

Age/Sex	Best Land	Poorest Land
1½ years/male	115.3	70
1½ years/female	116	60.5

What are a deer's chances of reaching full growth? That varies widely, of course, depending upon habitat conditions and hunting pressure. Records exist of deer living beyond 20 years, but few deer make it through 10 years, especially in the wild. Most great ages listed are for penned deer.

An Illinois study showed that whitetails have a life expectancy of 2½ years. A Pennsylvania study showed an average of two years for bucks, three years for does. Rue stated that only 3 percent of bucks and 20 percent of does reach 4½ years. Does live longer than bucks, hunted or not.

A Pennsylvania study showed that 60 percent of the deer killed were 1½ years old, 20 percent were 2½, 9 percent were 3½, 2 percent were 4½ and 2 percent were 5½. The remaining percentage to equal 100 was unaccounted for.

FEEDING HABITS

Whitetails consume about 2 to 4 percent of their live body weight daily in dry matter. This varies with the season, of course. Bucks eat most in the spring, decrease consumption a bit in summer, and increase it again after antler velvet is shed. During winter, they eat about half their normal amount for spring and summer. Bucks may lose 15 to 30 percent of their body weight in fall and winter, even when good food is available. They lose weight during the rut.

Does eat most in fall prior to the breeding season. Does in better condition reproduce better and have healthier and often more fawns.

Adult deer have a great need for high-energy foods during the breeding season and in cold weather. They will eat a lot of corn then. When acorns are abundant, particularly white oak acorns, deer may ignore just about all other foods.

The amount of terrain covered during feeding varies considerably with food availability. Deer will move beyond their home range for food but, usually, they return.

BODY STRUCTURE

A deer's body temperature is about 104°. The whitetail is a ruminant, meaning it has a four-chambered stomach. The rumen is the first chamber. It stores unchewed food and acts as a fermentation vat before the food is brought back up in cuds to be chewed for further digestion. The rumen can hold eight to nine quarts, which generally is 80 percent of the stomach contents. There are ordinarily 26 to 30 hours between eating and the resultant excretion. This system serves a deer well because the animal can eat and store food in a hurry, then chew the food in relative safety later while it's bedded down.

The adult deer has 32 teeth. There are no upper teeth in the front of the mouth. Deer pin grass against the upper pad and tear the grass instead of biting it. There are three molars and three pre-molars on each upper side. The lower jaw has 20 teeth, 10 on each side—three incisors, one modified canine, three pre-molars, and three molars. Teeth wear as the animal ages, so checking the amount of wear is a good way to get a preliminary age estimate. Tooth rings, the same as tree rings, are accurate.

The deer's eyes, located on the side of the skull, are angled forward about 25°. Their vision can be described as largely monocular but they can see in a great part of a circle. A deer's eyes bulge about one-quarter inch along the skull. Their bulging eyes help them see behind their head. Deer can see at least 310° of a full 360° circle. At least 50° of those 310° can be seen in binocular vision where the deer can perceive depth.

The nose, though, is the No. 1 defense system. The nostrils are lined with epithelium, which is composed of mucous membranes and sensory nerve endings. When these are kept moist, the animal can pick up scent better. That's why animals lick their muzzle a lot and why scenting is easier in moist air. The more epithelium, the better the sensing ability. A man's epithelium is about $\frac{1}{8,000}$ of the skin surface. A dog's is about $\frac{1}{80}$ of the skin surface, and a deer's is estimated to be about the same as a dog's.

The whitetail has about 24 square inches of reflective surface area per ear and the ear can swivel to help pick up sound. A mule deer has about 42 square inches. A man has about 3½ square inches.

On a live, 125-pound whitetail, skin will weigh 10 to 12 pounds, feet six to eight pounds, head six to eight pounds, and bones 16 to 20 pounds. Blood and entrails make up about 20 percent of the deer's weight. Blood is 7 to 10 percent of the total body weight in mammals, and is around 8 percent higher in males than in females. That's a lot of blood—possibly 12.5 pounds on a 125-pound deer. An average weight for an adult deer's heart, liver, and lungs is 10 pounds. The lungs are about three pounds, liver about five, and heart about two.

Tail length on a northern whitetail will be around nine to 10 inches from rump to tip of bone and 11 to 13 inches from rump to hair tip. When the white hairs on the underside of the tail are flared, they can spread 10 to 11 inches.

The front hooves usually are larger than the hind hooves. The outside hoof lobe is usually longer than the inside lobe because deer tend to walk on the inside lobe more—becoming a bit knock-kneed.

Much has been said about hoof size on bucks and does. Hooves, however, are relative to the size of the deer, for the most part. An old doe will have the big track and the rounded hoof lobes that are often ascribed to a buck. When you consider the fact that most bucks are shot at 1½ to 2½ years, you're looking at a condition that means track identification is difficult, at best.

A whitetail's walking stride is 18 to 19 inches and it can walk steadily at 3½ to four miles per hour— which is just a little faster than a man's steady walking rate. The trotting stride is 30 to 36 inches and the speed is 10 to 12 mph. Top speed for a whitetail is 34 to 40 mph.

Hair coloration varies with each animal. Black, a couple of shades of brown, and white appear in different degrees. The summer coat has solid, straight, thin hairs with no undercoat. There are many more hairs per square inch in a summer pelt than in a winter pelt.

Hair on a winter pelt is hollow, air-filled, and much larger in diameter than summer hair. It is also more brittle and can be easily pulled from the skin. The undercoat is fine, soft, and kinky and provides very good insulation. With the hollow, long hairs, this provides two layers of insulation.

Hair on the brisket points forward. All other hair points down or back. But hair is not simply hair. For instance, hair is generally darker near the top of the back than it is lower on the body. Hair on the stomach area is brownish gray, but the tips aren't as dark as the tips of hair on the spinal area. Navel hair is white, coarse, and curly, while hair from between the hind legs is white but finer, silkier, and not as curly. Brisket hair is stiff, grayish-black, coarse, and somewhat curly. Bow and gun hunters make use of this information when identifying a hit and determining the best waiting time before beginning to trail—and deciding the best manner in which to trail the animal, too.

Bucks may have good antlers at 2½ years, but the chances for a good or excellent rack after that are much better—all other things being equal. This whitetail has well-developed antlers. Photo by Erwin A. Bauer.

ANTLERS

Antlers have fascinated hunters since the dim past. They continue to fascinate, and much of the fog that used to surround antlers has been, or is being lifted.

Antlers are *not* for protection from predators. Otherwise, deer would keep them through times of deep snow when they are most vulnerable. Deer ward off predators by rearing up and slashing with their front hooves.

Age, heredity, and nutrition all affect antler growth and size. Well-fed yearling bucks with good genes can have antlers with a total of four to eight tines. A spike buck isn't necessarily a 1 year old. It can be genetically inferior, undernourished, or old— or a combination of those factors.

Bucks may have good antlers at 2½ years, but the chances for a good or excellent rack *after* that are much better—all other things being equal. That's simply because, from birth to 2½ years, the buck's first use of food is for body growth and well-being. After it reaches maximum body size, all food not used for body well-being can go into antler development. If the buck happens to be in an area that has the right minerals, such as calcium, it may be on the way to eye-popper size. Antler growth is triggered by the pituitary gland, which is stimulated by increasing hours of daylight.

Ian McTaggart Cowan of the University of British Columbia made an interesting study of this. He placed mule deer bucks in a controlled environment providing 12 hours of light and 12 hours of darkness daily year-round. These bucks couldn't shed their antlers and grow new ones. He kept another group of bucks in continuous light. They grew and discarded three sets of antlers in two years.

Antler tissue can grow as much as one-half inch per day, making it one of the fastest known forms of tissue growth. Antlers usually reach maximum size when the buck is about 5 years old. Bucks that reach greatest body size generally have the largest antlers, too. The dominant bucks are stronger, healthier, and grow the best antlers. They do most of the breeding, but not all of it.

Rue noted in *The Deer of North America* that "Most recent research indicates that the shape and number of points may depend chiefly on heredity, while the size of the antlers is the result of diet."

That makes sense. Countless bucks, especially those in controlled situations such as deer farms or parks where fallen racks can be easily recovered and checked, have been noted to have similar antler configurations from one year to the next, despite the size of the rack.

Older bucks generally shed their antlers before younger bucks. A falling testosterone level triggers antler drop. This decrease in the level of the testosterone hormone apparently occurs in older, dominant bucks first because they do most of the breeding. Dominant bucks use testosterone faster than they can manufacture it. Non-breeders will drop their antlers a month or so later than breeders.

When a buck gets old, its antlers may become smaller. The buck may maintain a large main beam, but the number of points or the size of the points may decrease. The whole rack will most likely, if not certainly, be smaller in the buck's last years—assuming it lives long enough.

This is a good indication of the mythical, mystical qualities assigned to whitetails over the years, the main one here being that you can tell a deer's age by the number of points on its rack. If that were so, the oldest deer would have the largest racks and the most points. Yet we all know that humans and their hunting dogs lose their robustness as the years advance.

Hunters and researchers have noticed that, all other things being equal, the larger and/or heavier the buck, the larger the diameter of the trees it uses for rubbing.

Antlers have a social significance for hunters and for deer. In most cases, the larger the antler the more dominant the buck. Bucks don't fight as much as we used to believe. They do more posturing and bluffing than fighting.

GLANDS

The whitetail has four major sets of external glands: preorbital (tear duct) in front of each eye, interdigital (between the lobes of each hoof), tarsal (on the inner sides of the hocks), and metatarsal (on the sides of the feet just above the dewclaws). There also are glandular areas of the forehead and tail. More and more people are looking into the possibility that the glandular area on the forehead is used for marking areas during rubbing. These glands and glandular areas are not fully understood—and may never be—simply because deer are a bit shy when it comes to telling us about themselves.

The preorbital gland is not well understood, but there's much speculation that the gland may be used in marking territory because deer rub the gland against twig tips.

The interdigital gland is each deer's individual marker. Each deer produces its own distinct scent, which it leaves every time it puts its foot down. This is the scent the doe follows to locate her fawn. Deer, however, don't track by scenting the air like dogs. They make good use of scents blown to them on off-the-ground air currents.

The tarsal gland isn't fully understood. It is the tufted, off-color patch on the inside of the hind legs at the hock. It isn't a gland in the typical definition of a gland because it doesn't have a duct opening. Instead, glands under the skin connect to hair follicles that work as ducts to bring the secretion to the skin surface. The deer can flare these hairs when alarmed. This is another warning signal to other deer.

Deer of all ages urinate on their tarsal glands. To identify each other, they smell the other animal's tarsal glands. The more dominant the deer, the larger and more active are its tarsal and metatarsal glands.

You don't need to trim off the tarsal glands when dressing a deer, either. They obviously didn't taint the meat when the deer was alive, so there's no reason to think they will taint the meat now. Just keep your hands off them and you'll be all right and so will the meat.

Metatarsal glands are about one inch long. They have a white hair tuft and they're found on the lower half of the hind feet. Their purpose is not well understood.

REPRODUCTION

The whitetails's initial breeding age depends mainly upon its health. For instance, does can breed at six to seven months but most breed for the first time at 1½ years. Bucks usually are about 1½ years of age when they first participate in the rut. And they usually do so minimally because they get run off by dominant bucks.

The peak of the rut or breeding season is usually in November. This peak may range from October to January, depending upon latitude, climate, and nutrition. In the states farthest south the rut normally occurs in late December and early January.

The doe is in heat (in estrus) for about 24 hours. If not impregnated the first time she is bred, she will come into estrus once or twice more at 28-day intervals.

The gestation period is approximately 202 days. It may vary from 195 to 212 days.

Bucks are physically able to breed earlier in the fall than are does but does do not respond to breeding attempts until the peak of estrus.

Habitat quality affects fawn production. Most does in the major breeding years—2½ to 7½ years—have two or more fawns every year. A Texas study showed that 65 percent have twins, 3 percent have triplets, and 32 percent have singles. This was on good range. A Pennsylvania study showed 1.8 fawns per doe on good range and 1.2 fawns per doe on poor range, which translates into 50 percent greater fawn production on good land.

A deer herd's capacity to increase is controlled by the number of fawns that survive the winter. Their ability to survive depends mainly on an adequate supply of decent food. If deer could be viewed as livestock, this would be easier for many hunters to accept. No rancher or farmer would attempt to feed twice as many beef animals over winter on the same amount of food and expect anything good to come of it. Nor would they feed twice as many dairy cows on the same amount of food and expect to maintain peak milk production. Yet a lot of the arguments about deer herd management have concerned objections to the harvesting of does.

The whitetail deer is one subject of which we'll never tire. It is and always will be a fascinating animal, not possessed of supernatural or mystical qualities, but extremely well adapted to its habitat and to us.

The Desert Mule Deer

By Jack O'Connor

In my trophy room, I have the mounted heads of two very good mule deer. At a quick glance they look much alike, almost identical, but a closer examination shows that they are, in some respects, rather different.

Both are magnificent specimens—big bucks a little past their prime and at the stage when they grow the most interesting antlers. One head would have been perfect and symmetrical with six points to a side except for one odd point. The other has a wider spread, is somewhat less symmetrical, and has six points on one side, eight on the other.

The coloration of these two bucks is quite different. The buck with the side spread has a bright, contrasty scalp. The brown triangle on his forehead is so dark that you might call it black. The light patch on the front of his neck below his chin is white. The dark spots on either side of his lower jaw are black and conspicuous, and the hair on his brisket is black. His coat is a brownish gray.

The cape of the other buck is much less vivid. The triangular patch on the forehead is definitely brown. The light-colored neck patch is yellowish white. The dark spots on either side of the lower jaw are brown and so small that they are inconspicuous. Incidentally, the farther north the mule deer is found, the larger and more conspicuous this jaw patch is. At the northern limit of mule deer range, in Alberta and British Columbia, the patch is coal black and almost encircles the lower jaw. At the lower limit of the range, in the deserts of the Southwest and Sonora, the patch is barely noticeable.

The hair on the brisket of my lighter-colored buck is brown, and the dark area is less extensive than that on the other buck. And the light buck's coat, instead of being a brownish gray, is definitely a grayish brown.

Both animals are mule deer with the characteristic large ears and evenly branched antlers of the species, but the buck with the contrasty scalp is a Rocky Mountain mule deer that was shot on the Salmon River in Idaho a few years ago. The lighter-colored buck is a desert mule deer, the best I have ever taken. He was shot on either December 30 or 31, in 1941, on the Sonora desert of northern Mexico.

At that time of year, the Rocky Mountain mule deer have pretty well finished the annual rut, but this old desert buck had just started getting interested in the does. His neck, as I remember, had not yet begun to swell. He did not have the odor of a rutting buck, and his meat was tender, juicy, and tasty. He was a very heavy buck. Several days later, when I delivered his four quarters to a meat locker in Tucson to be cut up, packaged, and stored, they weighed 175 pounds.

American zoologists are great classifiers and dividers. Consequently, they have listed many subspecies of mule deer in North America. I grew up on the Arizona desert and hunted desert mule deer in Arizona and Sonora for many years. I always thought that Arizona had only two subspecies of mule deer—the Rocky Mountain mule deer and the desert mule deer. I presumed that the deer found in the high country north of the great fault called the Mogollon Rim were Rocky Mountain mule deer and that those south of the rim, in lower and hotter country, were desert mule deer, or burro deer.

However, the last time I was in Arizona, I was

told that biologists had decided that the deer north of the Grand Canyon of the Colorado were Rocky Mountain mule deer, those south of the Mogollon Rim were desert mule deer, and those between were some sort of an intermediate subspecies. Just what they have decided to call them, I cannot say.

When I was growing up in Arizona, these desert mule deer were almost always called blacktails. Actually, like all mule deer, they have light-colored rump patches and little, dinky, off-white tails with black tips. The true blacktail deer of the Pacific Coast has a much larger tail that is black on top. It extends its tail to a horizontal position when it runs—or so I have read. (I have never shot a Columbia blacktail.) It never lifts it high and waves it around the way a frightened whitetail does. All I have ever seen a mule deer do with its tail is to wiggle it.

The Mexicans, too, sometimes call the desert mule deer a blacktail (*venado cola negra*), but the ordinary, back-country, Sonora Mexican simply calls it a *bura,* while he calls the whitetail *venado.*

In my youth, many Arizonans swore that there were at least two strains of desert mule deer. One, as I remember, was the bench-legged deer. It was supposed to be wide, blocky, and short-legged and to have antlers with a narrow spread. The other deer, the "regular blacktail," was supposed to have longer legs and wide-spread antlers.

Actually, wide-spread and close-pinched antlers are found in all subspecies of mule deer. If there is any important difference between the mule deer of the southwestern Arizona desert and those of the desert country of Sonora, I have failed to see it. The pale-colored big buck I shot in 1941 would plainly be classified as *Odocoileus hemionus eremicus,* as the type locality for this subspecies is not far from the area where I gathered him in. (The "type locality" is the spot where the "type specimen"—the animal on which the subspecific classification was made— was collected.)

Mule deer found in various dry areas of the United States are called desert mule deer. Some, such as those found in the dry, sagebrush flats and hills of southern Idaho and eastern Oregon are simply Rocky Mountain mule deer inhabiting arid country.

A desert mule deer is found in southern New Mexico, Chihuahua, and the Big Bend country of Texas. I have hunted these deer. They are a good deal smaller than the burro deer of southern Arizona and northwestern Sonora. From what I have seen, an average mature Big Bend mule deer buck with four points to a side will field-dress at about 150 to 160 pounds. The largest I have ever seen weighed 175. The antlers tend to be light.

The burro deer of southern Arizona and Sonora are heavy bodied and heavy antlered. Bucks field-dressing at 180 to 200 pounds are common and, now and then, one is shot that will weigh 225 to 250.

In Arizona, the desert mule deer are found not only out in the rolling hills and wide arroyos in the

Jack O'Connor.

lowland desert, but also in the canyons that break off the high plateau country and part way up the taller and rugged mountains. In the area of transition between the desert vegetation of the Lower Sonoran Zone and the live oaks, manzanita, and mountain mahogany of the Upper Sonoran Zone, the Arizona whitetail takes over.

In the deserts of the Mexican state of Sonora, however, the mule deer is entirely a low-country animal and even the little hills not over 100 feet higher than the desert flats have their complement of the beautiful, little whitetails (Coues deer). Often, I have seen whitetail tracks in the low country where the deer had come down to feed or to cross from one range of low hills to another, but I cannot remember

Heads in O'Connor's trophy room reveal differences between Rocky Mountain mule deer, left, and the desert variety.

ever seeing a mule deer or its tracks in the whitetail hills. (The tracks, incidentally, are unmistakable: Those of the whitetail are heart-shaped, those of the mule deer narrow and longer.)

How much work biologists have done on the ability of animals to tolerate other species I cannot say. In Africa, zebras and wildebeests habitually run together, and it is common to see several species grazing peacefully together on the same plain.

I think American animals are much less tolerant. In desert sheep ranges in Sonora, where there are few if any deer, the sheep habitually come down to feed out on the flats and sometimes even bed down in dry arroyos during the day. In areas where there are a good many deer, the sheep don't come down as often or stay down. On Tiburon Island, the mule deer range well up in the rocky cliffs and canyons. The reason, I am sure, is that there are no desert bighorns on Tiburon.

An interesting result of the whitetail and desert mule deer's ranging in adjacent areas is the occasional cross between the two species. I have never shot such a cross, but I have seen several hides from hybrids. The result looks just about like a Columbia blacktail. The tail is a blacktail's tail, the placement of the metatarsal glands is the same, and so are the markings of the face. For many years, a blacktail deer was listed for Arizona. It was called the Crooks' blacktail and was considered to be allied to the coast blacktail, but very rare. We know now that it was actually a cross between the mule deer and the whitetail.

For many years, Arizona had no open season on the desert mule deer, whereas the whitetails were hunted hard. The big, mature, buck mule deer did their best to keep the young bucks away from the does. At the same time, many unmated whitetail does were running around because there were many more whitetail does than bucks and the whitetail is much less promiscuous than the mule deer. Along the edges of the whitetail mountains, where the ranges of both species adjoined, an occasional romance occurred between an amorous young buck mule deer and a lonesome and neglected whitetail doe. I know of several hybrids that have been shot in southern Arizona and of two that were killed in Sonora.

The yearly cycles of the burro deer and all other desert, big-game animals are quite different from those of their relatives that live in colder climates. In high, cool country, from Arizona north of the Mogollon Rim clear to central Alberta, the mule deer are generally well into the rut by the middle of November. With their seven-month gestation period, their young are born in the spring. The desert mule deer, however, do not begin rutting until late December. Their fawns are dropped in late July or August.

Back to the story of the big buck I shot at the very end of 1941. My wife and I had a Mexican friend who owned a ranch, and we had arranged to rent a couple of horses from him and to borrow one of his vaqueros to take care of them and to show us around. We had driven up to a little adobe hut by a well in the desert, miles from anywhere, and were making camp when the vaquero rode up with the horses. He suggested that he and I take a turn to see if we could find a deer.

We had turned back toward camp about two hours later when we saw a couple of desert mule deer does about 300 yards away across a wide arroyo. We got off the horses and I was watching the does with binoculars when one of the horses reached up and yanked off a mouthful of ironwood leaves. A branch cracked. The does heard the noise and started to run. As they did, we saw a magnificent buck—but only for an instant.

Santiago, the vaquero, took off at a run and motioned for me to follow. I did. How he knew where the deer were going I have no idea, but he knew. We crossed the arroyo and went up the other side. A moment later, a doe came by, then another. Then the buck came into sight. My first bullet turned him around and my second put him down. He was so heavy that Santiago and I had to hoist him up into a tree with a riata so we could put him across Santiago's saddle. We tied him on. Santiago then scrambled up on top of the buck and, in triumph, we rode back to camp.

I do not know what the open seasons are in Sonora now but, when I lived in Arizona and hunted often in Mexico, the best time to get big, trophy, Mexican bucks was toward the end of the year when they were getting interested in the does. They have their minds on something more important than self-preservation then, and they move around more in the daytime.

West of the Santa Catalina Mountains, which loom like a wall north of Tucson, there is a stretch of rolling, cactus-covered hills, wide arroyos, and flats covered with grass, cholla, and brush. When I lived in Tucson, that area always held desert mule deer, and it was not difficult to find does, fawns, and young bucks. But during the hunting season, you could hunt hard and carefully for a weekend and rarely even glimpse a big, trophy buck, though you would see plenty of big buck tracks. There was just too much cover and they were just too smart. But in January, when the rut was in full swing, big, trophy bucks were all over the place.

I used to go out in January and hike back into the low hills to watch the deer. Each big buck would gather a harem of from five to a dozen does. Together, they moved restlessly uphill and down. From two to five young bucks always hung around the edge of the herd of does. Now and then, a bold youngster would rush in toward a receptive doe. The big herd buck would drive him off and, while the big buck's head was turned, another youngster would charge in and cover the doe.

I used to feel sorry for those poor herd bucks. Theirs was a hell of a life. They appeared to be exhausted. I never saw one eating. The lovemaking I saw performed was all done by the youngsters. The old bucks ran frantically around, overwhelmed by their cares, their mouths open, a wild and desperate look in their eyes. I have had them trot within a few yards of me and ignore me completely.

I have shot some desert mule deer at the beginning of the rut but never after it has got well under way. I would not consider it sporting to hunt in the middle of the rut. The meat is no good then, and I would not value a head taken under those conditions.

The mating season of the desert whitetails is even later than that of the desert mule deer but, just why this should be, I have no idea. When I was a professor at the University of Arizona back in the 1930s, I used to hunt in Sonora between Christmas and New Year. All that time, I shot only one whitetail buck that had begun to get interested in the does. My Mexican friends tell me that the whitetails do not start playing ring-around-a-rosy until late January or early February. Their whole cycle is later. I have seen desert whitetail bucks in April, when I was hunting javelinas, that were still wearing their antlers, and I have seen spotted fawns in November.

When I show friends the mounted head of my big desert mule deer buck, I tell them that he never had a drink of water in his life. If he did, he would have had to take it from a swift and briefly running arroyo after a violent summer storm. There is simply no natural open water in his country, which gets probably no more than from three to five inches of rainfall a year. The soil on the flats is mostly loose, large-grained sand from

O'Connor poses in Sonora with his best desert mule deer, shown mounted on page 10.

the decomposing, granite hills, and it soaks up water like a sponge. Mexican ranchers have dug some wells and have installed windmills, but it is rare for a deer to use this water.

Instead, the mule deer and all the other desert big game have learned to make out with the moisture they get from the dew on the leaves of the browse they eat and the water in the fruit of the various cactuses. Near the Gulf of California, the dew is often quite heavy and various plants contain considerable water. From my observation, I would guess that the desert mule deer, if suitable vegetation is present, can live and die without tasting open water.

You would think that in this dry environment, the flesh of desert game would be strong and dry. Actually, most of the browse is mild and delicately flavored and there is no better meat anywhere than that of a fat, desert mule deer or whitetail or a good, fat ram taken before the rut—or after the rut, when he has had sufficient time to recover his condition.

I have eaten a lot of desert venison in my day and I have also cooked a lot. One time, I arrived at a ranch and told the Mexican rancher that I would like to go deer hunting and would like to borrow a horse and a vaquero. He told me that he, too, was overcome by a desire to hunt deer and he would go along. His brother also felt deery, and so did a cousin who lived on a ranch about 15 miles away. By the time we got organized, our party consisted of about a dozen people. I had someone to make my bed, wash my sweaty shirts, round up and saddle my horse, and skin the deer. But there was no one to cook.

For two weeks, I fed the mob on coffee, pancakes, and syrup made of hot water and pinoche (unrefined Mexican sugar) for breakfast; at night, I made biscuits and gravy, and fried venison in Dutch ovens. I kept a big pot of frijoles simmering on the ironwood fire 24 hours a day. The camp handyman kept the fire going and watched the frijoles to see that they didn't boil dry. He also made a batch of tortillas every day. We took these with us when we rode out and, at noon, we would build a little fire, make a tin-canful of coffee, and heat the tortillas by tossing them onto the ashes.

My rancher host had brought along some tasty, homemade white cheese, and his brother had contributed a couple of cases of a delicious Hermosillo-made beer called High Life. One of the cowboys had foresightedly brought a jug or two of wild Mexican booze called sotol. It tasted like a mixture of high-test gasoline and horse liniment, but I discovered that, if I mixed it half and half with pineapple or orange juice, it became fairly potable.

My host was a very thrifty hombre who believed that a peso saved is a peso earned. And as fast as he, his brother, his cousin, and I collected deer, he had his henchmen cut the meat into long strips and hang them on the bushes to dry into jerky. He was laying in his winter's meat.

I used to come in dog tired. I'd have the boys put the Dutch ovens on to heat. Then I'd take a belt of sotol and pineapple juice and start cooking while my hungry Mexican friends squatted around watching me like starving vultures waiting for a sick steer to die.

It was December, and almost every morning we would awaken to find frost on the ground. My host, his brother, the cousin, and I slept on heavy Mexican cots we had brought in a truck from the ranch. They slept in blankets, I in a sleeping bag. Most of the vaqueros slept on saddle blankets near the fire. The camp boy who watched the beans was a tough, little Papago Indian about 12 years old. He simply took off his chaps, rolled them up for a pillow, lay down on the hard, cold ground, and slept like a baby!

The antlers of the burro deer compare favorably with the antlers of mule deer anywhere. I remember one magnificent and massive head taken near Ca-

borca, Sonora, that had eight and nine points and a spread of 42 inches. Clients of the late Charlie Ren who, for a time, operated a hunting outfit in northern Sonora, used to get some superb heads down on the deserts around Caborca and Altar. For whatever reason, I believe I have seen more outstanding heads from Sonora than from Arizona.

The outlook for the desert deer is, alas, not so good. In both Arizona and Sonora, it is receiving pressure from every side. In Arizona, most of its range is either leased from the state for peanuts by cattle ranchers or is Bureau of Land Management land leased from the federal government. The ranching interests are very powerful in Arizona—so powerful that they have fought off any attempt to regulate the use of state-owned land. As a consequence, most state land in Arizona is fantastically overgrazed and overbrowsed, and the desert deer must compete with cattle.

In Sonora, the story is about the same. Most of the land is public domain; some of it is privately owned. All is overgrazed and overbrowsed. Most southwestern ranches, whether in Arizona or Sonora, do not sell beef; they simply sell ambulatory carcasses that can be fattened and made into beef. Desert land is fragile. Growth is slow. Though the annual rainfall is only from one to nine inches a year, rains are often torrential and topsoil that has been laid bare by overgrazing is washed away. The desert was never intended to be cattle country.

For a long time, the dryness of the country in remote parts of Sonora protected the desert mule deer and the bighorn sheep from competition. But now, Mexican ranchers are developing water. They bring in bulldozers and throw up dams across arroyos to catch the occasional floods. The effect will be that sheep and deer, which have had a rough enough time anyway, will find it even harder to survive.

And, in many areas, the desert deer can be hunted from four-wheel-drive vehicles. In Arizona, there are probably 100 hunters today where there was one in the '20s and '30s. Country Mexicans have always hunted deer and sheep 12 months out of the year, and now big-game hunting has become fashionable in Mexico and rich Mexicans come from all the large Mexican cities to hunt desert bighorns and trophy mule deer. Some attempt is now being made in Mexico to enforce the game laws, but I understand that enforcement is still pretty sketchy.

In the southwestern United States, the desert bighorn has been saved for posterity by the establishment of rigidly patrolled game preserves administered by the federal government. Such a setup could be the salvation of the desert bighorn in Sonora and Lower California, too—and also of the desert mule deer.

I hope it is saved. It is one of the handsomest of the North American deer and it lives in the great, southwestern desert—my first love, the land where I grew up, and one of the most beautiful, unusual, and interesting regions on earth.

Runts To Mossyhorns

By Bruce Brady

ob Fulmer, president of the Miss-Ark Hunting Club, sat atop his tree stand and watched another dawn come to the Mississippi Delta swamps. A fox squirrel scampered down a nearby oak and momentarily diverted his attention from the buck's scrape that the stand overlooked.

When his eyes returned to the scrape, Fulmer spotted a deer slipping through the underbrush. His rifle scope revealed a big buck with a heavy, eight-point rack. Trailing a few yards behind the trophy deer was a second buck with five-inch spikes.

The big eight-pointer ambled closer, but Fulmer's crosshairs settled on the spike's neck. When his .30/06 roared, the little buck collapsed. Recovering from recoil, the hunter looked over his scope in time to see the eight-pointer bound away, his dark and heavy antlers laid back over his shoulders.

A witness to this scene might conclude that Fulmer had lost his mind in passing up a trophy for an 80-pound, five-inch spike. Actually, Fulmer was participating in a deer management program adopted by his club. The program has produced a large number of trophy bucks and has kept small spikes to a minimum on the club's privately owned land. The good news is that the program really works.

This deer management effort was initiated by Dr. Ross Shelton, formerly an extension wildlife specialist at Mississippi State University. Shelton earned his Ph.D. at Colorado State, where he conducted extensive research on deer and elk. His services were provided free of charge. Most states will assign a biologist gratis if the plot of land is large enough.

"Back in the 1950s, we shot some outstanding trophy whitetails on club property," Fulmer told me.

"But, gradually, the quality of our bucks declined. By 1971, a 120-pound four-pointer was the biggest buck of the year. I contacted Dr. Shelton about the poor quality of our bucks, and he agreed to make an analysis of our herd and the quality of our habitat. He found that an excessively high deer population had seriously overbrowsed the range and he urged the club to adopt a management program that almost caused a rebellion among club members."

Dr. Shelton recommended that the hunters reduce the total number of deer by harvesting a large number of does, which had been protected previously. But a second recommendation that caused eyebrows to lift was that members bag only spikes for a two-year period.

Shelton explained that a reduction in the total number of deer would permit regrowth of badly needed browse. The harvesting of spikes for two years would help eliminate genetically inferior deer and allow the best specimens to do most of the breeding. At the same time, forkhorn bucks would attain the age necessary to grow heavier antlers with more points.

His suggestions caused heated debate among club members, but they eventually adopted the program. Time has proven it was a wise decision.

"Actually, management for the production of trophy animals isn't new," Shelton remarked. "It has been practiced in Germany and a few other European countries for a great many years."

In much of Europe, the landowner, rather than the state, owns the wildlife. Many landowners manage their deer herds to produce quality bucks because that produces more income from the sale of venison

Two members of the Miss-Ark Hunting Club display bucks taken in 1978. They demonstrate the trend to quality whitetails.

in the public market and from hunting license fees. Bucks are classified "A," "B," and "C." The "C" bucks are young and need age to develop. "B" bucks are quality animals with good racks and a reasonable number are harvested according to a carefully conceived plan. The "A" group consists of outstanding male deer that are not harvested until their active breeding life has ended. This gives the best deer the chance to contribute their heredity to the herd. Defective deer are shot at any time, often by a paid gamekeeper.

"It's obvious that the American system tends to cull in reverse by harvesting the better animals and leaving the poorer ones to carry on the line," Shelton said. "This is particularly true in states that have laws that protect spike bucks."

Shelton issued a word of caution on shooting spikes: "Harvesting a large number of spikes on overpopulated range can virtually eliminate an entire age-class of bucks. Recent research at Mississippi State revealed that, on some ranges, spikes make up from 80 to 90 percent of the 1½-year-old, male age-class. Thus, if this age-class is hit too hard, too few deer will be carried through to provide a harvest during a later season. The advice of a competent biologist is required to assess the herd and the habitat and set the number of spikes to be taken. Conditions vary greatly, and the deer and the range must be managed accordingly."

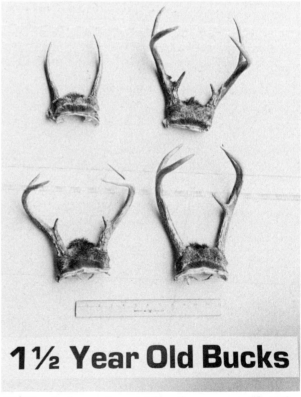

1½ Year Old Bucks

All of these bucks were harvested from the same range. The antlers demonstrate the variety of deer quality among same-age deer.

Dr. Shelton referred to the Miss-Ark Hunting Club, located on Archer Island near Greenville, Mississippi, as a classic case of just how effective a trophy management program can be.

"When I first visited the club in 1972, I found the worst overbrowsed range I have ever seen," Shelton recalled. "The club agreed on a program to improve body weight and antler size of their bucks. Antlerless deer harvests were increased in order to allow browse to regenerate. Club records for 1973 show that bucks shot that year had an average age of 2.1 years, average weight of 119.6 pounds, and an average of 3.7 points. Forty-eight percent of the buck kill consisted of spikes. Four of the spikes taken in 1973 were more than 1½ years old."

After a great deal of debate, the club members voted to shoot only does and spikes in 1974 and 1975. New rules made it clear that any member who shot a fork-antlered buck would pay a fine and face possible expulsion from the club.

In 1974, 14 spikes were harvested, none older than 1½ years; average live weight was 106.71 pounds. In 1975, 10 spikes were shot, only one older than 1½ years; it was a poor animal weighing only 118 pounds at 3½ years of age. The following year, five spikes were taken, none older than 1½ years, with average live weight of 120.6 pounds. There was a yearly reduction in the number of spikes older than 1½ years, a reduction in total spike harvest, and an increase in average weight of the spikes that were harvested.

In 1976, the club voted to allow members to take a limited number of fork-antlered bucks on a first-come basis. When a total of 12 fork-antlered bucks had been taken, club members who had not taken a buck had to hunt for spikes.

Above, Dr. Ross Shelton (right) shows how to age deer by jaw size. Right top, he and Miss-Ark Hunting Club members discuss preferred deer food for club lands. At right, he compares jaw sizes of the bucks to determine their ages.

MORE AND BIGGER BUCKS

Intensive management of deer herds and habitat on the Mississippi hunting clubs' land continues to produce dramatic results, as evidenced by the following data that were collected during subsequent hunting seasons.

Merigold Hunting Club harvested a total of 34 forked-antler bucks during the 1979–1980 season. The average age of these bucks was 2.8 years; average live weight, 165.5 pounds; average number of points, 8.4; and average inside spread, 15 inches. One of these bucks won the Mississippi Bowhunter's Big Buck contest for the season.

Ward Lake Hunting Club collected 15 forked-antler bucks during the 1979–1980 season. The average age of these bucks was 3.2 years; average live weight, 193.2 pounds; average number of points, 8.7; and average inside spread, 15.2 inches. Ward Lake Hunting Club member, David Holcomb, of Clarksdale, Mississippi, took a buck that qualified for the Pope and Young Club record book. Holcomb's buck weighed 210 pounds and had an 11-point rack with an 18-inch spread. During the 1980–1981 bow season, Holcomb took another huge buck with his bow; this one weighed 230 pounds.

The accompanying table shows the buck harvests in 1973, before the culling program, and in 1976. The improvement is self-evident. Does also improved in bodily weight. The average live weight of 1½-year-old does was 96.28 pounds in 1974, 103 pounds in 1976.

BUCK HARVEST

Year	No. Killed	Avg. Age	Avg. Live Weight	Avg. No. Points
1973	27	2.1	119.6	3.7
1976	13	2.9	150.2	5.2
Change		+38%	+25.5%	+40.5%

The habitat was enhanced by herd reduction and also by timber cuttings that allowed a significant increase in browse production. Dewberry and trumpet creeper, two of the best deer browses on club lands, made good recoveries.

To aid in antler development, members established deer licks containing salt, calcium, and phosphorus. When questioned about the benefit of these licks, Shelton said that definitive research on the subject was lacking but that "there is a distinct possibility such licks may aid in antler development. They certainly do no harm. It is a fact that such licks are heavily used by deer."

The success of the Miss-Ark Hunting Club management program became even more apparent after the 1977 season. Records indicated that quality bucks had been harvested in every age-class. A number of deer in the 1½-year-old class had had four and five-point antlers. Bucks in the 2½ to 4½-year-old class again produced the trophy racks that were totally absent in 1973.

During the 1978 hunting season, 14 forked-antler bucks were taken, which demonstrates that the trend to quality whitetails was continuing. Among the 1978 bucks, two that were 1½ years old carried eight-point racks. The largest buck in the 4½-year-old age-class was a nine-pointer with a 22-inch spread that weighed 228 pounds. Miss-Ark Hunting Club now has quality bucks in every age-class.

The club has 33 members and the group's goal is to permit 20 members to harvest forked-antler bucks on a first-come basis every year. When 20 bucks have been taken, the remainder of the members will have to settle for hunting spikes or does, if more does must be killed. In this way, there will always be a good carryover of older bucks and ample trophies.

As a result of the success of the program, four other hunting clubs in Mississippi adopted similar management projects. Shelton explained that, because of variance in deer populations, browse conditions, and relative size of the various tracts, each program must be tailored to the specific location. The advice of a competent biologist is essential before any program is adopted.

Merigold Hunting Club, near Rosedale, is one of the oldest organized deer camps in Mississippi. The club began a trophy buck management program in 1977 and harvested only does and spikes during the 1977 and 1978 hunting seasons. A limited number of forked-antler bucks were taken the following fall.

Club president Henry Hiter said members began to see results after two seasons.

"Heavy-horned trophy deer were once again being sighted by hunters," Hiter said, "and those were few and far between after the 1950s when a number of Boone and Crockett-class heads were taken."

He added that his club's deer herd was in reasonably good condition at the start of the program. Improvement was expected to be rapid.

Merigold members were in agreement that only does and spikes would be shot for two years. Still, a $500 fine and a one-year suspension of membership was the penalty for shooting a fork-antlered buck. None were killed.

Jim Humber is a member of Ward Lake Hunting Club near Clarksdale, Mississippi. His club had a trophy buck management program.

"Imagine yourself bowhunting and having 14 bucks with fine racks coming within 25 yards of your stand and not drawing your bow on a single one," Humber told me with a grin. "I had to settle for a spike. We were just moving into the second year of our program and I'd already seen more good racks than I'd seen in the past 15 years on club property. And while I couldn't take one yet, it was a real joy to see them and to anticipate future hunts."

Dr. Shelton has even instituted his trophy buck management program on a ranch in the Colorado Rockies.

"Mule deer pose a unique problem in that many herds are migratory," he said. "However, where a mule deer herd is resident, I see no reason the program won't work equally as well as with whitetails."

Dr. Shelton pointed out that, the larger the hunting area, the easier the program is to establish.

"If a number of clubs with small hunting areas are interested in establishing quality bucks in every age-class, they can join together in a cooperative effort and make such a program successful," Shelton said. "They can work together to control their deer herds and the number of bucks taken during the building program. Cooperation among the clubs will also lessen poaching, which tends to increase when word spreads that good bucks are being passed over.

"The significant thing about this particular management technique is that I believe it can be successfully applied to virtually any habitat where whitetails are found. Variations of this program have been used in Texas for a number of years."

By adopting this management program, members of the Mississippi clubs involved haven't been deprived of shooting or venison because they are allowed a reasonable harvest of both spikes and does when bucks with forked antlers are protected. While genetically inferior deer are being removed, the herd balanced, and the habitat restored, trophy bucks are in the making.

PART 2

HUNTING WHITETAIL DEER

Man Vs. Deer: The Lone Stillhunter

By George Mattis

Solo hunters are becoming the minority in the woods these days, for the trend is toward group hunting with its regimentation, fellowship, and varying degrees of fanfare. But, despite this tendency toward sociability on the hunt, there are always those few individuals who, like trout stream anglers, need no companionship to enjoy their day afield.

The unattached whitetail hunter has very definite advantages over the gang hunter, for he usually confines his efforts to deer territory with which he is thoroughly acquainted. Because any hunter's success is in direct proportion to the amount of time he spends under ideal conditions in good deer area, the lone stillhunter has the better odds. Unlike the organized party hunter, he puts in full time from the moment he enters the woods until the time he unloads his gun at the close of the day. This is in considerable contrast to the time-consuming procedure usually involved in group hunting, and especially in deer driving.

There is no doubt that the solo hunter fares better through the years than the individuals of any gang do, although this fact is not always recognized. If any group of eight or 10 hunters comes up with a full bag after the season's hunt, the story is related with considerable acclamation. Yet, if the lone stillhunter kills his deer the first or second day out to fill his quota, his success is not heralded in equal manner.

In group hunting, whether it be a drive or just a concentration of hunters in a given area each hunting on his own, the hunters strive to keep the whitetails

18

The feeding deer is preoccupied and, although he interrupts his rapid nibbling with furtive glances and ever-twitching ears, he is still less able to detect approaching danger as readily as when bedded down or idling along the trail. Illustrations by William Reusswig.

on the move so that all participants have shooting opportunities. These are mostly running shots and, all too often, are made at great distances. This is in opposition to the stillhunter, who strives to contain the undisturbed game in an area that he slowly and carefully probes. Under these ideal conditions, his single, well-placed shot at the unsuspecting quarry proves more effective than those staccato reports he hears in the distance.

Stillhunting differs as terrain and habitat vary. The hunter can be proficient in his own bailiwick but something less when he leaves his home grounds. Not every hunter has the same patience required for slowly covering a limited area for the duration of a full day, and you will find differences in method even among confirmed stillhunters in an equal situation. Regardless of their individual peculiarities, they all have one thing in common when they take to the field with their guns: They tax their eyes more than they do their legs.

THE WHITETAIL'S SENSES

The sense of smell is the most developed one in the whitetail, with hearing and sight following in close order. Yet, this is not always the order of their importance to the stillhunter. The deer's sense of sight is extremely keen in picking up a moving object at a great distance on a normally clear day, and this is what creates a problem for the hunter. At close range, however, say about 50 feet, the animal is unable to identify a motionless hunter, especially if the hunter's outline is broken by a tree trunk or any cover. Such a person, when seen in the open, arouses curiosity and suspicion in the deer and, while the strange object is under scrutiny, the whitetail might get a whiff of the hunter's scent or else catch a slight movement to complete the picture of danger. This weakness in a deer's eyesight at close range is of little benefit to the hunter if his quarry has detected him from a great range and already fled the scene.

Slow movements of the stillhunter are essential for an approach to his game.

I have many times come very close to whitetails that were bedded down under windfallen trees where they had little vision for any great distance. Their gifted noses and ears failed them because of such factors as very damp weather, adverse wind, or my noiseless walking.

The sense of smell in deer, practically nil in the hunter, is at least equally important for the hunter to surmount. It can detect danger when neither its eyes nor ears have sensed it. Sometimes, a scent alone puts the animal into flight, and it is a clincher when either sight or hearing has already alerted the deer. Here, the hunter's only recourse is to walk into the wind so that none of his scent will be carried ahead of his progress.

The deer's hearing power, though far keener than that of humans, might be classed last in importance to the deer for its effectiveness against the stillhunter. Here, the hunter has some leeway in selecting a route for a noiseless stalk with the aid of a favorable breeze or of quiet footing on soft snow or damp ground. Or, if he is trail watching, then the problem of noise is completely licked. The hunter cannot cope as effectively with the other two senses in his game. There is little he can do about the erratic air currents in the woods that so often betray his presence to the game, even in a well-planned stalk. Nor is there much he can do to keep himself from being seen while in the field, especially if his quarry is not preoccupied with browsing or loafing.

It is not often that the use of any one of these senses is sufficient to convince the deer of an immediate danger. A whitetail likes to see what its nose or ears have detected, and it also likes to smell or hear what it sees. And this delay in escape, slight as it might be, is advantageous to the hunter.

The snap of a twig alerts deer instantly, and they nervously search about for the source of the noise. It takes but a little time before they settle back to their former composure, however. Another snap of a twig and their heads are brought up sharply, and now they mill about definitely alerted to some intrusion. If I expose even part of myself at this point, they dash off with no restraint.

In like situations, I have often exposed myself to deer without making any noise. Now they appear just as alert as they would if they had heard a warning sound, but they seem more curious than startled. Here, the snap of a twig is all they need to complete the image of danger.

The whitetail's nose has caused many stillhunters to shake clenched fists in the direction of a whistling snort. Here, the quarry is well alerted even when danger is not seen or heard. The hunter is defeated, for he knows his stamping buck is waiting for any slight movement or sound from the intruder. And the animal is willing to expose its general location in exchange for any supplementary information the stalker might give. The whitetail usually wins out in the waiting contest, for it has the patience to wait and the advantages to see, while the hunter gains nothing by waiting, and he brings the situation to the usual end if he attempts to get himself in position to see his deer.

The slower the hunter travels, the more advantageous it is for him to move into any wind, however slight it might be. Scent accumulates about a hunter if he lingers for long in one spot and, if there is no breeze to carry it away or dissipate it, he will soon be surrounded by the scent for a considerable circumference. The effect of this concentration of human odor, when it is wafted to a deer's nostrils by some erratic air current, is experienced by most hunters. Such is the case when a hunter pauses on a vantage point for a few minutes. He hears and sees nothing and is about to move on. Then comes the loud snort of an alarmed deer that has just intercepted the spreading scent.

This scent problem holds true, too, in an area containing numerous hunters where the animals are pretty well alerted by human odor pervading the woods. The deer have learned to tolerate this threat to their safety, and they might even accept it with surprising calm. Nevertheless, they are aware of its presence, and the hunter will find it most difficult to surprise his game for a good shot under these conditions. Even those animals that are bedded down or resting, seemingly relaxed, are a bit jumpy. Any slight disturbance the stillhunter might make in their proximity is enough to trigger a hasty exit. This is why stillhunting in heavily driven areas is not too effective.

It is not always practical nor necessary for the hunter to move directly into the wind. Quartering into the wind in zigzag fashion gives more favorable coverage of a given area. If the hunter travels directly into the breeze, he might reach the end of his territory in an hour or so, and then he must return downwind to another starting point. A full, half day's stalking could be accomplished in one trip if the hunter made long, quartering thrusts to the right and left of wind direction.

HUNTING WITH YOUR EYES

The stillhunter works over the grounds with his eyes. He uses his legs only to carry him over the terrain he has carefully scrutinized. Each time he comes upon a change of grounds he must pause to scan the area about him. It is best to adopt a systematic procedure in searching the terrain effectively. A quick search from left to right will suffice to detect any movement of game within shooting distance, and a standing or browsing whitetail at close range should be spotted at once. Now a thorough study of the thicket should be made beginning with the foreground, sweeping back and forth in a wide arc, and extending the search farther into the background with each sweep of the head. Such an examination is best made from any convenient elevation, however slight.

After the survey is completed—and this could take several minutes—the hunter moves on at a slow pace, picking his way carefully in order to avoid snapping any twigs underfoot or brushing against overhanging branches. His movements, like those of a bird-watcher, must be smooth and slow, for such movements are less likely to attract attention.

It must be remembered that the stillhunter is looking for standing, browsing, or bedded-down deer. If he is just looking for *any* whitetails, chances are he will see them more easily—but they will be mostly out of range and running. There will be a difference in your mode of walking and searching if you make up your mind that you are seeking the stationary target only.

It is hardly possible for any person walking through the woods to refrain from making a disturbing noise sometime or other. The experienced stillhunter will pause for several minutes after such an incident, for he knows the whitetail, if within hearing distance, is now awaiting further evidence of an intruder. A deer's memory is somewhat short and, if there is no follow-up of disturbance, the animal will soon dismiss its anxiety. It is the series of man-made noises that is the bane of the hunter.

In canvasing deer country, the hunter should avail himself of any high ground along his course of travel. Those slight depressions on either side of him are worth some investigation even though they take him a bit off course. It is in these depressions, sometimes hemmed in by small ridges, that the whitetail can best be taken by surprise. These shallow basins, especially if located on high, flat ground, are ideal sanctums for the unmolested animals. Such spots are pretty well insulated against outside noises and odors. On many occasions during buck season, I have spent considerable time studying a group of antlerless deer in such seclusion.

A big advantage for the solo hunter is his ability to follow successfully in the wake of heavy group hunting. Deer driving can become very noticeably ineffective after the hunting season has progressed for some time. About the middle of the season, gang hunters start scurrying about, searching for fresh areas to infiltrate. After one unsuccessful group leaves a tract of deer country, another gang moves in with great anticipation—but often with equally poor results.

The fact is that, after the whitetails have been shunted about day after day in any territory, many of them gradually enter secluded pockets where they might remain for the duration of the season, if they're not molested. These odd spots could be the thickets in a small triangle of only several acres bounded by roads, lakes, or farmland. They could be points of land projecting into lakes or wet swamps, the thickets along a fence line adjacent to a pasture, or the wooded pasture itself, now devoid of livestock.

I remember finding many such hideouts, some of them practically in my backyard, after I had spent the season scouring the remote hinterlands. Once, an old buck had taken refuge for the entire season in a portion of the pasture scarcely 400 yards from the house. At night, he fed on a dense clump of sumac in full view of the farmstead. During the day, he withdrew to a thicket just outside the fence line. There was nothing here to disrupt his simple routine and, like a true slacker, he let the season go by sitting it out smugly on the sidelines.

The last day of one hunting season, I cut across a four-acre wedge formed by the intersection of a highway and a railroad. As I skirted a small swamp that formed the other boundary of this triangle, I started a veritable explosion of shaking brush and bobbing flags. Seven deer bounded out from this small retreat. There were no tracks leading in, and the snow was two days old, so it appeared the animals had hoped to see the season through in the safety of this confinement. This withdrawal to odd recesses is common among whitetails, especially the wily, old bucks, when the large deer areas are heavily and continually hunted. The animals seem to recognize patterns in the hunters' routines, and they find respite from disturbance by retiring to the edges. Most hunters, meanwhile, hopefully probe the depths of the big country, thinking that somewhere in the deep hinterlands they will find the whitetails concentrated in happy numbers.

Some of the older stillhunters I know carefully probe these lesser grounds. This strategy is especially successful when the legal bag is bucks-only, for any animal with a noticeable rack soon learns his hide is a prime target. The seasoned patriarchs long past their physical peak are often taken here. After a buck has attained a respectable age and becomes aware that he is a marked animal, he is willing to forsake his species and lead the life of a recluse. He has, perhaps, attained the age where he is less interested in does than in his own safety. He becomes fat and lazy from inactivity, his reflexes might be on the decline but, from his years of hazardous living, he has acquired the simple knack of self-preservation with a minimum of exertion.

Sometimes, if these refuges are partly open, like pasture lands, a buck will bed down on a hillside under some scraggly growth or alongside short shrubbery. From his elevated couch, he might occupy his time watching highway traffic or studying the movements of hunters as they gather in groups to plan an attack on the big deer area across the road. All the activity outside the sphere of the buck's limited domain causes him little concern. The whitetail becomes uneasy only when his immediate grounds are invaded. Even then, if the trespasser seems unaware of the deer's presence or makes no overt attempt to approach, it is likely the animal will trust to the security of his bed.

WHEN WHITETAILS FEED

It is generally accepted that whitetails stir about and feed mostly during the evenings, early mornings, and sometimes during the night. During the daylight hours, they confine themselves to inactivity and seclusion. Actually, it is the security factor that largely governs their feeding, and this would quite normally exclude the broad-daylight hours.

Whitetails usually venture on fields adjacent to busy highways after sundown or, if the fields are large, the deer might start to feed on the distant margins long before sunset. On isolated farmlands where there is little to disrupt their daily routine, the animals are sometimes not averse to feeding in the open hay lands in the light of high noon.

In the backwoods country, away from farmlands with their tender grass growth, the deer's feeding hours are also largely confined to early mornings and late evenings, but the hunter cannot hope to find a concentration of feeding animals in any one area. The feeding grounds are any relatively sunny spots conducive to young growth suitable for browse— the margins of swamps, the flats along streams, edges of old logging-camp clearings, logging slashings, or any glen where young growth is not hampered by dense timber.

The browsing hours are by all odds the best time for the hunter to find his game for the most favorable shooting. The fact that the animal is on its feet and not in its bed is a big advantage for the hunter. And the shaking of twigs or any slow movement of the browsing deer itself is sure to catch the eye of the alert hunter.

The feeding animal is preoccupied and, although it constantly interrupts its rapid nibbling with furtive glances and ever-twitching ears, it is still unable to detect any approaching danger as readily as when it is bedded down or idling along a trail. The strong factor favoring the stillhunter in remote or neglected areas is that here he might hope to find his game relaxed to the point where daytime browsing is not unusual for the species.

A group of whitetails feeding in a thicket is not too difficult to approach if the hunter keeps his eyes on them while he slowly advances under any available cover. Each animal seems to depend upon the others for detecting any signs of danger, for they constantly glance about to check on each other's

One of the best opportunities the stillhunter has for coming upon a walking or browsing deer is during a heavy mist or gently falling rain in the absence of any wind.

movements. When they do raise their heads to survey the outer area, this attempt at vigilance appears somewhat mechanical and routine. During the moment it is reaching for browse, the whitetail is completely off guard, and the hunter can now advance a few steps. It is probable that the deer does not hear well when chewing its browse, for often it will stop short with its mouth bristling with protruding twigs. Now it listens intently—but only briefly, if all seems well. It is only when it fidgets about without chewing its mouthful of browse that the deer is aware of some infringement on its privacy. This caution in one animal is contagious in the group. Now they mill about nervously, searching for the cause for alarm. Any slight movement the hunter makes at this point sends the animals bounding off.

WEATHER AND WHITETAILS

Weather conditions are an all-important agent in influencing the temperament of all game, and the behavior of the whitetail deer is especially susceptible to the elements. The hunter learns from experience that, on certain days, he finds less caution than usual in his quarry while, at other times, the white flicker of a tail over a distant rise marks the nearest approach he can make to his nervous game.

One of the best opportunities the stillhunter has for coming upon a walking or browsing deer is during a heavy mist or gently falling rain in the absence of any wind. The whitetail is farsighted, and any obstruction, however slight, moving through the air greatly impairs his vision. His sense of smell becomes considerably incapacitated in heavy atmosphere, and the moisture-laden air muffles the sounds the hunter makes in the soft, wet leaves. The animal seems to accept all this as a cloak for its own protection, and it leaves its bed to move about freely with little restraint or fear. If the precipitation is something more than a mere drizzle, the hunter might catch his deer flat-footed at very close range, and the once-high-spirited buck can become as gentle and mild-mannered as a farm deer.

Most hunters prefer to clear the woods during a rain, but the avid stillhunter properly attired for the occasion is willing to suffer some discomforts in return for the better odds of success. Here, the hunter seeks the animal's likely feeding grounds or, if he prefers to avoid the moisture-laden brush, he can walk the side roads, the logging trails, or the railroad tracks traversing the deer country. The animals are on the move now, and they leave the dense thickets for the browse of the open country. In their stirring, they spend as much time walking as they do feeding.

The reverse is true if there is a heavy rain, especially one accompanied by strong winds. The animals now retire to the back country where they bed down or just stand under what cover is available to them, often seeking shelter under the protective branches of evergreens. Here they await the passing of the storm with a minimum of activity.

Undoubtedly, the model hunting situation would call for about three to four inches of soft snow occasionally freshened with an added light cover as the season progresses. This is more idealistic than realistic. Sometimes the season opens with a deluge of knee-deep snow, perhaps followed soon by an additional blanket of the white stuff. Then there could be the other extreme of only several inches of fluffy snow followed by a thaw, a heavy freeze, and the subsequent noisy crust. In between, sometimes, you get tracking snow—that critical depth that does not hamper your hunting stride one whit, yet is substantial enough so that it does not evaporate before your hunting shakes have fully subsided late in the afternoon of your season opener.

Snow, generally, is not the magic factor that always works for the hunter's success. It is a definite advantage in spotting quarry that is within the range of vision. It enables the hunter to observe deer signs and to follow the tracks of a particular animal. But, most important of all, it mercifully reduces the loss of wounded animals. But these benefits of snow cover aside, the task of approaching game remains a problem for the stillhunter. The snow can grant his every wish or it can bring about his very defeat. It does give the lone hunter a wider spread of stalking conditions, both better and worse, than does bare-ground hunting.

Too often, in the aftermath of a snowfall, the weather turns abruptly colder. The deer have been feeding heavily before and during the snowing period so they now bed down and, like a mink after the first snow of the trapping season, they lay tracks with great reluctance. They might hole up for two days, leaving the hunter to suspect that his game has left the country. This could be termed the low tide in their activity. Then, as hunger urges them to their feet again, the whitetails emerge from nowhere during the night to track up the once-untrodden snow country.

The best snow condition the stillhunter can hope for—in fact, the best condition he can ever find in any weather situation—is a quiet-falling snow with a thin, white blanket already underfoot. This is it, and the hunter who leaves the woods at this time simply admits that his love for comfort is greater than his love for the hunt.

The layer of soft snow almost completely absorbs all walking sounds made by even the careless stalker, and the white blanket gives him the needed, contrasting background for sighting his game under the prevailing, poor light conditions. There is also the tremendous advantage of being able to ascertain when deer are in the immediate area. Tracks age rapidly during a snowfall and relatively fresh sign should put the hunter on the alert.

Now the whitetail is in no great hurry to cover ground. It feeds along an irregular course of travel and is led to the left or right by tempting browse, sampling but never deciding which shrubbery yields the most satisfying mouthfuls. Occasionally, it pauses to look about but its jaws continue working with the same rapidity as those of a nibbling rabbit. The whitetail is now thoroughly engrossed in its feeding. If ever the deer lets down its guard, this is

the time. The whitetail's response to an intruder on its domain now is one of surprise rather than of fear.

Even when the snowfall has ceased sometime during the night, if the temperature remains mild, deer will often browse throughout the next day if they have not been harassed. Fresh, fluffy snow and heavy air on a mild day always make for good stillhunting.

High winds affect the temperament of all game, and animal life now becomes nervous and retiring. Strangely enough, the whitetail often leaves its bed to forage or lounge about in the dense thickets during the days of extremely high winds. Some hunters prefer such days, with or without snow, to all others for stalking their game. The woods are noisy with falling branches, and both deer and hunter are handicapped in the game of hide and seek.

There is one strong point in favor of the hunter, however. He knows that his quarry is confined to the thickets, and he need not be greatly concerned with any normal walking noises he makes. Likewise, he cannot expect to be warned of any commotion a flushed animal makes. During a heavy blow, it is surprising how even a big, wide-racked buck can crash through a dense growth and not make a sound above the atmospheric disturbance.

The hunter, moving on any slight angle into the wind, need only search the lowland thickets. Tracking is not especially favorable now, for the whitetail does not travel a great distance across the country. The animal depends mostly on its vision for protection, and the hunter, likewise, depends on his eyes for finding his quarry. The hunter can ill afford to divert much attention to following tracks or making a stealthy approach.

Though the hunter can come within good shooting range of his target, the animals are now extremely fidgety and they do not hesitate to scamper off at the sight of an intruder. If snow is absent, there is little contrast in the woods, and each swaying clump of reeds, nodding ferns, or persistently rustling leaves of scrub oak stops the hunter's searching eyes. He will have some difficulty in discerning his game now, especially on a cloudy day and, by evening, his strained eyes will need more rest than his legs.

Heavy snowfalls come pretty often in the deer country of some of our Northern states—much too often to pass them off as unseasonal or unusual. The resourceful individual had best learn to cope with this condition. It calls for a brand of hunting that is not easily accepted by any but the more avid outdoorsmen.

An early, deep snowfall changes the habits of a whitetail overnight. It no longer makes those long treks from its bedding grounds to distant feeding spots. The rigors of oncoming winter are impressed upon it, and it expends energy rather niggardly. In fact, it will now most likely refuse to stir from its bed for a day or two after the big fall, as though it were unwilling to face its new, harsh world. Even before the snow has ceased falling, it has abandoned the open country and receded to the environs of its winter quarters. As the animal becomes uneasy with hunger and the snow becomes more acceptable, it moves about more freely. But the open field and edge country are largely neglected and the deer crossings along the roads are now virtually abandoned.

Only a stout-hearted and stout-legged hunter accepts the challenge of deep-snow hunting. Yet, it can prove very effective for the hunter acquainted with the country. The whitetails are in the back country but not necessarily a great distance off the road. The local lads who get around a bit know where the animals set up their winter quarters—the areas of swamps fringed with young evergreen growth, a mixture of thicket and evergreens, or any dense thicket usually along a flat or creek bottom. These are not the big deer "yards" given so much prominence, but they are the winter quarters of most of the animals in the North Country. Often, such spots are just off a road with little or no sign to indicate that a small band of animals is there.

It is likely the deer have not been shunted about lately, as few hunters are in the field and the animals feed somewhat securely in their new, snowy habitat. Most sere, short growth, so often mistaken for deer, is now covered and the hunter can easily spot the outline of his game. The whitetail is not all agog for leaving its recently established home at the appearance of a hunter, and its glassy stare at the intruder in its sanctum seems to reflect a measure of defeat in the animal. Even when roused from its bed, the deer hesitates a bit before plunging into deep snow and, after a short spurt, it prefers to stop and glance over its shoulder to reappraise its plight. The hunter willing and able to take deep-snow hunting in stride can put in some pretty good licks while the fair-weather boys are shaking their heads at the roadside drifts or are watering down their disappointment at some crossroads bar.

The stillhunter can adjust his strategy for most weather conditions as well as for the type of terrain he will hunt. There is, however, the extremely difficult situation of stalking the elusive whitetail on a relatively quiet day when the air is crisp and the snow is crusty, or when there is no snow and the forest floor is sere and the leaves underfoot crunch noisily with each step. Now, big game is as alert and spirited as it has ever been, and the stillhunter is probably licked. If ever he wants to take a day off from the chase, this is the most opportune time.

The undaunted and confirmed solo hunter will still play the lesser odds for, after all, he feels pledged to his lone role and he takes the days as they come. There is always the happy thought that he might chance upon a careless buck with his mind completely absorbed in romance, and this could be the day for such an anomaly in whitetail behavior.

Deer reduce their daytime activity to a bare minimum now, and they have a distinct advantage over the hunter by virtue of their roused sense of vision, hearing, and smell. An old buck, especially, likes to bed down just below the crest of a hilltop to command the view of the valley before him, with any light breeze coming from above to his back. Resting on this strategic point, he is as secure from his stalker as he will ever be. Every movement within his scope of vision is quickly picked up by his farsighted eyes. His ears constantly bend to catch any sound, and his nostrils are now quick to detect the faintest scent. It seems that much of the whitetail's response to possible danger stems from the animal's peculiar temperament rather than from any existing situation. The weather affects his moods, and his moods rule his fears.

THE DOWNHILL STALK

An effective method of stillhunting is the downhill stalk, especially when you are familiar with the terrain and have some idea where the deer are.

Even on a windless day, there are normally slight air currents moving over irregular terrain that can carry your scent to a deer's sensitive nostrils. These currents are especially pronounced on sloping ground where air tends to rise toward the summit. You may not notice the slight currents, but a deer resting on the slope above can easily pick up your scent. This situation can be turned to your advantage if you make the stalk downhill.

A deer in its bed is naturally positioned to watch the area below for any threat to its security. The animal is likely to select a bed site that offers protection from the ground above—perhaps below a low-branched evergreen or a fallen tree. If you are above the deer, you have a definite advantage.

You can move more quietly and smoothly down a slight grade than you can up the same slope. And, from the higher vantage point, you can better survey the area below and pick the best course for the stalk. This does not necessarily have to be directly down but can angle left or right.

You can pause frequently to search the grounds below during the descent with no concern that your scent will reach the deer. And there is no cause for heavy breathing, which so often hampers a hunter's sense of hearing in the stillness of the woods. As the gentle air movement carries your scent away from the quarry, it also helps mute any slight noises made by a careless step or the brushing of a twig. I have been able to surprise whitetails bedded down under evergreens at ranges as close as 60 feet away by simply idling my way down a mountainside.

Not all whitetail country lends itself to this type of stalk, but it is certainly available in much of the West, as well as the East. And, to a lesser degree, it can be found in other areas such as the slopes leading to river bottoms or the rugged mountains of Michigan's Upper Peninsula. Wherever you find such an opportunity to hunt this way, don't pass it up.

This article is excerpted from the book Whitetail, *by George Mattis. The book is available from Outdoor Life Books and is supplied to bookstores by Van Nostrand Reinhold.—The Editors.*

Deer Tactics That Really Work

Edited by George Haas

Deer hunting is a parochial sport. New Englanders can't understand why Southerners call deer hunting with dogs a sport. Southerners wonder how New Englanders manage to shoot deer without a pack. Then there are the stand-and-drive hunters of Pennsylvania, who can't use hounds because the law forbids it, and so use human drivers instead. And that state's law provides that there shall be no more than 25 men in the same gang. Twenty-five men! To a Western mule-deer hunter, that sounds like an army. Most deer hunters, though, have great respect for the lone stillhunter—

the man who goes out by himself and kills a deer simply by stalking. He doesn't use hounds or human drivers. He moves carefully and hunts quietly. Therefore, he is a stillhunter, a word we inherited from England, where noblemen hunted deer with hounds, horses, and hunting horns. The commoner—forbidden to kill the King's deer on pain of death—hunted very quietly indeed. On the following pages, four very successful practitioners talk about their methods. What they say might well spell success—wherever you hunt.

DOG DRIVES

Andy Dann

At 34 years of age, Andy has 30 years of experience in hunting deer with dogs. His father and grandfather began taking him along to deer camps on hunts in the Florida Everglades when he was 4. Assisted by his wife, Ellie, Andy took his daughter Andrea to deer camp

when she was 11 months old. Andy is a real-estate salesman in Tallahassee and a member of the Pinhook Hunting Club, which leases 14,000 acres. The land straddles the Georgia/Florida border on the edge of the Okefenokee Swamp. Most of the club's 30 members own beagles or larger hounds such as Walkers, redbones, and black and tans. The two state deer seasons total about nine weeks of hunting.

Our 30 club members, their families, and guests average about 20 bucks a season. The land is hunted by someone at least five days each week. The only way to move deer from the swamps is to drive them with hounds. We use packs of five or six dogs. We can put together four packs of beagles and five packs of larger hounds.

I'd no more hunt deer without dogs than I would hunt quail without a pointer. In this part of the country, the cover is so thick you have to use dogs to put the deer out. It's so thick that only good dogs can do the job because they have good scenting ability. A human driver wouldn't know it if a deer were standing 10 feet away.

I'm one of the huntsmen—I plan the drives, jump the deer, and try to stay with the pack while it is pushing deer. I have to be in really good shape when the season opens.

Six to 10 standers do all the shooting. We stop about eight drives out of 10 because the dogs are pushing does. Swamp bucks are tricky. When one is jumped by the hounds, he often heads for a bay-head where he knows there are does. When the dogs break out the other side, they're pushing a doe and the buck has vanished.

To plan a drive, we use aerial photographs that show logging roads, timber, water, and clearings. Starting a buck is the most important thing. The old ones have a home range of about a mile. We usually know where they are and have some idea of their escape routes. We've hunted some bucks for three seasons without getting a single shot.

At midnight or even as late as 5 a.m., I drag the sandy roads with leafy saplings tied behind a pickup truck to brush out old tracks. There's no hurry to start a morning hunt and we begin running the roads about 7:30 to scout for new tracks. I don't believe there is a sure way to tell a buck's tracks from a doe's. We usually assume that large prints are made by bucks.

My old beagle, Dixie, saves us a lot of time. She has a hot nose and she won't follow an old scent. Most of the big hounds will. I put Dixie down and let her test the tracks. If she wants to chase, I pick her up.

Usually, by the time we have located a good track, the deer are bedded. We check the wind and study the maps and try to figure out where the deer will go. Then I go and put the standers on their stations. Most of them are experienced and will stay where we put them until I get back after the drive. It's a lot safer that way.

Then I drive back to the tracks and put a pack down. Big hounds push deer hard in a fairly straight line. Beagles are slower and the deer may circle. You post your standers accordingly. Little hounds can't drive a buck out of a swamp.

When a buck outfoxes us, we may put standers in two different areas the next time. The first group may divert the buck to a gunner in the second.

It's hard to see deer sneaking through dense cover. Hounds make a lot of racket and the tendency is to look for the deer just ahead of the pack. The buck could be sneaking along several hundred yards ahead of the dogs. You almost never see the whole deer. The first sign is usually a flick of movement.

TRACKING

Larry Benoit

Larry Benoit hunts exclusively for trophy bucks, and he does it by tracking. A 52-year-old carpenter who lives in Duxbury, Vermont, he has taken 41 big bucks in 43 years.

I hunt trophy bucks—ridge runners going 200 pounds or better. I'm a tracker. So was my dad; so are my sons. We learned to do it that way in the Northeast Kingdom of Vermont, the same territory where my Iroquois ancestors hunted.

To knock down a mossyhorn every year, you have to think like a deer, know the country you are hunting, and be able to read deer sign.

Understand the patterns and habits of the buck you're after. In my territory—Vermont, New Hampshire, and Maine—the big trophy bucks are found on the remote ridges, in the hidden basins, or deep in the swamps. I know that most bucks travel in a circle and bed down every day near the same place.

Most deer hunters are scared silly of becoming lost. When you're on the track of a big buck, you can't worry about anything except that deer. If you fear the woods, you won't get him. Scout the land. If there are hills, climb them and remember the view—the basins, the ridges.

A big buck leaves deep prints. The deeper they are, the heavier the buck. From experience, I can look at a track and know whether the deer goes over 200 pounds. Is it a buck? It's not dewclaw marks that make the difference. Does have dewclaws, too. A heavy animal is usually a buck, although there are some big does. A buck tends to drag his feet and, in several inches of snow, you can see the drag marks. Bucks are built differently in the hips than does and a trophy buck's tracks are slightly staggered. He swaggers when he walks. A doe minces along. A doe creeps under low brush but a buck with a big rack walks around it. A buck will dribble in his tracks but a doe lets it fall in one spot. A buck in rut, of course, rubs his antlers, hooks brush or branches, and paws the ground. If there's snow on the ground, you can often spot tine marks in a buck's bed or where he's been feeding. In deep snow, it's sometimes hard to know in which direction the deer is going. It doesn't take long to scrape down in the snow and feel the hoof indentations so you can tell which way the front end of the hoofs were pointing.

Read the sign carefully when you're on the track. If you spooked the buck, he will run, lope, and stride. If so, sling your rifle and haul out after him. When he slows down, you slow down. When you see the deer track meandering and notice that he has been feeding on buds or pawing, sneak along slowly and peek. Don't make any mistake—that buck is up front, getting ready to bed down.

You have to use your eyes. Forget the wind. It blows four ways at once in the woods. The buck has smelled you if you spooked him and has been living with your scent. Just keep peeking and you may see him peeking at you. Unravel the woods with your eyes, step by step. If the tracks show the buck is close, it doesn't matter if it takes you 10 minutes to go 10 feet when the deer is browsing. He might be just ahead in his bed. Shoot well and quickly, and the trophy is yours. If you tracked him alone, it is *really* yours.

STAND & DRIVE

Sal Urso

Sal is a 43-year-old businessman who lives on Staten Island, New York City. He was raised in Brooklyn and started hunting deer when he was 17 by simply buying a surplus military rifle and a license, and driving upstate to a place that "looked good." He had never hunted anything before. Now he hunts with the Whitetail Sportsmen, a Pennsylvania deer club. He has taken a buck with the club almost every year since he started in 1960, and he is known as One Shot Urso.

We usually have 16 to 20 hunters and divide into two teams by pulling names out of a hat. The teams alternate standing and driving but, after you shoot a buck, you drive for the rest of the week. Our drivers maintain a fairly straight line when pushing through the woods. The orders are not to shoot to the left or right, but a driver can shoot back behind the line if a deer shows there. Standers do the same. We always know precisely where everyone is, and the ground is rolling, so it's easy to make sure there's high ground and not a man behind any deer you shoot. It's the only safe way for us.

Our team captains are very experienced and know where to post the standers and send the drivers. Our deer are so evenly cropped every season that really big racks are scarce. Almost everyone will settle for any legal buck.

I'm often asked why some club members get a buck almost every year while some haven't fired a shot at a deer in years. Our drives are slow so the deer often come through at a walk, but a hunter can spook a buck away from his stand. Don't move on stand once you have settled. First, kick away ground debris to form a bare patch; then you won't rustle leaves or break a twig if you do have to move.

Deer spot movement right away. Don't scratch, wipe your nose, smoke, cough, or belch. A deer's hearing is very good.

On dry days, you'll mostly hear the deer coming before you see them. The buck is usually a bit behind does and fawns but he may be alone.

Not moving can be almost painful after half an hour or so. If you can't stand it any longer, get it over quickly. Stretch, move all your joints, but don't make any noise. If you have a cold or sore throat, put a cough drop in your mouth.

Photo by Erwin A. Bauer

If a buck comes straight at you, let him come so close that he can't get out of range or into cover before you shoot. Deer can't see well straight ahead at close range, because their eyes are on the sides of their heads. If he heads between you and the next stander, left or right, it may be best to raise your rifle quickly and shoot for the near shoulder at an angle before there is any danger to your neighbor.

Another way is to let the deer go between you and the next man and shoot behind the line. Once the deer is 15 or 20 yards past you, he can't see you move. Angle the bullet in just behind the last rib. There are lots of people in our woods during small-game season, so the deer don't pay much attention to human scent.

Most of our deer are shot by standers, but some of us get quite a few while driving or even when walking to or from a stand. Go as slowly as kickoff time for the drive allows, and make sure you pause and stand still now and then. Look at the cover carefully and listen. I try to spot the white parts of the deer. If there's no snow on the ground, that's about the only white in the woods. I also look for the tops of their backs and the bottom line of the body. Most things in the woods are vertical or angled. Much of a deer's body is horizontal. I also look for the deer's glistening eye. If the woods are dry, it really stands out. Most of the time I don't really know what I see or hear first, but if I think a deer is there, I freeze and really stare. Then it's a matter of using your rifle just as though you were on stand. I really don't like to take running shots. It's possible to get a standing shot even on a drive if you can move quietly.

I use a lever-action rifle so I can fire a quick, second shot if I need it. I use a 2.5X-to-8X scope. I keep it on 2.5X when I'm driving because of the wider field. I set it on 4X when on stand, unless I have a long view, in which case I use 6X. If I spot a standing deer and can't see horns, I wait till the deer looks away and then jack the scope up to 8X. With that magnification, I can sometimes pick out antlers by looking between the twigs.

THE LONELY STILLHUNTER

Murry Burnham

Murry is a 47-year-old Texan who has been hunting whitetails since boyhood. As co-owner of Burnham Brothers, makers of game calls, both his life and livelihood have been bound up with hunting for many years. To him, the whitetail is the aristocrat of all game. He has hunted them from the Great Lakes region, to Nebraska, to Mexico, and has tried just about every possible hunting method. Long ago, he became convinced that the classic challenge is lone stillhunting. His uncanny ability in this, the toughest deer hunting method, is already legend.

I believe the big whitetail is the wariest of all game animals. That's why getting out among the deer on your own two feet to hunt a trophy buck is the ultimate challenge. I don't always win the match.

Stillhunting success requires a lot of patience. It's a mistake to say a stillhunter walks. Walkers succeed only by accident. You have to train yourself to move in slow motion—one step at a time, never out in the open, never skylined—even in the timber, always screened while you move by some outline-breaking cover, always placing each foot with great care so you don't clink rocks, break sticks, rustle dry leaves.

When I have a strong hunch a deer is nearby, I've often spent an hour moving 100 yards.

Because I move so slowly, I select my hunting areas very carefully. I look first for ample sign, especially buck sign such as rubs and scrapes. When I find them, I know a buck is probably within half a mile. I prowl edge cover at dawn and dusk. During the middle of the day I stick to thick bedding places. A successful stillhunter must be totally concentrated and an acute observer with all his sense. He must see the smallest sign, and that includes broken grass stems. I often listen intently while holding my breath. I even *smelled* one old buck.

In cover, I never look for a whole deer. I duck low and look for legs under the branches. I try to catch the glint of sunlight on an antler or the flick of an ear. Once, I bagged a bedded buck at short range because he had licked his nose shiny.

Still, overcast, damp days are best. If there's any air movement at all, note it well and walk into it, or keep it slanting across your front. If you can keep a low sun behind you, it will shine in the deer's eyes and prevent him from seeing you. But make sure you don't throw a long, moving shadow. Many hunters think they must have tracking snow. I prefer bare woods because the hunter doesn't stand out so sharply against a dark background.

"Quiet" clothing is important. I wear wool or soft cotton. I carry binoculars. In dim conditions, they gather a lot of light and compress depth tremendously. I intently glass timbered bedding areas at close range, moving the glass in slow motion. If I see a deer nearby, I often keep the binoculars in front of my face to camouflage it until the animal's attention wanders.

Even in dense cover I use a variable scope. With a good one, you can pick out the smallest shooting hole in brush.

Home Sweet Home For Whitetails

By John Weiss

When a hunter looks back over his years of pursuing whitetails, he can recall a few, isolated incidents when he saw so many deer his eyes widened in disbelief. Likely as not, he had been hunting long and hard without even catching a glimpse of buckskin, then he innocently pushed into a particular area and suddenly deer were all over the place.

I'll never forget the time I was stillhunting on our farm in southern Ohio. For two days, I had tramped along oak ridges and adjacent hollows that were choked with honeysuckle. I hadn't seen a thing. My enthusiasm was at a low ebb as I began sneaking through a cedar thicket, and what happened shortly thereafter can only be described as bittersweet. Up ahead, a sleek forkhorn stepped into clear view. Without hesitation, I fired and dropped him in his tracks. I instantly regretted my impulsive behavior because, at the shot, two other deer rushed from the cedars and bounded away, both of them handsome eight-pointers.

Another time, I was sitting in a tower stand in Texas where the intersection of two trails was worn trough-deep. During the first two hours of waiting, five different bucks wandered back and forth and I jokingly began to think it would be a good idea if someone installed a traffic light at the crossing. By letting so many deer pass, I knew I had pressed my luck to the limit, so when one of the bigger animals reappeared I squeezed the trigger and collected my winter's supply of deer meat. Strangely, however, my partner Jim Bielchek, who was stationed only half a mile away, later bemoaned that all he had seen were a couple of coyotes.

Photo by Leonard Lee Rue III

There are two logical explanations for these types of experiences in which hunters commonly go a long time without seeing action and then unexpectedly find themselves attending what seems like a deer convention.

A stark reality of deer hunting is that success often hinges upon luck, especially upon being in the right place at the right time. But even luck has its limits, and a hunter who consistently gets a buck each year can attribute a large measure of his success to knowing how to find concentrated sign and having the patience to wait for the deer to show.

All of this is based on understanding the home range of whitetails, particularly during the rutting period. Radio tracking studies conducted by biolo-

gists have shown that, no matter what the state, a majority of whitetail bucks live out their lives within an approximate 640-acre, elliptical-shaped area that usually is 1½ miles long and one-half mile wide. Yet, within this home range, there is a core area where the buck spends up to 90 percent of his time.

Core areas average less than 40 acres in size. They are deer magnets of the highest order because they possess the right combination of food, water, and security cover that a mature whitetail prefers. And, because this is where a buck spends the vast amount of his time, it stands to reason that his signs—tracks, droppings, browse lines, beds, rubs, and scrapes—will be more prevalent in the core area than anywhere else.

It also stands to reason that, because these special areas are not plentiful, numerous bucks may be drawn to each one. Consequently, the deer congregate in rather close quarters.

Therefore, it's easy to understand how a hunter can leave boot tracks across miles of acreage without seeing a deer, then suddenly and unwittingly enter a core area and be flabbergasted to see deer everywhere.

A good example of this phenomenon occurred once when my hunting friends and I were staging drives in western Kentucky's Land-Between-the-Lakes. For our maneuvers, we had four different tracts of terrain staked out, each of which was about 75 acres in size and could be driven in an hour's time. During the first drive, a single doe was pushed to the hunters waiting on stand. During the second drive, nothing was seen and, during the third drive, a spike buck popped up but was not shot at. On the fourth drive, however, three impressive bucks showed themselves and two were taken.

But that is not the end of the story because, the following day, we made drives through the same areas. Again, the first three drives proved uneventful but, on the fourth drive through the same rolling brush country that previously gave up two bucks, two more splendid bucks were taken.

Obviously, there was something very special about that particular area. Likely as not, it was the bucks' home turf, a hotspot where the core areas of numerous bucks overlapped. But exactly what it was that made the place so overwhelmingly attractive, compared to nearby and apparently similar areas, is not certain. That is of no consequence, however, because it is extremely difficult to pin down which types of food deer may prefer in certain areas, the type of security cover they may choose or any of the other nuances of their behavior. We no longer even bother to try to second-guess what's going on in the deer's minds. We simply let them come out and tell us what they're doing and where, by reading the signs they've left behind.

The easiest signs to dope out are those made in conjunction with mating activities, but there is an unusual twist to this that many hunters are unaware of. Scientists firmly believe that times are changing and that, nowadays, during the rut, bucks no longer behave the same way they did when our fathers and grandfathers pursued them.

Decades ago, when deer were far less plentiful, bucks going into rut immediately began expanding their home ranges, traveling widely in search of does in heat. In fact, this so-called "search and find" mating behavior is typical of most animal species when their population levels are relatively low. Some mysterious cosmic signal or genetic instinct tells them to disperse over a wider-than-usual range to ensure maximum reproduction.

In the case of whitetails, the effect of this natural law resulted in the toughest stand hunting imaginable. When does were few and widely scattered, an amorous buck might have his line of scrapes strung out across two or more miles of countryside. And, because it might take him two or three days to check his scrapes, hunters quickly became discouraged and eventually abandoned their posts.

Although it's pure speculation, I believe it's this type of deer behavior that caused our fathers and grandfathers to disdain "stump sitting" and, instead, stillhunt and track deer. Even now, though, there still are a few pockets—usually in Northern states where there are vast tracts of unfavorable deer habitat—where deer populations are not very high and local hunters characteristically pray for opening day to reveal a new skiff of tracking snow.

Fortunately, however, almost everywhere else the opposite situation exists. In a majority of states, deer numbers have soared. During the past 20 years, Ohio's whitetail population has more than doubled and in Texas, Alabama, and many other states it has almost tripled. The result of any mushrooming animal population is that it greatly restricts the species' travel tendencies. Not only do deer begin adopting much smaller home ranges, but the competition arising between substantially increased numbers of bucks causes them to tenaciously cling to far-smaller mating territories. Consequently, this has fostered a generation of hunters who choose to wait on stand and who, not surprisingly, are seeing greater success than their stillhunting and tracking counterparts.

On countless occasions, my hunting partners and I have seen evidence of this increased homebody tendency of whitetails. On our farm, certain bucks are often sighted several times a day in virtually the same place. It's clear they are staying put. With bands of resident does sometimes numbering a dozen animals or more, there's no reason for bucks to scour the countryside in search of mates.

There are two important keys to finding, and then capitalizing on, the core areas used by whitetail bucks. The first is to be willing to do as much scouting as possible and the second is knowing what to look for.

Studies have shown that any particular whitetail buck will make approximately 105 tree rubs each mating season. Biologists say rubs are signposts a buck creates to establish his presence in the area. At the same time, the rubs proclaim his ranking in the local pecking order. Further, once a rub is made, a buck may pass through the same area at a later time, but this is only happenstance, not intentional.

It has been learned that younger, inferior bucks typically rub saplings of small diameter while dominant bucks usually rub larger trees, sometimes up to six inches in diameter. New evidence, however, has shown there are sporadic periods of heightened sexual activity when a buck's hormonal secretions reach such intensity that he may thrash his antlers against both large and small trees and even on bushes, shrubs, and fence posts.

As a result, finding rubs on only small-diameter trees is usually an indication of a small buck working the area. Yet, if you find large-diameter trees that have been damaged or a combination of large and small trees in close proximity to each other, the discovery almost foretells a trophy buck is in the area.

Keep in mind that bucks make an average of 105 rubs each rutting season. This makes it imperative to disregard the occasional rubbed tree one finds during scouting missions. Instead, be on the lookout for what biologists refer to as "concentrates," places where dozens of trees have been demolished. This is the best indication that you are in a buck's core area.

During Ohio's 1982-83 hunting season, my dad and I were looking for a place to install one of several portable tree stands on the "back 60" of my Morgan County farm. After pushing through a thornapple thicket and finally emerging on the other side, our eyes almost popped out of our heads. There before us, on a tag alder hillside, were rubs almost everywhere. Big trees, little trees, even multiflora rose bushes looked like they had been attacked by a runaway lawnmower.

After counting 62 rubs in an area only one-quarter acre in size, we searched nearby areas for scrapes. Later, after finding a good ambush location, we flipped a coin to see who would get the stand. As it turned out, luck was on my side and by 8 a.m. on opening morning, there was a 10-point buck hanging in my barn. The important thing to note about this experience, however, is that the buck was not taken right where we found the many antler rubs but more than 200 yards away.

Finding concentrates of rubs is only the first accomplishment of an enterprising hunter. A buck generally makes the rubs in clusters roughly surrounding the perimeter of the core area as a type of "marking behavior" to warn other bucks that this is his turf. Because rubs are not returned to on a regular basis, but instead serve as boundary markers, the hunter's next task is to find scrapes so he can decide where to place his stand. In other words, "before you can find the king, you have to find his castle."

During the rut, whitetail bucks make an average of 27 scrapes that serve as mating invitations to receptive does in estrus. The vast majority of a buck's scrapes—and the ones he revisits most frequently—

are, of course, within his home range but concentrated more heavily within his core area. They're also customarily made in groups of two to five.

Consequently, finding a lone scrape somewhere is not likely to reward a hunter with venison unless he's very lucky. Most likely, the hunter has found a peripheral "secondary" scrape and now it's necessary to continue searching for places where there are a series of scrapes located within close proximity to each other. How close is close? Well, if I found several scrapes somewhere, I'd have to find another group within 100 yards, then still another series within 100 yards of that, to get even mildly excited.

As with antler rubs on trees, most biologists agree that it's possible to examine the size of a scrape and make an educated guess as to the size of the animal that made it. Young bucks that have not yet reached sexual maturity generally make small, half-hearted scrapes only six inches in diameter. Middle-aged bucks ranging from 1½ to 3½ years old, which usually carry six to eight-point racks, construct scrapes averaging 12 to 18 inches in diameter. And the biggest trophy bucks sometimes produce scrapes that are so awesome the sight almost makes your hat lift off your head.

I'll never forget the pin oak tree my hunting partner, Mike Starkey, once found in Potter County, Pennsylvania, where, beneath an overhanging limb, a buck had made a scrape about 20 inches in diameter. A day later, Mike returned and found the buck had begun work on a second scrape several feet away from the first. Two days after that, he returned and almost had a seizure at what he discovered. The buck had pawed away at the ground separating two scrapes until he had made one giant scrape about six feet in diameter.

Even better, Mike found seven more scrapes in the immediate vicinity, leaving no doubt as to where he would be perched at first light on opening day. Later, at that same spot, he tagged the biggest deer he'd ever taken. Although the buck's body weight was only 180 pounds, the massive non-typical rack missed qualifying for Boone and Crockett recognition by only eight points.

Another way to examine a scrape and guess the size of the buck that made it is to look closely for antler drag marks. After trampling the ground, pawing away grass and sod to bare soil, and rub-urinating on the scrape to deposit tarsal gland scent, bucks usually drag their racks through the muddied dirt. If the distance between each tine drag mark is at least five inches, with each drag furrow measuring at least half an inch wide, you can be certain you've found the courting grounds of a very fine buck.

The importance of finding a buck's core area cannot be overemphasized. As elementary as it sounds, scouting before the season, especially during dawn and dusk when deer are most often about, is an excellent starting point. If you spot a buck, there's a good chance you are seeing him somewhere within his core area. A subsequent study of the terrain may reveal concentrated sign such as heavily worn trails connecting a series of scrapes. After that, you can decide on the best location for a stand or blind.

It's also wise to use maps because you can cover far more ground. You can eliminate from consideration pieces of land that are not likely to prove productive, too. If your map does not possess grid marks, draw your own with a ruler, with each square representing one-quarter mile. Then explore the areas covered in each, one by one. Move along quickly until you begin to find sign, then slow down and search the area methodically to determine whether the sign is only incidental or whether you've entered a buck's core area.

It's very helpful to mark on your map the location of each sign you discover—particularly rubs and scrapes. Sometimes the irregular nature of the landscape can make it quite difficult to figure out the significance of rubs and scrapes found here and there. But if you've marked them on your map it's often possible to see how the pieces fit together like a jigsaw puzzle, giving you a clear idea of how the buck is using the area.

Several other tips are also worth mentioning. Through radio telemetry studies it has been learned that the core areas of whitetail bucks are many times—but not always—delineated by natural or man-made boundaries such as wide streams, rivers, lakeshores, superhighways, and similar features that deer are reluctant to cross on a regular basis. Consequently, if there's a swath of real estate bordered on two or more sides by such obstacles, it's worth checking out in detail.

You should also be continually on the lookout for does. If you're not periodically spotting them, chances are the animal population in that particular region is not high. This means bucks will also be fewer in number and those that are present will be traveling great distances from one day to the next.

Another tip is to avoid doing your scouting too early. Many hunters make the mistake of starting earlier than they should in an attempt to learn as much as possible. Although their intentions are admirable, they are often self-defeating. The time when fall blends into winter is a period of transition in which whitetails make adjustments in their home ranges and core areas in accordance with changes in food availability, cover density, and growing competition among bucks for prime mating grounds. It is best to wait until about a week before the deer season opens, then cram in as much scouting time as possible.

On occasion, anyone may luck out and find himself collecting a handsome deer because he happened to be in the right place at the right time. But if you want to consistently tilt the odds in your favor, remember that whitetail bucks spend 90 percent of their time within a 40-acre core area. This means there is no other whitetail hunting strategy as effective as going after deer on their home turf.

Hunting North Woods Bucks

By James E. Churchill

I nocked a four-blade broadhead, hung the compound bow on a forked stick pushed into the ground near my right hand, and relaxed on my shooting stool. Evergreen limbs arranged to form a ground blind concealed me. A deer trail ran along a hogback ridge 25 yards downwind from the blind. My watch said 3 p.m., and I expected a fat forkhorn to pick his way down the trail at about 4:30 because I had timed him and knew he was as regular as the sunset.

At 4:20, I slipped the bow off the forked stick and got ready. First, a bald, brown head came into view as a doe walked and fed about 40 yards away. From the corner of my eye, I saw the forkhorn walking briskly down the trail. I released the arrow and the buck swapped ends and trotted back down the trail.

Surprisingly, the doe paid no attention to the string noise or the antics of the buck, but she did bound away when I went to look for blood. A few yards down the trail I found it—a good trail that I followed. Half an hour later, I found the buck where he had fallen while apparently trying to get through a cut-off treetop.

North Woods bucks don't come easily, and each of the deer I have taken in northern Wisconsin was the result of hours spent scouting and studying their habits. Although I hunt in the North Woods with a bow, the methods I employ are useful to gun hunters, as well.

North Woods whitetails live north of the farm belt and they are an especially hardy and wary breed. The weak strains have long since been culled out by waist-deep snow, tree-splitting cold, scarce food supplies, and relentless predators. I believe a North Woods buck older than 2½ years is the most difficult North American hoofed animal to bag when he is hunted on a one-to-one basis. This is doubly true when the hunter uses a close-range weapon such as a bow.

Yet, like other animals, they do have certain weaknesses that make them vulnerable to a dedicated hunter. I have studied these animals for years and have discovered that they are much more restless than is generally believed. When the deer population is less than five animals to the square mile, they forage far and wide, nibbling clover in an abandoned farm field today, aspen leaves in a recent cut-over area tomorrow, and pond weeds the next day. Each area may be a mile apart. However, they move in a large circle through home territory and they almost always move counterclockwise.

Once the typical deer movement in a certain area is known, it is useful year after year because the herd continues to follow the ancient trails as long as the forest cover remains. Thus, the hunter can build permanent blinds or go quickly to a certain ridge or wooded marsh point and be fairly certain that deer are using it.

During a typical year, there are long stays in certain areas. For instance, two or three does stay around our 15-acre pond and marsh from the time they drop their young in May until about July 1 when the fawns start feeding on their own. Then they move in a huge circle that seems to take them about a week to complete. However, when the acorns start falling, most of the does, fawns, and small bucks stay close to the oak trees that are bearing the heaviest mast crops. The largest bucks don't seem to

Photo by Leonard Lee Rue III

trouble themselves by moving away from their favorite backwoods clearing or swamp fringe just for acorns but, when the rut starts, they suddenly develop an interest in any place where does congregate.

The rut starts in northern Wisconsin in early or mid-October and, when it does, the bucks change from docile, retiring creatures to earth pawing, tree-gouging, belligerent rounders that grow more interested in breeding and less interested in food. Beginning about the second week in November, they only snatch a mouthful now and then.

The bucks patrol their territories on a more or less continuous basis, making scrapes to mark their home areas and attract does. Most scrapes are located under an overhanging branch that the buck chews and rubs with the glands that are located under his eyes.

Deer have other external glands on the insides of their hind legs above their feet, between their toes, and on the insides of their hind hocks. They all play a part in the mating game. The hock glands provide scent for the scrape because the buck humps his back and urinates over them when he is standing in or near the scrape. A receptive doe interprets this scent as belonging to a prospective mate and, when another buck scents it, he knows he is in a buck's territory and is risking combat.

To the hunter, a scrape means that a buck is probably in the territory and he can start looking for more scrapes to determine the deer's regular patrol path. Don't make the mistake of hanging all your hunting time on one scrape. I once watched a deep, active scrape for 14 consecutive days for two hours in the morning and two hours in the evening and never saw the deer that made it, even though he did visit several times when I wasn't there.

I believe the most effective way to hunt scrapes is to determine the pattern that the buck has laid out. Then watch a trail somewhere along the route where natural obstructions guide the deer into a certain path whenever he comes along. This may be a trail along a ridge, a skidding trail through log-cutting debris, or a wooded point in an open marsh.

Finding the pattern is not difficult if you realize that most scrapes are made on old logging trails and roads, in treeless draws, at the edges of small clearings, or on bare ridgetops. If the territory isn't familiar, probably the best way to find the pattern is to study the topographical maps. After you find and analyze a few scrape patterns, you can almost read them on a topographical map without actually walking the entire route. They are almost always laid out in a circular pattern around a huge marsh, a big hill, or a series of clearings—or they follow unused logging roads.

Once the scrape pattern is established, the hunter has a rough idea of where the buck is going to be, but it is important to realize that the deer will move along this route by staying in the thickest cover available. He might only come out to visit the scrapes after he has circled downwind to check for the scent of does, predators, human beings, or a bigger buck.

Tales of foolish, rutting bucks abound and, when he is trailing a ready doe or has just left one, a buck sometimes does lose his caution. But if you base your tactics on a buck doing something stupid, your life-time score is going to be very low. It's better to hunt as though the deer never lost his usual caution. Make as little noise as possible, wear camouflage if you are a bowhunter, and keep free of disturbing scents.

North Woods bucks are paranoid about human scent. Farmland deer see or smell people nearly every day but a North Woods buck may encounter only one or two people in a year's time—except during the firearms hunting season. Human scent scares the heck out of them. Two examples come to mind. Standing on the rim of a ravine last season, I watched a good buck coming down from the opposite rim. When he got to the bottom of the ravine, he came to the tracks I had made. He would not cross my foot scent trail. Instead, he changed directions nearly 45° and headed south instead of in the easterly direction he was taking. A doe and two fawns ran back the way they had come when they smelled my scent on a leaning treetop that I had touched on my way to a stand.

Yet airborne scent is the most common culprit. When conditions are just right, a deer can wind 100 yards away, probably much farther. I try to counteract this by staying as scent-free as possible. This can get very involved but, from a practical standpoint, your clothing should be clean and should be hung outside the house for at least two hours before you hunt. You should keep clean by bathing with unscented soap just before the hunt.

Don't eat onions, peanut butter, or other foods with strong odors, or carry highly scented foodstuffs with you. Brush your teeth with salt instead of toothpaste, don't chew gum or tobacco and don't smoke while hunting or just before. Don't overeat or drink alcohol, and try not to work up a sweat getting to your stand.

Even so, stay downwind of the buck's expected approach route. Sometimes this isn't as simple as it seems. Wind currents swirl around trees, around and over hills, and tumble in all directions through ravines. In some places, it is virtually impossible to find a location that won't allow scent to be blown in many directions. A buck coming into these air currents will catch your scent and probably sneak back the way he came, even though the hunter has every reason to believe he is downwind.

I have found a simple little device that will save a hunter from using a tree stand in such places. I fasten a perforated metal can to a 10-foot pole and put a small fireworks smoke bomb in the can. Then I light the bomb and hold it up at the height of the tree stand. The direction the smoke takes will tell me exactly where the air current is going. If it swirls in all directions, I change my location.

Cover scents are widely used today and I believe skunk odor helps to some extent, especially if it is fresh and placed downwind of the hunter. Scents used for trapping predators also seems to be effective cover-up agents. However, these scents don't smell the same as a live predator and, after awhile, the deer may catch on. Besides, deer avoid some predators, too. In my area, the smell of a live coyote causes fawns and does to quickly move one-quarter to one-half mile away from the source of the scent. I have seen this happen many times.

Even after a hunter has found a trail on the buck's scrape route, the buck may abandon the trail to keep track of some nearby doe. Because leaves cover up the tracks in a short while, the hunter may spend several days watching an unused trail. I handle this problem by carrying a small rake with me. Every morning when I'm done hunting, I rake the leaves off part of the trail and rough up the top layer of soil so that any passing deer will leave easily seen tracks.

An amazing amount of information can be gathered in this way. By checking the raked portion several times during the day, you can tell about what time deer are coming by, how many deer are using the trail, in what direction they are going, and their approximate size. I used this trick to set up an ambush for the deer that I told about shooting at the beginning of this story. Of course, if the deer abandon the trail entirely you become aware of that too.

Some hunters tie thread across a trail. By checking several times a day, they find out if deer are using the trail and at about what times. Carrying this one step further, there are electronic devices that also record the time a deer comes by. They stop the hands of a clock at the correct time. These devices are most useful if you don't care what sex or size deer you hunt.

After you have found out where a buck is coming by and at what times, and you have correctly located your downwind tree or ground stand, you will probably have to call on the greatest asset a deer hunter can possess—patience. I have talked to many deer hunters who have said they couldn't stay in one place because they were too active by nature. They seemed proud of that fact. Patience is a virtue very few men possess, but it can be learned and most good hunters have worked on it for years. Staying silently in one place results mostly from having confidence in your location. If you believe a deer will come, you can keep your mind on hunting and avoid thinking about unfinished work, next month's mortgage payments, car troubles, or whatever. Focus your mind on what you are doing until you know for sure that any second a North Woods buck will step out of the cover and offer a shot.

In some areas, the combined bow and gun season on North Woods deer starts in September and extends into the tree-popping cold of late December. The deer herd may yard up sometime after the gun season opens. This provides a very good opportunity for the late-season hunter to score if he can locate deer concentrated in a sheltered yard. Trails and feeding areas can be easily pinpointed in the deep snow because they are heavily used. Dress warmly, wear white clothing if you are bowhunting, and aim carefully. A late-season deer is a real triumph if you have been hunting all season without putting meat on the table.

How To Hunt Farm Bucks

By Monte Burch

Standing at the aluminim gate to my field, I stared dumbfounded at the dangdest sight ever. A huge buck was munching contentedly on my alfalfa.

Nonchalantly, he tossed his head up occasionally to watch the passing trailer trucks and cars on the busy highway not 40 yards from where he stood. But when the gate rattled in the wind, he saw me.

For a second or two, we stared at each other. Then he turned and bounded down into the draw toward the creek bottom. It was two days after the close of the Missouri deer season.

"Where were you a couple of days ago?" I muttered to the disappearing whitetail as I continued my search for a strayed calf. The small four-pointer I had collected several days earlier already seemed insignificant as I daydreamed about meeting the big buck during the coming year.

Farmland bucks aren't new to me. Even before I bought my Ozark farm several years ago, I had hunted the farmlands for bucks.

The rich prairies, woodlots, and fields of soybeans, corn, and milo hold concentrations of deer that many hunters don't even dream of.

When I was a kid growing up in central Missouri, a deer sighting was a rare occasion. I can remember Grandma cranking the old wall phone to tell everyone in the neighborhood about the lone doe that was walking a hedgerow between the neighbor's fields. All the folks got pretty excited in those days. Today, it's a common sight to jump a buck or two from those same prairie fields while hunting for quail.

Deer are extremely adaptable critters, and they have discovered that the small woodlots, creek bottoms, and even sparse, clumpy prairie spots in the middle of a huge expanse of grain can be a real haven. Many times, these deer literally live in the farmer's backyard. In some areas, deer can eventually become so overpopulated that they eat the farmer out of business.

Several years ago, we had this problem in our county. A certain part of it became overpopulated with deer that literally stripped soybean and alfalfa fields at night.

This was before Missouri started a zone system of management. The bucks-only rule just wasn't keeping up with the exploding deer population. In fact, whitetail deer are so adaptable that I have often seen farmland bucks in places where you'd swear you couldn't hide a jackrabbit. Yet deer not only adapt to the sparse cover but also seem to thrive on the rich grains available in farm country.

One good reason for hunting farmland bucks is that they're usually bigger, healthier, and fatter than other deer. A buck living off soybeans, corn, and alfalfa won't starve during the winter, regardless of how bad the weather gets. His woods cousins, on the other hand, may run into hard times, especially if the mast or acorn crop is bad one year. Most farmland bucks will have a minimum of gamey flavor because their diet consists principally of grains, rather than wild foods and nuts.

Perhaps the most important aspect of farmland buck hunting is that it's economical. You don't have to drive great distances. A close examination right near your home may reveal some mighty good hunting areas.

That's what I found several years ago when I lived in Kansas City. Almost within sight of the skyline in both Kansas and Missouri was some fantastic deer

A whitetail buck stands alert in an Ohio farm's meadow. Photos by Erwin A. Bauer.

hunting in the overgrown belts of farmland surrounding the burgeoning suburbs. Although some of this land was closed to gun hunting, a bowhunter had a literal haven of deer to choose from. By contrast, a pilgrimage of deer hunters leaves the city on the eve of each season, headed for faraway hunting grounds.

Hunting for farmland bucks is somewhat different from hunting the backwoods. Farmland is privately owned, and getting permission to hunt on it is your biggest challenge. Deer hunters can be problems for farmers and ranchers. I know. I've been on both sides for many years.

Most hunters respect other people's property and are safety-conscious about the direction in which their guns are pointing. But it only takes one accident to cause shudders to the farmer or rancher who must be out in the field looking for a calf or repairing a fence during gun deer season.

Nevertheless, responsible hunters will probably be welcomed by farmers who have deer depredation problems. Check with your local conservation commission for an idea of what parts of your state or county might be good prospects. The local officer in those areas can name places to start your search.

If you're serious about finding some good private

hunting land, start well before the season. Don't drive up to the door on the first day and ask if you can hunt the woods behind a farmer's house.

Local chambers of commerce can often give you advice on where to look for hunting areas. Orchard owners are another excellent choice for some prime deer hunting leads. Deer can literally wipe out small fruit trees. Also check Christmas tree farms.

A drive through the country should give you an idea of what type of hunting is avilable. But let me repeat: Make sure you do this well in advance of the season.

Once you've spotted good-looking hunting areas, stop and ask the farmer or rancher. Quite often, if you can prove you're a responsible hunter, you can get permission—perhaps even on land that is posted.

If you don't get permission, there may be several reasons. One that few hunters realize is that often the farmer and his family like to hunt. Most farm youngsters are devout hunters. Many farmers also have friends who hunt their property.

If you do get permission to hunt, remember that it's a privilege. Treat it with all respect. You might consider giving something in return to the farmer or rancher. Probably it will be the first time a hunter has offered, and the landowner will be pleasantly surprised.

In some areas, farmers are deluged with hunters who want to hunt. A farmer can get so tired of hunters pounding on his door that he just starts saying no to everyone. When I first bought my farm, I'd get a dozen calls or have guys showing up early Saturday morning wanting to hunt my back 40 for squirrels. I just gave up and said no to everyone. Eventually, as I made friends in town and decided who would be responsible, I began to allow hunting by a few. This kind of situation is even more common in prime deer hunting country.

When you do get permission to hunt, it's a mistake to think that taking farmland bucks is easy. In fact, they're sometimes much harder to collect than their cousins in wilder areas. A trip to north Missouri several years ago revealed this truth to me with frustrating clarity.

We were hunting on a friend's farm north of the Missouri River. This farm had almost no cover at all. The woodlot in one back corner, separated from the rest of the farm by a small creek, consisted of huge white oaks amid intensively grazed brush. The area looked like a well-kept city park.

The rest of the farm consisted entirely of row crops. Milo, the main crop that year, was interspersed with some soybeans. Around part of the farm were typical hedgerows and a latticework of small draws that wouldn't hide a Brittany on point. Yet for two weekends, four hunters pursued a huge buck around and around that open country without seeing anything but glimpses of white as he used the rolling farmland to continually elude us. The farmer's son and I ended each night of the season sitting around a warm stove plotting the next day's strategy. But we were outwitted each time.

On one trip back to the house after an unsuccessful drive, we saw where the huge deer had lain under a multiflora rose at the top of a draw, allowing us to walk within a few feet of him. Then, after we had passed, he'd turned and sneaked on his belly down the draw. The story was easy to read in the soft gumbo mud of the gulley.

A week after the hunting season, the farmer saw the huge buck almost in his garden patch, along with a couple of does. Just such a sighting a few weeks before the season and the resulting phone call from my friend had been the main reason I'd hunted the place.

I have seen whitetails do some mighty unusual things, but the most unusual one happened a few years ago. I was driving over to help a neighbor and saw two bucks standing on a pond dam about 100 yards from the house. The season was well under way, and I had already collected my buck. But I stopped the pickup to watch them, as I always do. Both heads came up with a snap, and the bucks stared at me for a second. Then they turned and streaked for the nearby woodlot. The smaller buck cleared a barbed-wire fence with an easy bound, but the bigger buck, with a huge rack, merely went under the fence at a dead run.

Amazed, I went to examine the fence. The bottom strand was barely a foot off the ground, yet that old buck went under it as if it weren't even there. He never even faltered a stride of his streaking run. No blood or hide was on the fence, just a few gray hairs.

Probably the biggest mistake most novice farmland hunters make is to hunt the fields. Your first scouting trip around the edge of a grain or alfalfa field in prime deer country will reveal enough deer tracks to give the most stouthearted hunter the shakes. Obviously, deer use the fields, often quite heavily. Unfortunately, though, most of this action happens at night. I have frequently seen deer bedded right in the middle of soybean or alfalfa fields at night. Then, just before daylight, they slip back into surrounding timberland and stay until evening. An old buck loves cover, especially the heaviest. He will use it to every advantage when traveling from his feeding field to his bedding area.

Granted, many deer are killed on opening morning while they graze in fields. But, as soon as the first shot is fired, the deer usually stop using the fields except at night. This pattern is especially prevalent during a full moon. Exceptions do happen, though, and I have taken a couple of deer by taking advantage of these exceptions. Small, hidden fields deep in wooded hills such as those found in the Ozarks are usually used during the entire season. Many of these are less than 100 yards wide and snake along the bottom between the ridges. Such a field usually has lots of nearby cover and easy escape routes, so the deer continue to frequent the place throughout the season.

An excellent method of hunting these small fields is to stillhunt them, slipping quietly into the edge of the field and following the contours of the valley,

watching the field sides closely for feeding deer. The deer can be hard to spot in fields such as standing milo or corn. Quite often, these small, isolated fields will occur in a chain that follows the steep Ozark ridges. So, if you quietly hunt from field to field, you can get some mighty good results.

Most farm and ranch country, however, is much more open. I have never had much luck stillhunting in open farm country. Stand hunting seems to be the best and most other farmland hunters I've talked with agree.

Location of the stand is, of course, a most important aspect of farmland hunting. Select a spot that allows you to watch the edges of a field and that is also near a main deer route to or from the field. Don't be confused by the number of tracks. Careful scouting will reveal a main route for entering and perhaps one for leaving the field.

Locate your stand off to one side of these major routes. If possible, locate two stands, one on each route. Then, depending on time of day, wind and so on, you can use the better site.

One problem is that farmland bucks can see you even more readily that you can see them. Many times, they lie watching the field. I have seen where bucks have lain up in a woodlot and watched me walk to my stand.

If possible, choose a stand that offers you good cover going to and leaving it. I recommend locating the stand about halfway between feeding and bedding areas. There you'll have a chance to see deer relatively later in the morning and earlier in the afternoon.

I've watched deer take as long as an hour to cover a quarter of a mile from their bedding area to their feeding field, stopping to nibble on a branch or blade of grass, or to play, running a few yards, then turning and chasing each other. They seemed to time the trip so they hit the edge of the field just at dusk.

Sometimes the biggest problem connected with stand hunting in open country is how to build a stand. An elevated deer stand is probably the most effective but sometimes you find no suitable tree. In flat, treeless farmland, your only choice may be to hide in the standing grain or a clump of bushes. One farmer I know takes his deer each year while sitting on a comfortable camp stool in a clump of multiflora roses that border a 200-acre bean field. Sometimes, hay bales are left along the edges of a field and these make an excellent blind.

If trees are available but are too small or weak to support a stand, a lightweight, leaning stand is an excellent choice.

Most of the routes deer travel in farm and ranch country are well established. Once you determine the routes used *during the season,* you can count on them to be used year after year—unless the habitat is substantially changed, say, by bulldozing.

When you plan your next deer hunting trip, consider hunting the farm or ranchland close to home.

You not only save a great deal of travel expense but you may also find some great hunting.

13 Do-It-Yourself Tree Stands

By Richard C. McGee Jr.

Take a look into the treetops during deer season and, chances are, you will see a hunter peering down at you, feeling quite comfortable and confident with his bird's-eye-view vantage point of the cover below and several hundred yards around. It's also likely that, while you're busy marching through the woods chasing deer to other hunters, that tree-stander will be busy marching back to camp—buck in tow.

There is no denying a tree stand's effectiveness when hunting whitetails, bears, wild hogs, turkeys, and other game, but modern-day hunters are faced with a choice in stands—portable or permanent. Each has distinct, desirable traits.

In some cases, you cannot choose which tree stand to use. But, where they're legal, permanent or semi-permanent build-it-yourself stands offer an inexpensive, secure shortcut to putting venison in the freezer.

There are many and varied ways to erect these permanent stands and to gain access to them from the ground. All of these platform ideas and tree steps can be built and erected with basic tools, inexpensive materials, a little know-how, and time.

All these stand types are commonly used by hunters and, if properly constructed, there are no problems with structural failure. Hunters, though, are cautioned to build and use these stands at their own risk.

For more information on portable and permanent tree stands, tree steps and how to hunt from these elevated platforms, send for *The Original Tree Stand Handbook*, available from Sportsman's Studios Publishers, Box 10830, Jacksonville, FL 32207.

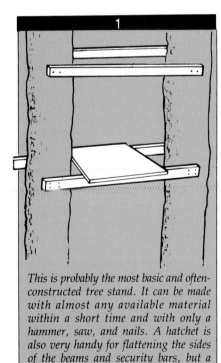

1

This is probably the most basic and often-constructed tree stand. It can be made with almost any available material within a short time and with only a hammer, saw, and nails. A hatchet is also very handy for flattening the sides of the beams and security bars, but a good hunting knife will do the job with a little more time and effort. Always use the largest nails possible without splitting material.

2

Typical "I" bolt and washers. 3/8" x 4" bolt with 1" eye

Typical turnbuckle

This is the basic ladder tree stand constructed of 2x4 and 2x6 material with three-quarter-inch plywood platform. It can be carried by one hunter for a considerable distance so long as thick brush is not encountered. Considered to be a semipermanent stand, it can be moved easily within the hunting area. This stand can be left in the deer woods and used for several seasons if built with treated material. The recommended height of this ladder stand is eight to 10 feet. As shown in the illustrations, a turnbuckle may be used in conjunction with a screw-in tree step to gain an even-stronger lockup.

3

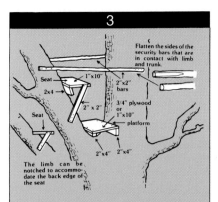

Flatten the sides of the security bars that are in contact with limb and trunk.

Seat

2x4

Seat

1"x10"

2" x 2" bars

2" x 2"

3/4" plywood or 1"x10"

platform

2"x4"   2"x4"

The limb can be notched to accommodate the back edge of the seat.

This is a very comfortable and stable tree stand, but it must be built with the seat on a limb that comes off the trunk at an angle so that the hunter can avoid excess reaching. If the limb angle is too low, the seat can be extended to make sitting and standing convenient.

4

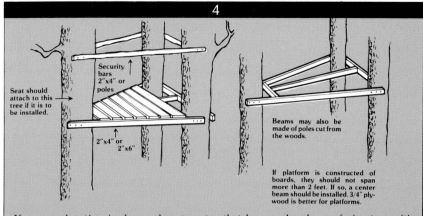

Security bars 2"x4" or poles

Seat should attach to this tree if it is to be installed.

2"x4" or 2"x6"

Beams may also be made of poles cut from the woods.

If platform is constructed of boards, they should not span more than 2 feet. If so, a center beam should be installed. 3/4" plywood is better for platforms.

If you are hunting in deer or bear country that has an abundance of pine trees, it's easy to find three trees growing near each other in a triangle. That's the best place to build this spacious tree stand. The same principle could make an even-roomier stand if built using four trees. To make for comfortable waiting, it is best to erect a seat against one of the trees. A milk box could also be used, but standers should be sure to use a safety belt in conjunction with any tree seat or stand.

5

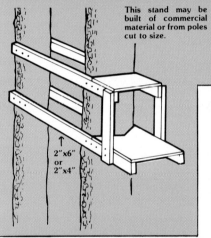

This stand may be built of commercial material or from poles cut to size.

2"x6" or 2"x4"

The seat situated on the outside of the tree makes this a favorite among bowhunters who need a greater range of movement to shoot effectively from a tree stand. This stand is quite simple and is easy to construct. It may be assembled on the ground and hoisted into position and can be either nailed to tree trunks or lashed with a nylon rope. Nails offer added security. Bowmen can also nail a bowhanger to the tree to avoid fatigue from holding the bow.

6

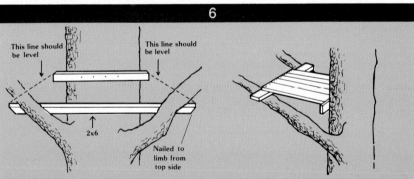

This line should be level

This line should be level

2x6

Nailed to limb from top side

No more than a platform constructed in a tree, this stand can be placed in almost any tree that has large limbs that grow out from the trunk at approximately the same level.

Support beam against tree trunk should be level with beam across limbs. This, too, is ideal for the bowhunter. Platform should be made from 2x4 or 2x6 material.

7

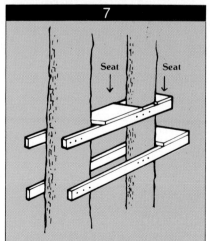

Seat

Seat

If you would like to take a companion or photographer into the stand with you, try this variation of tree stand number 5. Simply nail a piece of plywood across the support beams for a comfortable seat. Steps can be nailed between trees.

8

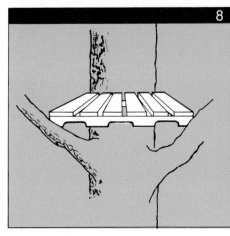

This is basically the same type of stand described in number 6, except the platform is an average loading pallet available from any warehouse. It may require an additional board or two to form a platform with solid footing, however. You will probably need a hunting buddy to help you get it up into the tree and into position. The use of a simple pulley attached to a limb of the trunk can make the hoisting job quite a bit easier. Again, secure the platform with nails.

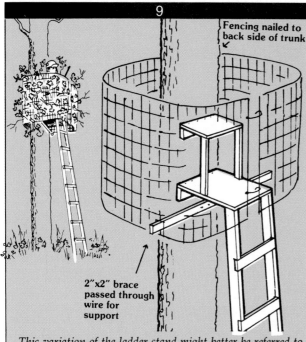

9

Fencing nailed to
back side of trunk

2"x2" brace
passed through
wire for
support

This variation of the ladder stand might better be referred to as a tree blind because, as the illustration shows, it is a combination of a stand and a blind. In many hunting situations, you must, by necessity, be located in an open area. If there is no other foliage to break up your shape, you can be easily spotted by approaching game. A 2x2-inch brace passed through the chicken wire at its bottom is essential for added support. Camouflage fabric can then be secured to the wire mesh. Limbs and branches are less-expensive camo.

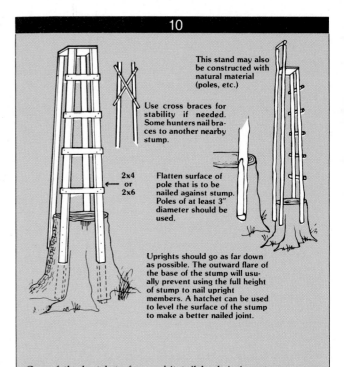

10

This stand may also
be constructed with
natural material
(poles, etc.)

Use cross braces for
stability if needed.
Some hunters nail braces to another nearby
stump.

2x4
or
2x6

Flatten surface of
pole that is to be
nailed against stump.
Poles of at least 3"
diameter should be
used.

Uprights should go as far down
as possible. The outward flare of
the base of the stump will usually prevent using the full height
of stump to nail upright
members. A hatchet can be used
to level the surface of the stump
to make a better nailed joint.

One of the best bets for a whitetail buck is in cut-over areas with a profusion of treetops scattered about. This kind of area provides good bedding cover and food. The tree-stump stand is the perfect stand to use in this area. A stump of about 18 inches is a minimum size on which to erect a stand, while 24 to 36 inches is ideal. The stand should be no higher than 10 feet and builders should be sure to use large nails to secure uprights to the stump. Inspect before using a second season.

11

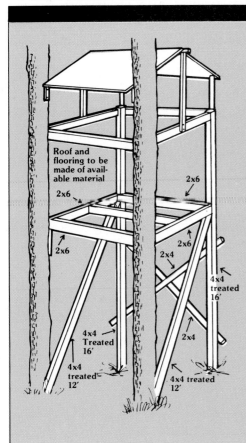

Roof and
flooring to be
made of available material

2x6

2x6

2x6

2x6

2x4

2x4

4x4
treated
16'

4x4
Treated
16'

4x4
treated
12'

4x4 treated
12'

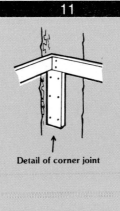

Detail of corner joint

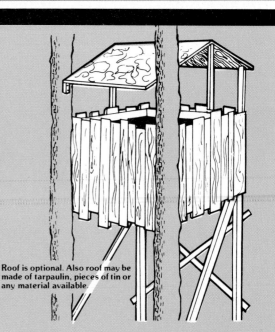

Roof is optional. Also roof may be
made of tarpaulin, pieces of tin or
any material available.

This elaborate permanent blind is one that must be built months before the season to allow the game an opportunity to become accustomed to it. This type of stand is best placed near the edge of a field or wide-open territory where long-range shooting is possible. It is best to build this stand with the beams fastened to the inside of the trunk. This helps keep it from being too obstructive. The inset shown in the middle is the corner joint in detail. This stand becomes a virtual tree house when enclosed with boards. A roof can also be added—constructed from wood or tarpaulin.

12

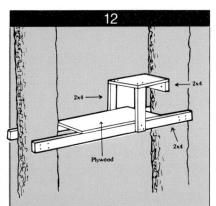

This structure can be previously assembled and secured in the tree with nails or nylon rope. When the hunter is shooting in the direction he is facing when seated, he can use the tree as a rifle rest. Security bars are recommended, but bowhunters may find them a hindrance and should use some sort of safety belt.

13

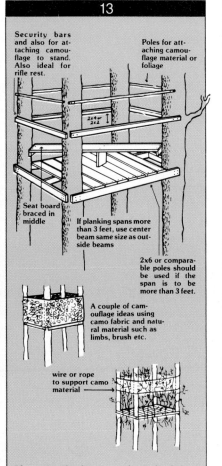

If you're lucky enough to find four evenly spaced trees, you may want to build this stand. Notice the seat board running diagonally across the platform. This will enable the hunter to face any direction while seated and still have adequate room to stand and move about the platform.

TREE STAND STEPS

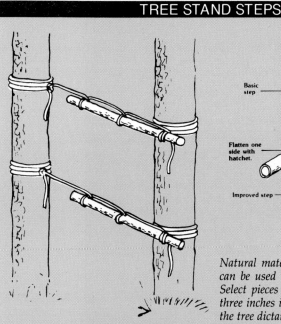

There are various ways to gain access to permanent tree stands. These steps are made with the use of one to two-inch thick poles. You will also need a length of one-quarter to one-half-inch rope for each step. If rope is tied securely to tree trunks, it will slip very little when applying your weight. When climbing, place foot close against tree and on ladder rung.

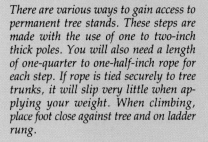

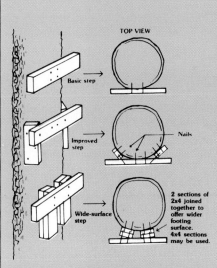

Aside from large nails or spikes driven into the tree trunk, the most simple step is a length of 2x4 or 2x6 material, from 12 to 24 inches long, nailed to the tree trunk. When erecting these steps, be sure to use strong lumber and be sure that the nails penetrate deep into the tree trunk. And never build a stand in a dead tree. The higher up you climb, the safer the steps must be.

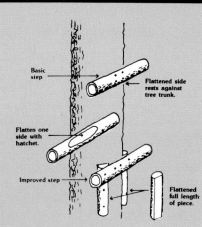

Natural material, usually small trees, can be used when building tree steps. Select pieces for steps that are two to three inches in diameter and as long as the tree dictates. Use a hand saw to cut the sections you'll be using and use an axe to flatten the side that fits against the tree trunk. With a bag of nails and a few tools, you're ready to build a basic stand and basic steps with material that is at hand.

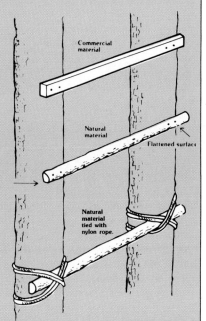

This is also a well-known step to hunters who build tree stands. When using this type of step, always place foot as close as possible to tree, thus putting less stress on the center of the span where it is more likely to break. These steps are very adaptable to being secured to the tree with rope. The steps can be built with natural or commercial materials.

Solving The Whitetail Puzzle

By Kathy Etling

It's opening day and there you sit, high in a tree with a perfect view of several scrapes and rubs. The ridgetop setting is perfect. The wind is right.

"It won't be long now," you think to yourself as the sun slowly rises.

Just a few hours later, the first nagging doubts begin to tug at the corners of your mind. Where is that buck? You know you did everything right. You scouted this trail right before the season and found tracks all over it. The scrape in that clearing literally reeks of a buck in rut.

But still no deer. So you wait. And wait. And wait some more, while a barrage of rifle shots echoes through the neighboring hills. Deep inside, you know that every deer in the woods is several miles away by now. You can picture the deer clustered together chuckling at all the fool hunters skulking through the forest hoping to rout them out.

Sound familiar? Every whitetail hunter has had a similar experience. And it's these same hunters who have heard and read lots of things about deer. I know I did. And I began to wonder just how much of what I'd read was theory based on one-time observation and how much was backed up by solid evidence. The kind of evidence that might be provided by the supersleuths of the animal world—the behavioral scientists.

All state game and fish departments employ wild-life biologists. Very few, however, have the funding to conduct the kind of research most whitetail hunters would like to see. Therefore, the truth about rubs, scrapes and whitetail disappearing acts goes largely unknown.

Some recent research projects attempt to lay to rest many questions about the habits of whitetails. One such study, researched and written as a master's thesis by Don Autry of Illinois, *Movements of Whitetailed Deer in Response to Hunting Pressure on Crab Orchard National Wildlife Refuge,* monitors the everyday wanderings of deer. Deer were tagged, released, and then observed by researchers every day for seven months before, during, and after an intensive split-season hunt.

Georgia researchers Terry Kile and Dr. H. Larry Marchinton co-authored another study on the significance of rubs and scrapes. Terry is the game management chief for the state department of natural resources and Larry is associate professor of biology at the University of Georgia. Their study concentrates on the social role rubs and scrapes play in a whitetail's life.

A second Georgia study was conducted by Dan Marshall and R. W. Whittington of the state DNR's game and fish division. Their research included the use of radio tracking devices to confirm behavioral patterns of whitetails during several types of hunts.

46

There are certain territories within a buck's home range where the dominant animal will not allow others to tread. Photo by Leonard Lee Rue III.

Deer were exposed to varying degrees of pressure during the study.

Findings from these studies and others are nothing short of incredible.

RUBS

Every whitetail hunter knows what a rub is. But, to understand the role rubs play in a deer's life, it is necessary to first explain the term "home range." Home range is to a whitetail what a neighborhood is to a hunter. It's the deer's stomping ground and the place the deer is most familiar with. A whitetail knows every nook and cranny of its home range.

Home ranges vary in size depending on several factors: the deer's sex, age, the population of an area, and the carrying capacity of the land. A buck's home range is generally larger than that of a doe—sometimes twice as large. The bucks that range the farthest are most often the 18-month-old bucks. Older bucks

are more sedentary and their home ranges are smaller.

Don't confuse the term home range with territory. A buck won't defend his entire home range. He couldn't. He'd wear himself out because it is far too large. In fact, several bucks may share portions of the same range because of overlap. (Imagine several long, flattened ovals meeting at a common center and you'll get the general idea.)

Within each buck's home range, however, there are certain territories he'll defend. The buck rubs trees bare with his antlers to form visible signposts for these territories. Rubs act as warnings to other bucks. A rival buck may travel through this area without a fight if he assumes a subordinate posture. That is, if he keeps his head and tail down and refuses to look the dominant buck square in the eye. If the visitor fails to conform, a fight for dominance will follow.

Rubs are generally made on small, aromatic trees

There is some relationship between the size of a buck and the size of his rub or scrape. Photo by Gary Knepp.

with relatively smooth bark. Pine, cedar, shining sumac, and cherry are all favorites. Rub trees vary in size from pencil thin to about three inches in diameter. Rubbing begin one month prior to the onset of breeding, then declines dramatically before the rut actually starts.

Rubs are signposts in two senses of the word. The exposed wood of a rub acts as a visible indicator to other bucks, while a glandular secretion from between the whitetail's antlers serves as an aromatic signpost, according to Marchinton.

"This tissue contributes the buck's own individual scent to the rub and so increases the value of the tree as a signpost," he said.

Check the next rub you find. More than 75 percent of all rubs studied have hair other than antler velvet adhering to them.

There is some relationship between the size of the buck and the size of the rub, according to Kile.

"When I find a big, old tree rubbed high up on its sides, I can't help but get excited," he said. "But I've seen very small bucks rub very large trees and huge bucks tackle small trees."

So there's really no way to be sure if the rubs you find were made by a monster mossyhorn or a youngster.

Rubs are usually found in clumps and they crop up in the same general area year after year. But bucks rarely rub the same *tree* year after year. Rubs tell other bucks: "This is my breeding ground and I'll defend it if necessary."

SCRAPES

Scrapes, on the other hand, are a buck's way of communicating with does.

As Kile so aptly put it, "They're sort of like love letters in the sand."

Scraping parallels breeding activity and usually starts a month after rubbing begins. Scraping and breeding peak at the same time and then drop off

dramatically. All breeding activity is triggered by the release of a hormone from the pituitary gland. This is directly related to the decrease in the amount of daylight so, the farther north you hunt, the earlier breeding will occur.

Scrape locations are predictable. Look along established trails or old roads in fairly open woods. Grouping of scrapes, like rubs, is common. About 86 percent of all scrapes studied were beneath low-hanging limbs. The next time you find a scrape, locate the lowest limb and examine it closely for damage. Why? A buck will walk through the woods with his head up. When his antlers strike a limb it elicits a scraping response. The buck will then take the offending limb in his mouth and chew—but not eat—the limb. This limb is now marked with his scent. Of all scrapes studied, 66 percent showed such damage to overhanging limbs.

Next the buck will paw the ground with his front feet to create a bare spot. Then he'll squat over the scrape and urinate, often allowing the urine to flow over the tarsal glands located on the inside of his hind legs. Sometimes he will dig his antlers in the scrape, and horn the branch that triggered this response, as well, marking the limb once more. Although researchers have seen bucks defecating in scrapes, they believe this is just a random behavior in answer to nature's call and has nothing to do with the actual scraping response.

The buck will defend his scrape against other bucks. One aggressive buck even attacked a University of Georgia research biologist who wandered too close to his scrape.

When a doe finds such a scrape, she'll urinate in it and leave. The buck will check his scrapes periodically and, if he senses that the doe is in heat, he'll follow her with his nose to the ground sometimes grunting, snuffling, and even squealing.

All this may be common knowledge to most hunters: Everyone knows bucks make scrapes and then return to check them out. But there are some variables that will completely alter how you regard scrape hunting from now on.

First, don't look for that mythical line of scrapes that will lead you right through the woods. Scrapes exist in clumps. While strings of scrapes will occur occasionally for a short distance, there may sometimes be as much as a mile separating two of the same buck's scrapes with no additional scrapes in between.

Second, if a buck makes 90 scrapes and only five attract does, which do you think that buck will return to? Nothing succeeds like success. The buck won't waste his time visiting scrapes that don't attract does.

Third, human acitivity may frighten a buck off. How much activity is too much?

Ollie Torgerson of the Missouri Department of Conservation says, "Even one walk through the woods in an area generally unbothered by man may be enough to send a wary old buck fleeing to another part of his range."

Fourth, if the population is out of balance, and

Marchinton believes most are, the doe-to-buck ratio will be high. Social structures break down. The bucks continue to rub and scrape, but it loses its significance. The does want to breed and are coming in on their own.

As Kile so aptly put it, "The salesmen have as much business as they can handle, so why advertise?"

WHERE DO THEY GO?

The big question remains: Where do deer go? After opening day, it gets downright discouraging. Soon, hordes of disgruntled hunters lumber out of the woods mumbling, "There are no deer around here." Then they jump in their trucks to try their luck some place else. Farmers shake their heads and refuse newcomers permission to hunt on their land because they fear they might run off all their deer. But the facts are in. A home range is exactly that. A "home" range. Several independent studies have proven that, under ordinary hunting conditions, whitetail deer won't leave their home range.

Infiltrate their hollows and ridgetops, spread your scent all over the woods, drive them, stillhunt, stand hunt—it makes no difference. If a deer was there before the season, it'll be there during and after the season.

There are a few exceptions. If a deer is chased with dogs, for instance, it'll run as far and as fast as it can. One study observed a deer traveling 13 miles from its home range during such a chase. Yet that same deer went straight back to its home range as soon as the hounds were called off.

Another exception is if a deer is wounded. Several deer involved in the radio tracking study left their home ranges after receiving an ultimately fatal wound during one of the seasons. Shock is a possible factor in such cases.

Photo by Leonard Lee Rue III

Cultural knowledge is a third reason why a whitetail will leave its home range. When a doe finds a spot within her home range where it's possible to escape hunting harassment, a place such as a wildlife refuge or a large tract of posted land, she'll return there year after year, always taking a new generation of fawns with her. When these fawns grow up, even though they now have home ranges of their own, the memory of the safe place shown to them by their mother appears to motivate them to temporarily abandon their own home ranges in favor of the refuge. After a period of time, many deer share in this knowledge. It's a cultural learning phenomenon.

What does this mean to the average hunter? Take heart! Unless you're hunting quite close to a wildlife refuge, the deer are still around. And, even if you do hunt near a refuge, not all deer will share in the cultural knowledge—only those whose ancestors' home ranges were part of the refuge.

How big is a home range? It varies. The smallest home ranges belong to does with young and the largest to 18-month-old bucks. The actual area covered runs from 40 to 360 acres. While the study areas involved all had excellent carrying capacities, most home ranges aren't as large as is popularly believed. And, the greater the deer population, the smaller each individual home range.

Home ranges are most often elliptical or linear in nature, rather than circular. A deer will generally traverse its entire home range once every 24 hours using favorite paths and trails. Generally: That's the critical word. As whitetails adapt to human activity within their home ranges, they soon realize what constitutes normal human activity and what doesn't. If deer are used to finding human scent around fence rows or on certain paths, this isn't likely to scare them off. But, if you do your pre-season scouting in an area where there normally isn't much human activity, you're asking those deer to change their habits. Deer won't shift their home range but they may start concentrating in a different part of it. Although sign is everywhere, deer may not be.

To avoid scaring deer away from their usual haunts before the season, use the same precautions while you're scouting that you use when hunting. Torgerson advises hunters not to walk on their trails or even upwind of their trails.

"Be sure you're free of as much human scent as possible," he explained. "Use a masking scent if the rut hasn't started yet. Don't approach scrapes too closely; observe from a distance. And, travel quietly through the area you're planning to hunt."

If you have a stand to build, do it well before rubbing begins. Then get out and stay out. The deer will calm down, get used to the stand, and return to their normal areas of activity.

Trophy bucks are doubly hard to bag. Once the season starts, mature bucks move less than any other deer studied. They stick close to home. Does move about the most, but not the farthest. Bucks 18 months and older move the next-greatest amount.

The number of hunters and the types of habitat also affect how and when deer move. To keep deer moving in mature woods with little cover requires at least five hunters per 240 acres. To obtain a heavy kill requires 10 hunters per 240 acres. Even so, deer moving under such conditions are masters at evading humans. One radio-collared deer moved continuously during six days of moderate to heavy hunting pressure in open woods, and yet was sighted only once during that time.

More hunters per 240 acres are required to keep deer moving in areas of dense understory. If deer can find a good undisturbed hiding place within their home range, this is where they'll stay until hunting pressure lessens or they're disturbed again.

Once deer find such hiding places, they immediately decrease their daytime activity. This is a short-term adjustment to hunting pressure. In one study, the number of deer sightings decreased by more than 42 percent between the first and second days of hunting. And this figure was adjusted to exclude deer killed. The moral here is: Catch deer unaware and the odds are in your favor.

Before the season, deer will flush if you get within 50 yards of them. They'll bound off noisily in every direction. But, once a deer suspects the hunters are hot on its trail, it will become incredibly tenacious, holding tight until the hunters pass by.

Don Autry observed a doe for two consecutive hours during a particularly trying any-deer hunt at Crab Orchard National Wildlife Refuge in Illinois. The doe remained bedded in a heavily overgrown field even though hunters almost completely circled her position. Eleven shots were fired during this time and all were within 250 yards of the doe. Yet she held tight except for four minutes when she stood, pivoted around, and stared at another group of hunters. (Brush obscured her so she went unnoticed by the other party.) Finally, she rebedded in the exact same spot, alert but apparently undisturbed.

Marchinton told of a similar experience. He was tracking a radio-collared buck and knew exactly where the deer was bedded.

"I walked steadily toward him and he never moved a muscle. Finally, I got to go within three feet of his hiding place and still nothing. I slowly circled him but he hugged the ground. The only way that deer reacted to my presence was when I deliberately made eye contact. Then he flew out of there."

Only the eye contact succeeded in flushing this deer.

Facts about the whitetail are on the increase. Researchers will know more tomorrow than they do today. But, even if they could tell us every single detail about a deer's existence, the whitetail would still remain the premier big-game animal. Cunning, adaptability, and unpredictability combine with its incredible senses to make the whitetail a formidable adversary, and well worth the trek into the woods each and every autumn.

New Ways To Hunt Scrapes And Score

By Tom Opre

Bagging trophy whitetail bucks is only as difficult as finding the scrapes they make to attract does, right?

Many deer hunters have believed this ever since wildlife researchers confirmed the role that scrapes and rubs play in the whitetail's fall breeding process.

But researchers at upper Michigan's Cusino Wildlife Research Station now say that hunting near scrapes to help tag your buck is not so simple. After a decade of studying the social structure of whitetail does and fawns, researchers have found that locating scrapes is no certain route to locating bucks and improving hunting success.

Scrapes, however, are important in the world of whitetail deer. They are the chief signposts used by breeding bucks and does and can therefore be useful to the hunter. But the new Cusino studies show, for instance, that a prime-aged dominant buck may make dozens, perhaps *hundreds* of scrapes each fall—returning repeatedly to only a few—usually the ones that generate the most encounters with does.

Some scrapes are meant simply as warnings to lesser bucks—markings of a breeding area for a dominant animal.

But the dominant animal may not be the one that shows up while you're waiting near. Other bucks—along with almost every other deer in the neighborhood—will visit most of the scrapes they wander across, wherever they are found.

Even if the scrape is one of a very few "key" scrapes—ones a dominant buck uses repeatedly—the buck that made it may not check it for days. This is especially true if he's accompanying a doe on the verge of coming into estrus, the 36-hour period when does are receptive and breeding can be successful.

Sometimes, that big buck may check a key scrape several times in one day without coming close as 100 yards. Glandular scents of breeding does and bucks carry a long way on fall's breezes and will alert the big buck to any scrape activity in his territory.

So what does all this new information add up to? It seems to mean that scrapes are a useful but not very precise tool for hunters.

John Ozoga, a 20-year veteran of deer research at Cusino, believes that, as far as Northern states are concerned, only bowhunters can benefit from scrape hunting. Peak scraping activity tapers off drastically before gun seasons open in the North, he points out. In Michigan, scraping activity peaks in late October and early November—almost two weeks before the state's traditional, November 15, firearms season opener. Breeding, however, doesn't peak in Michigan until mid-November.

Southern states generally schedule their gun seasons earlier. In Georgia, for instance, peak breeding comes only two weeks later than it does in Michigan (according to a University of Georgia study by Terry Kile and Larry Marchinton).

But, by then, the state's gun season has been underway for almost a month.

"Scrape-making starts about two weeks before breeding begins, whether we're talking about Northern or Southern whitetails." Ozoga said. "The peak of scraping usually occurs nearly two weeks before breeding peaks."

He believes that, for hunters to fully understand where scrapes fit in, they must first acquire a knowledge of the rather complex social order of does.

51

Whitetails are part of a truly matriarchal society where life revolves around the most mature females. Bucks are kept outside this social order for most of the year.

"There's no question that whitetails operate mostly in two separate groups," Ozoga explained. "Does and their young do not associate with older bucks— those males 1½-years-old or older. The bucks, meanwhile, run together throughout spring, summer, and fall. The dominant ones tolerate younger males, except during the rut's most intense breeding activity."

It is the does' well-defined territorial habits that dictate where deer concentrations will be found each fall. Here is where most of the breeding will occur. Although does become highly active just prior to estrus and actively seek out bucks, they do not move to scrapes created in a helter-skelter fashion. Bucks purposely build scrapes in areas where several does' territories overlap (usually those of mothers and daughters). This, then, is where female activity is highest.

"There may be as many as 100 scrapes concentrated either where territories overlap, or in feeding areas or along routes does frequent going to and from feeding or bedding areas," Ozoga explained. "But less than half of those scrapes will be revisited even once by the buck that made them."

Ozoga, studying a herd of wild whitetails in captivity at the mile-square Cusino enclosure, began concentrating on does' social structure several years ago. Each individual deer was marked for recognition with large, numbered ear tags. Because the entire herd is live-trapped each February for blood samples, X-rays, and other data-gathering processes, researchers have been able to restructure the herd to meet whatever research requirements were set.

Ozoga has always been able to recognize each deer in the herd. He has known which fawns belonged to which does. And, as those fawns have matured and produced more fawns, he has come to recognize each individual in every new generation. He knows which older does are the matriarchs, which are the prime breeders (highly successful at raising their young to adulthood), and which ones are their sons and daughters.

"I feel we have confirmed here what European game managers have said about deer for years," Ozaga emphasized. "There are, within the female system, five distinct social classes."

Class 1 is composed of young female fawns. They don't often breed in upper Michigan or other northern climes.

But, farther south, as many as half of them will have matured enough to be bred by December of their first year. They remain close to their mothers and they tend, Ozoga discovered, to give birth to a higher percentage of male fawns.

Although scrapes are important to breeding deer, researchers have found that locating scrapes is no certain route to improving hunting success. Photo by F. Eugene Hester.

These young breeders make up Class 2, along with the 2-year-olds that are bearing young for the first time. They will set up housekeeping in a territory adjacent to, and often slightly overlapping, that of their mothers. One that is, nonetheless, distinctly their own—with their own precise 20-acre "safe" patch used each spring for actually bearing fawns. Each fawn-bearing doe tends to establish one of these patches, keeping all other deer—even earlier off-spring—from moving inside it for a period of nearly a month after fawns are dropped in June.

Class 3 is composed of 3-year-old does and those having their second fawns. Ozoga calls these deer the "dispersers." They leave their familiar range to establish their own territories farther away.

Class 4, then, is the group of prime-age animals, the 4 and 5-year-old females that are established in a new territory and are successful at rearing fawns. These are among the most prolific does. Rarely do they lose fawns through their own mistakes, although predation is always a problem. They will almost never desert a fawn—simply walk away and leave it to die—as Class 2 does will do when stressed.

Last in order are the matriarchs. These are does 6 years old and older who have perpetuated, by this time, a rather large surrounding clan of daughters. These older does are very productive, too, and their

A three-inch tree "rubbed" by a rutting buck.
Photo by Leonard Lee Rue III

ability to rear fawns does not wane with age. The "dry" old doe concept, Ozoga said, is just a myth.

"We have many records of does up to 14 and 15 years old bearing lots of healthy fawns," he said. "The only difference is that they, like the youngsters, tend to provide more male fawns."

Male offspring in these family groups are tolerated by their mothers and sisters only so long.

"The year-old buck hangs at the edge of his mothers' small fawning territory the next summer, along with his sisters," Ozoga said. "But as fall approaches, he's constantly hounded by his siblings and by other subordinate bucks within that range. So, he leaves to find and form a bond with another non-family group. It may be near or far away, but there he is received differently. He does have a chance to eventually become dominant—if he survives long enough."

The regrouping of the female clan members and their fawns with all the local bucks begin in late August, according to Ozoga's records. It intensifies in early September when the peak shedding of antler velvet occurs. Whitetails of both sexes may travel together then to feed and bed, and positioning for dominance among the bucks begins.

"Pre-rut socialization is vitally important in setting the stage for events to follow, namely a smooth and efficient breeding season," Ozoga observed. "It is my view that an open habitat is psychologically important for pre-rut activities like the female regrouping, buck display, buck combat, dominance hierarchy formation, and individual recognition of dominant bucks through sight and odor."

So, hunters observing whitetails in open hay or cornfields, come October, may mistakenly think that the only reason they're present is for food. But the does and fawns stand off to one side feeding while watching the bucks spar. They are learning which bucks will be dominant, Ozoga said.

He also firmly believes that, once strict male dominance hierarchies are established—usually by mid-October in the North—every buck's status is known and its odor and appearance recognized by all other deer in the area.

"All antlered bucks engage in some fighting in October," Ozoga stated. "Older and larger bucks may have been tolerant of yearling bucks early on, even sparring with them in a gentle manner in September. But, when the interactions become more serious in October, the results can be more violent, even among more evenly matched bucks. That's what I call fine tuning the system."

Antler rubbing against tree trunks, saplings, and bushes has been going on since September as the bucks busily scratch off velvet. But rubbing activity surges again in mid-October as the hierarchy of dominant bucks establishes itself. Biologists seem to agree that this rubbing is done mostly by dominant bucks as a display of their status.

"Remember that rubs are not only visual signs," Ozoga added, "but are also marked with the glan-

In upper Michigan, rubbing activity surges in mid-October as the hierarchy of dominant bucks establishes itself. Photo by F. Eugene Hester

dular secretion from the forehead. Therefore, such marks carry the specific odor of the maker, which is recognized by other males and females alike."

Data from Cusino shows that yearling bucks only made about half the number of rubs made by more mature animals. Occasionally, one dominant buck got carried away and accounted for nearly all the rubs in a given area.

When it comes to building scrapes, Ozoga said he suspects that often most of the scrapes are made by these same dominant bucks.

"So a hunter can be pretty sure that, if the area he is scouting shows scraping activity early in October and the scrapes are numerous, large, and well-constructed, it probably signals the presence of an older and larger buck," Ozoga said.

Most deer hunters are familiar with what scrapes look like. The "key" scrapes, though, will usually be oval in shape, three or four feet long by two or three feet wide. The ground will be well churned up, raked mostly with hooves but sometimes with antler tines. The scrape will normally be positioned underneath low-hanging branches that the buck

thrashes with his rack and even chews while he rubs the branches to cover them with glandular scents. Without this overhead branch, the scrape is probably not a serious effort, Ozoga said.

An earlier Gerald Moore and Marchinton study from Georgia showed that bucks urinate on scrapes. Does that find scrapes urinate on them also. Apparently, a doe in estrus can then be easily tracked from the scrape once the buck returns to find that scent. Ozoga's observations confirm what was recorded in Georgia.

He also emphasized that does become very active around the time of estrus and that "a paired buck and doe will frequently be seen as much as a mile from the doe's normal, small home range when breeding."

Earlier studies by Ozoga and Cusino Supervisor Lou Verme showed that does become 28 times more active than normal on the night prior to breeding.

"That's measuring our captive herd." Ozoga added. "In the wild, such activity levels would assure contact with a buck."

What that means, of course, is that, while the scrape serves as the loose connection between buck and doe for breeding, the pair often won't stay around a scrape once contact is made. A buck may even use a few scrapes located close to one another for a week or two and then suddenly put more emphasis on another set of scrapes not far away. Biologists have theorized that the bucks switch because the does have moved their center of operations slightly.

How then can scrapes be used to help you get your buck?

"Remember that, while the dominant buck is gone with a doe, other deer are visiting that scrape—including other bucks," Ozoga explained. "Some of our observations suggest that, while a top buck may not be willing to expose himself often in daylight hours, the lesser bucks will, and they can be found around various scrapes. The buck a hunter shoots off a scrape may not be the dominant one that made it. I suppose that some hunters are willing to settle for something less or else they are unaware that a bigger buck was involved with that scrape."

Lesser bucks are more than willing to use the major scrapes of bigger bucks. In fact, Ozoga says he has seen several examples of this behavior. If the larger animal catches a smaller buck on his scrape, he'll chase him off and redo the scrape himself immediately.

Dominant bucks use the same favored locations for scrapes year after year. Certain specific scrape sites may be re-established each fall for generations, Ozoga observed.

"The spots where many of these key scrapes are found have similar chracteristics, too," he said. "If they're in edge country, a mixture of woodlots or timber and open meadows or fields, the bucks seem to prefer edges where second-growth or high-canopy brush has blocked out sunlight and kept ground cover to a minimum.

"For Michigan and other Northern states, that might include second-growth aspen edges around a field, a place where the bucks find no grass beneath the overhanging limb, or it might be in sumac," Ozoga observed.

More open farm country often means bucks will build scrapes at the edge of open fields, under low-hanging oak or maple branches.

One of the Georgia studies listed tree types most often associated with scrapes there. Sweet gum was favored overwhelmingly, although red cedar, dogwood, and loblolly pine were popular, too.

The territory or home range of a dominant buck will often cover a square mile or two—some 1,300 acres at most. But bucks are capable of wandering over much larger areas if does are scarce, Ozoga believes, perhaps as much as four or five square miles. To cut down the unproductive area, Ozoga said, the hunter ought to do intense scouting during the hunting season.

"They should do it methodically, the way I did my studies," he suggested. "Every few days, I would make a precise circuit of the scrapes I had located, covering each one lightly with whatever nearby material seemed most natural: leaves, pine needles, or dried ferns. As I rechecked them, I would keep track of which ones had been reopened by the bucks."

Eventually, a pattern emerged, showing which scrapes were worth the hunter's effort. Assuming the hunting area holds lots of whitetails, productive scrapes would be the half-dozen or so that the larger bucks returned to again and again in their search for does.

With this knowledge about scrapes and the habits of deer, where should a hunter place his stand or blind? Ozoga shakes his head.

"It's a real crap shoot for the hunter," he explained. "Generally, my observations show that dominant bucks will approach a scrape from the safest way. Where hunting pressure is evident, that may mean coming upwind toward the scrape from positions in cover. Or the buck may just wander in across an opening, or pass by downwind and check it out without ever setting foot within 100 yards of the scrape."

For a gun hunter, uncertainty over the buck's approach route is not a big problem. A gun blind situated to oversee as much of the home territory around a group of active scrapes isn't that hard to position and should do the trick. Bowhunters must get much closer, however. Whether a blind or an elevated platform is used, it should be built within bow range of the scrape itself or on one of the several approach routes a buck might use.

Some hunters swear that afternoons are the best for scrape hunting, no matter where the blind is located. The does will become very active in late afternoon on the day before they breed, these hunters theorize. If the hunter is on stand by midafternoon, he should be there not only before the does, but before the bucks come to scent the does' presence. If a hunter arrives at dawn, these hunters say, he'll generally spook off both does and bucks working around the scrapes.

Conversely, if the area hunted is mostly private or is remote, with the prospect of competing hunters relatively slim, rutting activity may go on throughout the day. Hunters with this advantage can justify staying in their blinds all day. A buck may show up at noon.

The advice, obviously, is not precise—largely because whitetail activity is not absolute. Rutting activity between does and bucks is never all that predictable.

Deer hunting's best trophies will always go to the hunter who has the greatest ability to learn his hunting area—and who has the patience to spend long hours hunting it. Scrapes will help but they will not be foolproof. They are, however, a key to getting within range of a big buck.

Small Drives For Big Bucks

By John Weiss

Many deer drives are disorganized and they can be dangerous because of all the confusion. Sometimes, there are 20 or more participants. Half of them form a long line and then shout, whistle, and stomp their way through the woods in hopes of pushing deer out to the other half, who are on stands. I remember such drives not very fondly, because very few of them were successful, and many of them frightened the wits out of me.

The din of the drivers often enables the deer to pinpoint each of the drivers. The big, crafty bucks frequently sneak back through the line, skirt around the ends of the line, or simply remain hidden in their beds in heavy cover until the drivers pass and then bound off behind them. Sometimes, on the other hand, the noisy drivers stampede the deer so that they don't follow the familiar escape routes where the standers are posted. As a result there are very few shots and very few kills. Standers who do see deer that are running full out usually miss.

Even a blind hog finds some acorns but, compared to really sophisticated drives, the usual stomping, shouting push is a real mess.

I have hunted whitetails in the East, Midwest, and South for many years. Because many of the best deer states have long seasons, I've participated in countless drives and most of the variations. All my experience boils down to eight very effective drives. They will work almost anywhere, but they are especially suited to cover and terrain where the largest bucks commonly live. These eight drives are based on the fact that whitetails follow set routines and it's therefore possible to eliminate guesswork and employ intelligent planning. These drives almost always result in more shots at trophy bucks than do the more usual, big, noisy, unorganized efforts.

In some of these drives, several drivers will remain silent while others let out a yell once in awhile. The idea is that the deer may avoid the noisy driver and run right into a silent one. A silent driver is in a dangerous position unless everyone knows exactly where he is. Therefore, it's best to keep the number of hunters involved to a minimum so that everyone can keep track of everyone else's location. It's much safer that way.

BUTTONHOOK DRIVE

This drive is designed for rather small patches of very heavy, yet isolated cover such as stands of pines, brush, honeysuckle, or other nearly impenetrable ground-story growth that is surrounded on all sides by open fields, meadows, low crops, or country roads. Typically, these patches of cover are rectangular because of the shape of the surrounding agricultural land.

With this type of cover, an old-fashioned, noisy drive wouldn't work because the deer are enclosed in rather tight quarters (about eight acres or less). The animals would become alarmed early at the start of a big, noisy drive and would almost always spurt out anywhere along the edges of the patch in an attempt to make a run for it across the surrounding roads or fields. If the standers weren't posted in just the right places, they would probably get only fleeting glimpses of vanishing white flags.

To drive these small patches, try the semisilent

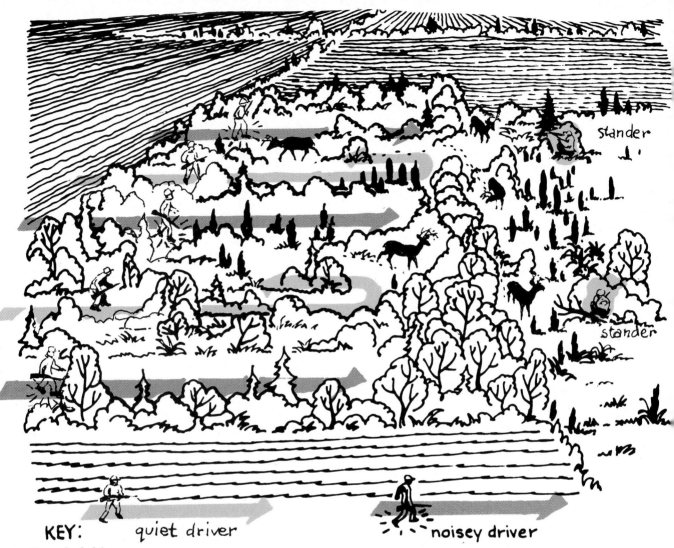

KEY: quiet driver   noisey driver

Buttonhook drive

buttonhook drive. Only seven hunters are required and, for safety reasons, all should be wearing fluorescent orange.

Two standers are positioned on the far side of the cover, out about 50 yards from the edge. The best bet is to put the standers in trees. If that isn't possible, station them behind any convenient brush or other cover. The deer are pushed slowly through the cover and they will be concentrating mostly on what is behind them (the five drivers).

The drivers start out from the opposite side of the cover after the standers are in place. The drivers are an equal distance apart. As they begin moving very slowly through the cover, the two end drivers and the one in the center sound off, but only once in awhile. The two other drivers remain silent.

With this drive, the deer are less likely to spook and spurt randomly out along the sides of the cover. They aren't pushed too hard and, when whitetails aren't really alarmed, they are very reluctant to expose themselves in the surrounding open areas. Instead, they usually attempt one of two evasive tactics, both of which allow them to be intercepted. The deer may gradually drift all the way through

the cover to the opposite side and eventually find they have to run out of the cover and make a break for other cover in the distance. Typically, the standers see the animals sneaking slowly toward the edge of the cover, hesitating or nervously milling around before deciding what to do. Usually, the deer present themselves along the edge in full view of the standers. There is almost always more than enough time for one or both of the standers to pick out a good buck and score.

If the drivers are carrying out their duties as they should, however, it is even more likley that the deer will attempt to pinpoint each driver's location. Then they'll dodge, circle, or sneak through the line of drivers to get behind it. Because they can pinpoint only the noisy drivers (human scent is everywhere), and the three men sound as though they are very widely spaced because the two other drivers are silent, the deer often try to sneak back through the line right where the silent hunters are coming through. In most cases, one of the quiet drivers is suddenly confronted by a buck that materializes right in front of him for a quick but almost point-blank shot.

Big old bucks are master tacticians and will try anything, including crawling on their bellies. Thus, they do sometimes succeed in getting behind the line. That is where the buttonhook maneuver comes in. When the line has gotten about three quarters of the way through the cover, the two silent drivers reverse direction and quietly stillhunt toward their starting positions. Often, both men spot bucks that are sneaking away or even standing still with their senses tuned in on whichever noisy driver is closest. The deer seldom even suspect the presence of the silent stillhunters until they fire. In all stand-and-drive hunting, wind direction is less important than the terrain. Because scent often comes from several directions, it doesn't mean much to the deer. Noise is the important factor.

FUNNEL DRIVE

It is seldom wise to drive large woodlands or brushy tracts. The deer simply have too much room to roam and circling the drivers is very easy. It's much better to concentrate on smaller chunks of broken, irregular terrain where the smallness allows the hunters to control the direction in which the deer move. The funnel drive is one way to do this. The method also takes advantage of the whitetail's reluctance to venture into open areas.

The funnel drive is best where cover gradually necks down into a much smaller cover area through which the deer must pass in order to reach another big patch. Perhaps a thick stand of evergreens is surrounded on all sides by open fields with the exception of one corner where brush or high weeds lead to the edge or corner of a woodlot. Maybe there is a triangular piece of cropland, the sides bordered by meadows with one corner touching the head of

a hollow tangled with greenbriers. In such cases, you can place bets on where the deer will go. When pushed by drivers, they will almost always head for the funnel leading to other cover.

Because the funnel drive is suited to rather small patches of cover, five hunters are sufficient. Two standers should be positioned just beyond the neck of cover where it begins to widen out again to merge or connect with the next big patch. Or the standers can be posted wherever there are good vantage points overlooking the narrow neck.

The drivers space themselves equally among the widest opposite edge of the cover. If the drivers move too fast, however, or if they are too noisy, the animals may panic and dart out of the cover at almost any point. Or they may bound through the neck so fast that accurate shooting is impossible.

The drivers must move very, very slowly, and they must not be too noisy. A yell now and then—mostly to keep everybody current of each man's location—is enough. The deer will gradually funnel through the narrow neck as though sneaking out the back door, and they should provide the standers with relatively easy shots at slowly moving targets.

FUNNEL DRIVE IN A BOTTOM

The second type of funnel drive is similar in that the animals are gradually pushed through a narrow neck of cover—but there are differences. This funnel drive is designed for draws, hollows, canyons, and similar bottomland terrain with fairly heavy cover and rather steep sides. The ideal place is a bottom where two hillsides or steep slopes almost touch.

Seven hunters are required—four standers and three drivers. Two of the standers position themselves on each side of the narrow neck. The other

Funnel drive

OPEN FIELDS

DENSE PINES

WOODLOT

OPEN FIELD

Funnel drive in a bottom

two standers are on the slopes or rims overlooking the bottom about one-half the distance from the starting point of the drivers and the narrow neck.

The drivers are close together so that it is absolutely impossible for the deer to sneak back through the line. The drivers sound off occasionally as they move toward the neck. In most cases, the deer will move through the cover, and the standers overlooking the neck should get shots an unsuspecting, loping animals. On occasion, though, when the deer are jumped from their beds, the bucks go straight away for only a short distance and then try to sneak around the ends of the drive. If so, the two standers on the slopes will get shots at slow-moving bucks.

LINE DRIVE

If your hunting party consists of only a few men and you spend the early morning and late afternoon on stands watching trails, you can stage drives during the middle of the day when deer are usually bedded and trail watching is useless. There aren't enough hunters to stand and drive in the usual way, so your best bet is the line drive.

A four or five-man line drive is best in a rectangular chunk of terrain with two long sides where there are clumps of very heavy cover interspersed with clearings. The hunters start out on one of the long sides. They are quite far apart so that each hunter can just barely see an occasional flash of orange from his neighbor or neighbors in the line. They move very

slowly and each man stillhunts on his own behalf. There is no yo-ho-ing.

When a buck is jumped from his bed, he is usually afraid to run toward the other long side of the cover because he will come to the open field beyond it in a very short time. Instead, the buck will usually run a short distance ahead of the line and then turn to run across the face of the drive in order to stay in the woods. As he crosses in front of the drive, he often will be forced to cross a clearing (usually near an edge) and will present a shot to one of the drivers. When this happens, the hunter gets a good chance.

TWO-MAN DRIVE

Let's suppose you're in a two-man deer camp and most of your efforts are dedicated to waiting on stands overlooking deer trails early and late in the day. With only two men, there's no chance to stage drives during the middle of the day. That's what most hunters think.

Actually, a two-man drive is very effective. It's especially good in very heavy patches of cover, large or small. But, the surrounding area should be open on all sides because that encourages the deer to circle and sneak rather than bolt out into the open.

The first hunter enters the cover and very slowly and quietly stillhunts in a straight line. He walks five or six steps, stops for a full minute to listen and study the cover ahead of him, walks a few more steps, and so on.

After the first hunter has gone about 75 yards into the cover, the second hunter enters. The second man also stillhunts in a straight line. He moves on a parallel course behind the first man about 50 yards to the right or left and perhaps 150 yards behind him.

Whether out of instinct or the pure joy of it all, whitetails like to play games. They often circle a lone hunter in order to get behind him and eventually close the distance enough to see what's up. When the buck finally determines that the hunter is really a man with lethal intentions, he often gives a loud snort and bounds away—usually to the man's rear. Sometimes the buck simply sneaks away. Whatever the case, the trailing hunter frequently gets an extremely easy shot. The deer is concentrating on the leader and seldom realizes the second man is there.

Line drive

Two-man drive

Both hunters should wear Blaze Orange and both men must carefully refrain from firing toward each other. Shots to the left or right are safe, and those are the ones that are most likely to present themselves.

If you modify this drive by putting in a second trailing hunter, you restrict them both to firing off toward the outside. It's usually not worth it.

DRIVE WITH FLANKERS

If you watch football on TV, you know what flankers are and how they move. This system is great for a fairly large tract of mixed cover with some clearings. Eight hunters are required—three standers, three drivers, and two flankers. The standers position themselves on the far side of the cover in places where they can see into clearings along that edge. The five other hunters line up along the opposite side of the cover. The two flankers are on opposite ends of the line.

In driving this type of cover situation, deer moved from their beds may go all the way through the cover and make easy targets for the standers. But they may angle away from the drive line to the sides. If so, the standers won't get shots.

The flankers are the first to jump off at the beginning of the drive. They are silent and stillhunt straight ahead. When they are about 50 yards into the cover, the other drivers kick off. When the drive begins to approach the standers, the left flanker flares to the left and the right flanker flares to the

right. All the middle drivers sound off now and then, but the flankers remain silent.

With this system, the flankers often have a better chance to get a shot than the standers. They are in position to intercept any bucks that angle off to the left or right instead of heading straight for the standers, and they are also in prime position to spot bucks that attempt to circle widely to get behind the line. Frequently, the deer sense the standers—another good break for the flankers.

A glance at the diagram shows that the standers and drivers wind up in a roughly circular position. If it's a tight circle with deer inside, everyone concerned must refrain from shooting until the deer move out and are going away from the hunters.

TWO-MAN DRIVE ON A RIDGE

This drive is designed for long, steep ridges with dense cover. In many regions, the biggest bucks bed down in such places during the middle of the day.

A buck will seldom travel the length of the ridge. He knows that he will eventually reach the end of the ridge, where there is no place to go but downhill toward more human activity and more hunters. The

Two-man drive on a ridge

WOODED RIDGE

big bucks usually prefer to run uphill and remain at higher elevations.

One hunter takes one side of the ridge about two-thirds of the way up the slope and the second hunter does the same on the other side. The ridge itself separates them so shots can be taken in any direction, though skyline shooting must be avoided, of course.

Both men stillhunt quietly along the ridge. If one man jumps a buck from his bed and does not get a shot, the deer almost invariably lines out straight away for a short distance and then cuts sharply to one side and goes up and over the crest of the ridge.

Drive with flankers

When the buck is greeted on the other side, it is often unnerved, and the deer often stands there and gawks long enough for the second driver to make an easy kill.

When a buck goes over a ridge, he usually turns backward because he does not want to be driven to the end of the cover. Both drivers should therefore be alert for a deer that turns as soon as he crosses.

ONE-MAN DRIVE

The one-man drive is just the ticket when all members of the hunting party prefer to wait on stands but one man has already taken his buck and wants to help his partners fill their tags.

If this one-man drive is to be successful, the terrain must be scouted thoroughly or known in advance. The cover may be heavy, only moderately dense, or dotted with many clearings. All members of the party must know exactly where all the deer trails are lo-cated. Stands should be taken or blinds constructed at places where two or more trails cross or come to-gether to form a major runway. The stands should not be so widely spaced that the lone driver is faced with seemingly endless miles of walking. If there are four stands, for example, they should be within 800 yards of one another.

Standers take their positions and the lone driver begins hiking a methodical pattern. He doesn't make a lot of noise but he isn't entirely silent. For safety, he should be wearing a lot of Blaze Orange. I often whistle softly to myself as I go along as though on a routine summer hike. I know the deer trails, but I make an effort to walk in heavy stands of cover to kick the deer out. Because most deer frequently see farmers, loggers, and campers, a single driver doesn't usually alarm them too much. They simply get up and move before the lone driver gets too close and they often follow an established deer trail to a stand. One driver can keep deer moving all day.

One-man drive

A Scent For A Buck

By John Weiss

Nick Selsy, a member of our annual deer hunting group, has never been enthusiastic about using commercially prepared buck scents even though other hunting party members have sworn by them. But, last year, he decided to try a popular brand.

On opening morning of the deer season in southern Ohio, Nick was headed for his stand. Having previously scouted the area, he had found a worn trail through thick cedars. Nearby was a towering maple and that was where he planned to install his portable stand. Because of the dense cover, Nick had to walk the final 75 yards directly alongside the trail. The scent he'd bought claimed to hide human odors and to attract deer. So, when he came upon the trail, Selsy stopped, took a small plastic squeeze bottle from his pocket, and squirted a few drops of the scent on his boot soles. Then he went to his stand and squirted more drops on nearby bushes and tree trunks.

Less than an hour later, a six-pointer and a yearling spike materialized in the distance. The cover was much too dense for a clean shot, so Nick had no choice but to watch and wait until the bucks got closer. Then something happened that he will never forget.

A few yards short of where he had squirted the deer scent on his boots the bucks slammed to a halt, their noses tight to the ground like nervous bird dogs. They snorted and repeatedly stamped the ground with their front feet. Then they threw their tails high and, loudly blowing air, bounded off back down the trail.

Selsy claims that he's never seen whitetails so spooked. And now he's more convinced than ever that using deer scents is a waste of time and money.

Another friend, Rick Scott, takes the opposite point of view. It's his belief that some modern deer scents not only effectively mask human odors but actually attract deer.

Scott claims that, wearing scent, he has often hiked to his stand, situated himself, and soon saw deer following not their own trail but his. Once, an eight-pointer showed up minutes after he sat down and the buck acted very strangely. He held his head and nose high in the air, strained his neck forward, and wagged it back and forth. He seemed entranced by the pungent aroma wafting downwind from the scent-saturated felt band on Scott's hat. Rick killed that deer with an arrow through both lungs.

And so it goes. Some hunters swear by scents, others swear at them, and still others have no opinions about them. It had long bothered me that I belonged in the no-opinion group. So, a few years ago, I decided to try to find out as much as I could that would help me make up my mind whether scents are any good or not.

The first thing I did was to buy the 12 most popular brands of deer scent on the market (based on the amount of national advertising each manufacturer did). Then, I got in touch with each manufacturer and asked some pointed questions. I wanted to know what types of ingredients they used in their scents, and whether they'd made any experiments or studies to determine the effectiveness of their products.

I spent many hours testing the 12 scents on whitetails—41 bucks, 80 does, and 26 fawns. One series of tests took place at the Bob Evans Farms near Gal-

A few drops of skunk scent on soles of boots mask human odor. It wears off after a while.

lipolis, Ohio, and another at the Francis Marion National Forest in South Carolina where many deer roam unmolested. But most of my tests were conducted at the Waterloo Wildlife Experiment Station near my hometown of Athens, Ohio.

Some results of these tests were revealing. Some weren't. In others, there were too many unknown factors involved to reach any reasonable conclusions. So, it would be unfair to list specific brand names of scents and state unequivocally that certain ones were effective and others were not. But here is what I learned about the various *types* of scents being offered.

First, there are hunter's soaps available in both concentrated, liquid (tube) form and in bars. It is claimed that these soaps, used while bathing the night before the hunt, remove as much serine (an acid secretion of the skin), perspiration, and other human odors as possible. In addition to using such soaps, their manufacturers suggest that a hunter wash his hair, air out his hunting clothes to free them of human and household odors, and refrain from eating spicy or strong-smelling foods the day before hunting.

Masking oils are intended to disguise man scent with aromas thought to be less alarming to deer. Ce-

dar oil, clove oil, oil of wintergreen, pine oil, and other similar "woodsy" concoctions are popular. Typical instructions are to use them sparingly because they are highly concentrated. A drop or two on each boot sole is commonly recommended to hide any scent the hunter may transfer to the ground. It is also suggested that a few drops be added to the hunter's clothing, preferably on some type of absorbent felt, cotton, or wool pad pinned to his coat, and a few more drops be deposited around any stand site.

Attractor oils are intended to lure deer by appealing to their senses of taste and smell. The most popular are apple, wild grape, and acorn, but there are many others. Most come in concentrated liquid form in squeeze bottles. But, one brand consists of highly aromatic dry pellets in a small pouch, and another comes in an aerosol spray can.

Many scents are dual-purpose. They are intended to lure deer by appealing to their sense of smell (in finding food) and also to mask human odors.

Finally, there are glandular scents intended to capitalize upon a whitetail buck's vulnerability during the mating season. To understand how these work, it is necessary to know something about the behavior of deer during this period, which lasts from two to four weeks in late fall and early winter.

The ritual begins when does become receptive. The bucks then stake out mating grounds and mark the borders of them with waxy secretions and oils from glands at the base of the eyes and between the toes of the hoofs. These secretions warn other bucks to stay away or risk a fight.

Bucks also paw the ground in many areas, creating what are known as "scrapes." These usually are circular and from one to four feet in diameter; they have

Attractor scents that simulate or reproduce food odors work well when placed on trees and brush near the hunter's stand.

When a buck follows a sex or food scent, he eventually identifies the source as a hunter. That's why it's better to put the scent away from your stand. With the deer's focus on the source, you'll have a better chance to get off a shot. Photo by Erwin A. Bauer.

a muddied texture, and are marked by hoofprints and antler-tine scratchings where the buck has cleared away leaves and other debris. While making each scrape, the buck hunches and urinates on it. The urine runs down his hind legs and over moist tufts of hair (known as tarsal glands) on the hock. In doing so, the urine transfers a musk to the ground. The scent of this musk is attractive to does that are willing to be serviced. When drawn to a scrape, a doe will deposit her glandular secretions in or near it and then hang around until her suitor shows up.

Most sexual attractor oils or scents are intended to simulate the smell of does in heat. Most come in plastic squeeze bottles. But, one company, a maker of handwarmers, has developed a small, sponge-filled aluminum cup that clips to the front of a handwarmer. The sponge is saturated with scent, the handwarmer is lighted, and then the device is slipped into a flannel carrying bag. The maker says that the heated aroma given off is more realistic than "cold" scents and is much more representative of the smell of a living animal.

Just what ingredients these attractor oils and other oils and scents contain is something manufacturers are reluctant to reveal. When I asked about them, I invariably got evasive answers. Among them were: "Made from rare ingredients that can be obtained only at certain times of year," "Made from an old family recipe passed down through generations from a great-grandfather who was a famous hunter and trapper," and "Made from an old Indian secret that few know about."

Several companies, however, stated that their scents were made from 100 percent pure musk or glandular secretions. They said that this makes their scents more effective than those offered by competitors.

"Not so," says J. Rushton Baily, president of Rush-Hampton Industries, a Florida-based company I contacted that specializes in odor control and air treatment. "Pure musk costs about $75,000 per kilogram, and that alone prevents any company from marketing a totally natural musk scent."

One scent manufacturer admitted to me that in nearly every case the "old family recipe," the "rare ingredients," and the "old Indian secret" concoctions consist of a deer urine base to which synthetic additives or natural vegetable or animal oils (not from glands) have been added.

This is not to imply that all commercially made deer scents are worthless, though claims concerning their ingredients may well be exaggerated in some cases. It is important to keep in mind, though, that whitetails have an acute sense of smell. If the scent is artificial, it has to be a very good imitation. The best any hunter can do is to try several different kinds and note the results. And, it may be that the results will differ from region to region or even when used by different men in the same place.

The hunter should understand the purpose of each scent. Whitetails are always suspicious of anything that is not a natural part of their environment. To use a sex scent effectively, for example, the hunter must know that the local whitetails are in rut or will be shortly.

I tested one sex scent that is supposedly made of doe estrogen substances. During a 12-month period in Ohio, I saturated cotton pads with the scent and

This brand of glandular scent (sex lure) is used in a handwarmer. The warm odor is like that of a living animal.

put them where I could watch the reactions of the deer. I noted three different reactions.

From March through June, no bucks came to the scent. Does are not in heat then, so that's what you would expect. Curiously, however, does and fawns *did* come to the scent.

From July through the second week of October, the sex scent did not attract bucks or does. That could be important for bowhunters because their season opens earlier than the firearms deer season.

From the second week in October through January, bucks from 1 to 4 years old, as estimated by their antlers, came to the sex scents. The greatest number of visits were made during the first two weeks of November—the peak of the rut. Only a few big bucks came and they were not very enthusiastic. It's only an educated guess, but the lack of reaction by big bucks may be because older animals are not as active sexually as the youngsters.

Another sex scent, supposedly also made of doe glandular secretions, had no effect on does and was only minimally effective in attracting young bucks during the rut. It didn't attract a single trophy buck.

Still another sex scent attracted no does or big bucks and seemed to alarm small bucks. I don't know why, but every buck that got a whiff of this scent almost turned himself inside out to leave the area.

During these tests, I learned that attractor oils (sex or food) should *not* be used on a hunter's clothing or at his stand site. This is contrary to accepted practice, but my reasoning may in part explain why some scents are used ineffectively. When a buck follows a sex or food scent, he pinpoints the source. Eventually, he identifies the source as a hunter and spooks unless the hunter can get a shot first. It's much better to put the scent source away from the hunter, perhaps in a clearing near the hunter's stand. With the deer's attention focused on the scent source, the hunter has a better chance to get off a shot.

My best results with sex scents came when I squirted a few drops into a breeding scrape and waited in a tree stand about 50 yards away.

With food scents, the best results were obtained by squirting a few drops on leafy bushes, tree branches, or other cover that stood at least a few feet above the ground so that the odor carried downwind.

A dual approach can also be effective. Use a sex or food scent to attract, and use a masking scent to hide your own odor. Murry Burnham, a well-known manufacturer of animal calls and scents, told me that skunk scent is an effective masking agent. I tried it four times. It was highly effective once but I could observe no noticeable results the other three times, except that the doors of my home were locked when I got there.

Apples and acorns are preferred whitetail foods, but are their scents effective where there are no apple or oak trees? How about other food scents? In the arid hill country of south Texas, for example, would a deer spook if it suddenly smelled apples? Or would the buck approach out of curiosity? Would a Michigan deer spook if it smelled clove oil? I made only a few tests, so I don't have firm conclusions, but it seems that scents that are not native to the immediate area alarm deer.

Three times, in one location near a southern-Ohio orchard, deer came to an apple scent (or drifted through and didn't detect my presence because of the scent). During two tests in another area where there were no apple trees, deer were very wary and jittery during one test with apple scent and showed only mild curiosity during another.

In an evergreen swamp in South Carolina, using an acorn scent cost me a shot at one of the biggest bucks I have ever seen, and the scent also unnerved does that came by six different times. In Ohio, on a ridge behind my home where oaks are plentiful, deer have often come to acorn scent I put out. One doe tried to eat the cotton scent pad. Twenty minutes later, a fawn picked up the cotton pad and carried it off.

I recently used one pine oil masking scent in a brushy hollow between two cornfields. A dozen does shot out of the hollow like puffed wheat from Gabby Hayes' cannon when they got a whiff.

Some hunters are so sure that certain scents spook deer that they use them in reverse. A good example is Georgia deer hunter George Jarbrinski.

He read all of the advertisement testimonials, talked with experienced friends, and finally tried one popular brand not long ago.

"The stuff was so putrid it would gag a polecat," George said. "I followed the instructions on the bottle and the deer skirted my stand even if they had to leave their regular runway."

But George found a use for that scent. Now he sprinkles it on nearby trails and takes his stand overlooking one where there is none. In every instance, he says, the deer immediately abandoned the scented trails and came down the remaining one to his stand!

Do deer scents work?   You bet they do, for the guy who knows how and when to use them.

The Fox Gets The Deer

By William Johns

Many hunters who dislike the crowds that hunt near where they live strike out for faraway places. But they can only go so far in any direction before they run into hunters fleeing from another metropolis for the same reason. Other disadvantages of travel include hunting time lost, the expense, and the fact that if you stray from home turf you will not be familiar with the terrain.

Instead, a few canny hunters are playing their cards to enjoy fine whitetail hunting close to home, even if home is near a large metropolitan area.

One reason for it is that whitetails don't like to live in climax forests where there is little low browse. They fare much better in fringe areas near mankind. In these places, there are orchards, lush agricultural croplands, and plenty of the whitetail's favored "edge" cover. There is no lack of hunting land in the agricultural belts surrounding most cities. They include state parks, national forests, game management units, and private company tracts. The rub is that public land closest to big cities gets exceedingly heavy hunting pressure. Everyone who can buy or borrow a gun seems to be afield on opening day. But it is possible to get your buck, even if there is a madding crowd.

The hunting tactics are much the same, but you outfox the other hunters and use them to your own advantage. There's nothing dishonest or unsporting about this; it simply makes good sense to stack the odds in your favor. Because fixed-acreage public hunting lands must accommodate more and more hunters every year, outsmarting the other fellow is becoming as important as pre-season scouting, choosing a place to take a stand, or planning a stalk.

There is a whole passel of these little tricks, and foxy Tom Norris of Columbus, Ohio, uses some of them well before the deer season begins. His favorite hunting cover is the Hocking State Forest, which is not far from Columbus and is carpeted with hunters during the season.

Norris' ploy is to milk other hunters for information, but he seldom prods other deer hunters because he knows they are tight-lipped. Some even fabricate tales to steer other deer hunters in the wrong direction (a foxy trick in itself).

Norris spends a good deal of time hunting other game in the state forest prior to the deer season—turkeys, rabbits, squirrels, and grouse. He often encounters other hunters who, unknowingly or uncaringly, tell all.

Many sportsmen are specialists. Some are upland bird hunters. Others hunt turkeys exclusively or shoot nothing but quail or whatever. These outdoorsmen can often be maneuvered into giving information that Norris values. Recently, I hunted rabbits with him in the Hocking forest. When we chanced upon another rabbit hunter, there was a brief, mutual introduction, and then Norris steered the talk along these lines.

"You know," Norris said, "I've had a lot of problems with my dogs picking up deer scent in here and chasing them instead."

"Yeah, mine, too," said the rabbit hunter. "Always chasing trash of one kind or another."

"But for some reason, we haven't run into a single deer here this year," Norris went on. "Just lucky, I guess. Lordy, they can wreck a good trailing dog in nothing flat. Nice looking beagles you've got there."

A GREAT OPENING MOVE

Most opening day hunters just tramp around in the brush close to roads, so if you have a stand close to a wide place in the road where they like to park, they'll stir up the deer for you. A tree stand works well—and it's much safer than sitting on a log or the ground.

Of course, your stand is near a well-used runway chosen before the season. Keep the parking situation and your "volunteer" drivers in mind when you make your choice.

THE SECOND ACT

After opening day and maybe a few more, most of the deer leave the roadside circus and make for deeper woods. You do the same, having set up two or three stands in advance.

The local deep-woods deer will be there, plus the newcomers, so you'll see plenty of deer. Mostly, they'll be seeking hideout cover, so choose stands accordingly. There will be other hunters, but not so many. Good, thick bedding cover may be the very best bet.

"Thanks a heap," replied the other hunter. "Let me tell you to stay away from the north ridge. You know, over by Township Road 53. More acorns up there this year than ever before and it's been like a magnet to the deer. If your dog cuts a hot scent, you'll spend eternity trying to find it."

"Hey, thanks for the tip," said Norris.

"Another thing," the other hunter went on, "stay away from the cranberry bog over by the big power line. Jumped eight deer in there last week and my dogs didn't come home until after midnight. Jumped six more there this morning. Tracks and droppings all over the place. Rabbit hunting there is ruined."

Tom tied his tag on a nice six-pointer only half an hour after first shooting light on opening day. He killed the deer in the cranberry bog.

Pre-season chicanery can be carried out in many other ways. For example, it pays to hang around a local sportsmen's club. Turn a deaf ear to most of the deer talk, however, or you may find yourself victimized by hunters cleverer than you are. Mix with other small groups rapping about coon hunting, turkey calling, squirrel forays, and even anglers who dote on finding hidden trout streams. It's almost a certainty that all of them will be disguising their coon, turkey, or squirrel-hunting secrets, and perpetrating other frauds on fellow coon, turkey, and squirrel hunters. It is equally certain that all of them at least occasionally encounter deer, and making a quietly provocative remark now and then may garner many clues that will put you onto a trophy buck.

Another gambit is the "two-stand" approach. It is often used to take advantage of the way novice deer hunters typically deploy on opening day. It involves nothing more complicated than recognizing the fact that most hunters will be in predictable places early in the season. Afterward, the picture changes.

Simply choose two stands, one in the middle of the hubbub and the other somewhere in the hinterland. The opening-day stand is chosen after careful scouting of the cover to find out how deer are moving and using terrain within 500 yards of some county or township road.

Because of easy access, and also because an overwhelming majority of deer hunters won't venture more than a quarter of a mile away from where they park, you will have plenty of company the first day or two. There will be loud talk all around, car doors slamming, and crowds of hunters traipsing past your stand. But it's all to the good, because the other hunters unknowingly push deer in your direction.

The deer haven't been subjected to much human activity during the long closed season. Because they hate to leave their preferred range, it takes a good deal of commotion before they vacate the premises. During the first day or two of the season, many deer stay near the road but they continually circle and dodge the many moving hunters. With the hunters keeping the deer in circulation, you may get a shot at almost anytime of day, if you are patient enough and sit in the right place without fidgeting, coughing, or smoking.

In fact, deer are likely to pass your stand between 8 a.m. and noon, a time when they usually would be bedded. Most deer hunters tramp around looking for deer and most of those who take stands become restless after only an hour or so of sitting and seeing nothing.

That kind of hunter first gets up to stretch his legs. Then he sits down again. He's up again and maybe has a smoke. Down again. Then he's up and milling around. Hearing a shot in the distance helps to get him moving.

As my friend George Mattis of Birchwood, Wisconsin, explains in his book on deer hunting: "They soon come to believe that in this veritable oasis of deer country, they alone have . . . selected the desert."

This kind of hunter often sits early in the morning and walks around in the middle of the day. The

Photo by Erwin A. Bauer

crafty and persevering hunter who is able to stay quietly on stand can benefit from all that commotion.

I have been a first-hand witness to this many, many times. Just last year in an area near Mammoth Cave National Park in central Kentucky, 47 hunters—I counted them—walked by my stand on opening day. Most of them were like old ladies rushing to a yarn sale. Seventeen deer also crept by like wisps of thin smoke. I counted 14 does, some of which may have circled and come by more than once. For sure, there were three different bucks. The first was a forkhorn, the second a spike, and the third was an eight-pointer. Its head now hangs on my office wall.

By the time the second day of the season is over, and if you haven't scored, abandon the roadside stand. The heavy traffic is over. Physically unaccustomed to two full days of hiking, some hunters give up and go home. Many are able to get away from their jobs for only a day or two and they have gone back to work. Some of them may reappear the following weekend for a final go at it.

The close-to-the-road deer covers are quiet. There

CAMPGROUND DRIVERS

If hunters must park or camp in supervised areas, you can bet that most of them will head for the nearest patch of woods in the morning. Plan ahead—and be on the other side of the cover just before shooting light and let them push the deer to you.

In many such places, you don't even have to build a stand. Just sit or stand inside the edge of the cover but, in most cases, it's best to get out of there well before the mob reaches you. You can shoot the buck, gut out, and leave before they get there.

are no mobs to keep deer moving and the shy bucks that lived there have probably retreated anyway. Two full days of ruckus have encouraged them to drift into more distant, heavy cover within their usual 1½-square-mile home range.

Now is the time to use your second stand. Of course, you scouted the terrain thoroughly beforehand and located your stand overlooking well-worn trails that lead to or from dense undergrowth and other security cover the deer prefer.

From my experience, a hunter who does this often sees twice as many deer as before. The resident deer of the deep woods are still present and there are also the refugees seeking temporary quarters after having been pushed out of the edge areas. Hunter activity is usually very light in such places, so the best time to get a shot is during the two-hour dawn watch and the two hours at dusk. During the middle of the day, the deer will be bedded and stillhunting might pay off, if you can move quietly enough to get a shot.

If most of the hunters have been unsuccessful near the roads, a few of the more energetic ones may decide to try the thick cover, and their random explorations could keep the deer moving for you. There's also a chance that groups of hunters may begin staging drives, and that, too, should encourage you to stay on stand longer than usual.

Having as many as four good stands available is a good idea. Alternate stands are insurance against the discourtesies of some hunters and provide an escape if their plans inadvertently conflict with yours.

In Potter County, Pennsylvania, I once found a three-acre oat field. The entire perimeter was pep-

pered with so many scrapes and rubbed trees that I knew the place was smoking hot. I chose the best tree for my portable stand, cleared some brush to provide three, unobstructed shooting lanes into the field, and went home to wait for opening day. A week later, in the pre-dawn darkness, I hiked confidently toward the stand. Then I heard voices, laughter, and the clatter of pots and pans. It was sad. Two other hunters had set up a tent camp smack in the middle of the field. They didn't know about my stand. As it turned out, I collected a fat forkhorn on the second day of the season only because I had readied an alternate site about half a mile away.

An alternate stand is also good insurance against the man who deliberately robs you of your hunting place. Face the facts—he's out there, the unsportsmanlike clod. This kind of hunter is so ignorant that he can't read deer sign himself. When he comes upon an unoccupied stand, he takes over and tries to benefit from your scouting.

This has happened to me several times. Just saying "You're on my stand" is often enough to get the dolt moving but, once in awhile, it's not enough. The interloper may ask if my name is on it, and then I say "Yes, my name is William Johns and my signature is written in ink on the board you're sitting on." That may do it. But, if not, having an alternate stand saves the day.

All of this makes a good case in favor of not building a permanent stand. It's often best to carry a portable, climbing tree stand with you. If there's no physical clue, the dolt will never locate the site. You can eliminate the trouble of toting the portable stand back and forth to your car by painting it in a cam-

THE FOLLOW-UP

Sometimes you can get a shot by following another hunter. Most of them don't even know that they are moving deer. Follow along behind him, or off to one side. A buck may circle right across your front. It works best if the other hunter's the usual Bigfoot and you are a feather-soled deerslayer.

If you try the follow-up, be very careful about where you shoot. Keep the other man's location in mind. Shoot when the buck is coming or when he is going, not when he is between the other hunter and yourself.

ouflage pattern and hiding it nearby under leaves and forest duff.

While waiting on stand, another hunter may spot you and amble over for a chat, which does absolutely nothing to increase your chances of killing a deer. If you can, nix this right away by putting your index finger over your lips to silence him and wave him away. Most hunters will comply. Stay alert, because a deer may be keeping tabs on that moving hunter and may circle and sneak past your stand.

Sooner or later, a real dolt will insist on speaking to you. Just whisper, "I haven't seen a thing." You're on your own if he continues to hang around. To get him moving, I'm not above telling him that I saw deer two miles away.

Sometimes a hunter sits down nearby without noticing me. I don't worry about it. If he hasn't installed a tree stand or built a ground-level blind, the chances are that he'll soon get itchy and move off. That's all to the good. Any deer in the vicinity will have their attention riveted on him. They will be unaware of your presence and may blunder right into you as they slink around the moving hunter.

Jimmy Marcks is a very sly whitetail scout. I've known him to deliberately use other hunters to drive deer. He hunts Ohio state parks where campsites are jammed during deer season. He knows the lay of the land and which direction most of the hunters will take when they leave camp on opening morning.

If one side of the campground butts up against dense woodland, for example, and the other sides face fields, scrub brushland, and the like, it's almost guaranteed that most of the hunters will head for the woods.

Looking at a map, Marcks brainstorms some way to get to the back side of the woodland and scouts it for a suitable stand site.

"More times than not," he says, "the deer stampede in my direction at first light, pushed by a crowd of hunters entering the woods on the other side."

Marcks also takes note of favorite parking places on woods roads. Most of them are wide places on the berm. Hunters park there and walk in predictable directions toward the adjacent deer cover. Marcks installs his stand accordingly and, at dawn, he is aided by unsuspecting drivers.

A similar tactic works well on a smaller scale when you are stillhunting. Whenever you notice a hunter-orange-clad figure walking ahead of you, angle off to one side or the other and then parallel his route. There's an excellent chance of seeing deer that are circling to get behind him.

I see a great many deer simply by trailing another hunter. I don't get so close that I interfere with his chances, but I follow 200 or 300 yards behind him. Deer frequently cross directly in front of me or I see them in the cover off to one side while they eyeball the hunter moving ahead of me. I think these deer are either pushed out of their beds and are circling to get behind the hunter or they are waiting for him to pass. If you do this, you have to be very careful not to shoot toward the other hunter.

Just ask Tom Norris or Jimmy Marcks. I even swear by it myself. On crowded public hunting lands, a knowledge of basic whitetail hunting techniques is essential. But, if other things are equal, it's often the fox that gets the deer.

Blackpowder Bucks

By Bruce Brady

The hardwood ridge I was walking fell away into a great, shadowy bottom. From the high ridge, I could see the sun sparkling on a spring branch far below. Several large white oaks promised an abundance of acorns, a preferred mast for whitetail deer.

My .50-caliber muzzleloading rifle was in the crook of my arm, charged and ready. It was midmorning and my two hunting partners weren't expecting me back at the pickup truck until noon. I looked around and selected a place that would give me a full view of the bottom and the ridges to the west. Quietly, I scraped away the leaves at the base of a young oak and sat down.

I glanced at my rifle to be sure the percussion cap was still firmly in place on the nipple. When I looked up again, I was staring at a deer that was moving into the bottom below me. I saw no horns, but the deer had the stiff-legged trot and the flat back of a buck.

I stayed motionless while the deer crossed the hollow. I was determined to allow the animal to come as near as possible. At the foot of my ridge, the deer paused, and I judged it to be a doe. Then the ears moved, and I saw a spike. The young buck was perfect for the family larder.

I slowly depressed the trigger and then thumbed back the big hammer to prevent the usual click of cocking. After releasing the front trigger, I pulled the set trigger and waited for the right moment. The buck ambled uphill toward me and then paused to look down his backtrail. That gave me a chance to shoulder my weapon. I took a fine sight, put the white bead on the buck's chest, and touched her off. The rifle boomed, blue smoke rolled, and the little buck bolted as though the very devil had him by the tail. I missed him clean at 30 yards! Just why it happened, I'll never know.

It was opening day of Mississippi's primitive-weapons season. From a meager beginning in 1971, the popularity of deer hunting with frontloading rifles has grown steadily in this state.

I live in Brookhaven, Mississippi. I began planning this muzzleloader hunt by calling Frank Davis, a district manager for the St. Regis Paper Company. The company has more than 300,000 acres of woodlands in the state, and almost all of it is open to public hunting. Frank is an ardent deer hunter and I knew he could suggest a good place to take a buck with a muzzleloader.

"I can do better than that," Frank replied. "I'll be hunting on opening day myself and you're welcome to come along."

He told me that he'd be hunting on company land near Natchez and suggested that I bring a friend.

Bob Stamps and I drove 60 miles from home and were waiting for Frank at 4 a.m., when the headlights of his car came into view. Bob is a hometown hunting pal of mine. We cranked up and followed Frank for two or three miles. Finally, he pulled over and signaled me to park my truck. Then he put me on a logging road that led to deep hollows and rugged oak ridges. After we all agreed to meet at noon, he and Bob took off on two other trails. Later that morning I missed the spike buck I mentioned earlier.

After missing such an easy shot, I was disgusted

The author recently shot this four-pointer with a muzzleloading rifle. The popularity of deer hunting with frontloading rifles has grown steadily in Mississippi during the past fourteen years.

with myself. Shots at whitetail bucks are hard enough to come by but, if you blow a shot with a single-barrel muzzleloader, you may very well wait until next season for another.

At about 10 a.m., I began working my way back toward my truck. I was within 200 yards of the road when I came to a fork in the trail that I hadn't noticed at daybreak. After glancing at my watch, I decided to make a short hunt along the other trail. New country always intrigues me, so I was moving very silently when I came to a finger ridge that joined the

hogback I was following. I paused to study both sides of the ridge.

A deer was walking up the ridge toward me and I could see horns—a fork buck, at least. Silently, I cocked my rifle and waited. The buck stopped among some saplings 60 yards away. I had to wait for a clear shot. Suddenly, his head whipped around and he cupped his ears in my direction. His tail flipped nervously and I knew he was going to break.

The deer was already in motion when my rifle boomed. I ducked in an effort to see under the cloud of blue smoke, but the deer was gone. I ran to the spot where the buck had been and found blood and hair.

I reloaded my piece and waited 15 minutes before I took up the blood trail. Frothy blood indicates a lung shot, but these drops were dark red and no larger than a dime. Either the wound was superficial or the buck was gut shot. A gut-shot deer usually bleeds very little externally and can travel for miles. My fears were confirmed when I found bits of rumen in a dot of blood. Because I knew the animal was gut shot, I had to stay on his trail until I got him, in order to prevent a lingering death and a wasted deer.

I took my time and often got down on my hands and knees to search for blood or a fresh track. Every time I found sign, I marked the spot with a blaze mark on a nearby bush or tree. It was slow going; by 11:30 I still hadn't come upon the buck. Once I found tracks where he had stood motionless for several minutes. Just as I marked the place with a blaze, I heard the distant boom of a rifle. I guessed that Bob or Frank had venison.

My buck wasn't avoiding steep hillsides, so his strength was holding. I lost his trail several times and had to backtrack to my last blaze and work in a circle to find a sudden turn to one side. The value of marking each bit of sign was obvious.

The signs finally became so difficult to find that I decided I needed help. It was almost 2 p.m. when I got back to the truck, where Frank and Bob were waiting. Frank had fired the shot I had heard but he had missed.

It was a simple matter for us to follow my blazes back to the last sign I'd found. We spread out and Bob soon discovered a drop of blood on a huckle-

NOTES ON MUZZLELOADERS

The author uses a .50-caliber caplock rifle made by Thompson/Center and that company's lubricated, solid-base bullets. A cloth patch around the bullet isn't necessary. A measured charge of blackpowder is poured down the barrel, and the bullet is simply rammed down on top of it. Then, a metallic percussion cap is placed on the nipple, and the arm is ready to be fired. At 100 yards, it's possible, the author reports, to keep most of his shots within a 12-inch circle. But, at longer range, holdover becomes very critical.

Many blackpowder shooters use the traditional round ball, which is loaded in rifles by enclosing it in a greased cloth patch. The patch "takes" the rifling and spins the ball. The patch drops away after the ball leaves the muzzle.

Minie balls are also used. They are actually round-nose bullets with hollow bases. The skirt of the bullet expands when the rifle is fired, and takes the rifling to impart spin. No patch is needed.

Flintlocks discharge when sparks caused by friction between flint and steel ignite the priming powder in a flashpan. The system is slower than caplock ignition and it is subject to malfunctions because of dampness, but some hunters prefer flintlocks anyway.

MUZZLELOADER MUSTS

To participate in Mississippi's primitive-weapons season, residents must have a special $7.50 archery/primitive-weapons license in addition to the regular hunting license. A non-resident must have a $25 primitive-weapons license as well as a non-resident all game hunting license, which costs $60. Due to reciprocal regulations, a non-resident all game hunting license costs Alabamans $99 and Tennessee residents $115.

Hunters may take one antlered buck per day, five per license year. Legal bucks must have antlers visible above the natural hairline. In addition, one antlerless deer per day is allowed, with no more than three per license year. This 12-day season is customarily scheduled for mid-December.

In Mississippi, primitive weapons are defined by law as muzzle-loading rifles or smoothbores using blackpowder and firing a single projectile of at least .40 caliber. Use of telescopic sights, dogs, or sidearms is prohibited. Hunters may use longbows during the season, though archers have a special two-month season of their own that begins early October.

Primitive-weapons hunting is usually permitted in 20 or more specially designated wildlife-management areas (listed in literature issued with the hunting license) and in any other part of the state normally open to deer hunting. Obtain permission before entering private land, whether posted or not. Among the best WMA's for blackpowder bucks are: the Adams County WMA near Natchez, the Red Creek area near Wiggins, the Choctaw WMA near Ackerman, and the Upper Sardis WMA near Oxford.

All deer hunters in the state must wear hat, cap, or vest of Blaze Orange during any gunning season for deer.

berry leaf. Six eyes are better than two and we were able to move along rapidly.

After half a mile we came upon a thicket where the buck had bedded down—the first indication that his strength was ebbing. Then the trail turned downhill and we entered a bottom laced with spring branches and ditches. I was searching for sign when Frank called out, "Bruce, here's your deer. It's a big doe!"

My heart jumped into my throat for a moment, but the smile on Frank's face gave his joke away. My buck was finally down, hidden in a narrow ditch. A neck shot finished him.

The little buck carried five points. I field-dressed him and dragged him out to the truck.

We had the rest of the afternoon to hunt. Frank directed Bob to a tree stand. I had a bonus deer tag in my pocket that entitled me to a second buck, but I decided I would fill it only if I hunted up a real trophy. Frank showed me a logging road that ran along one of the highest ridges on the tract.

"There are some tremendous hollows off the sides of the ridge," he told me. "It's big buck country, so keep your eyes open and take your time."

Frank tried the same trail he had taken at daylight, hoping to get another crack at the buck he had missed.

By the time I eased half a mile up the logging road, I'd found a dozen large rubbing trees and four smoking-hot buck scrapes at least two feet across. All that fresh sign added up to one thing—a buck in full rut. Judging by the size of the saplings he was hooking, he had to be big.

I decided to take a stand and watch one of the fresh scrapes until dark. I had been there for half an hour when a shot boomed to the west. A minute later, there was a second. I was sure someone had knocked a buck down and then fired again to finish the job. Thinking help might be needed, I left my stand. A short time later, I found Bob Stamps dragging a spike down his logging road.

"I took a running shot," Bob said, "but I missed. I reloaded and, just as I was pulling my ramrod, here comes the spike back through the plot again. I didn't miss that time."

Bob shoots a round, patched ball in his .45-caliber rifle.

Soon Frank came up and we started dragging. We had two bucks tagged and Frank had shot at an eight-pointer. It had been quite a day in the deer woods.

"Look," Frank said in the fading light, "I'm coming back in the morning for another try. You guys are welcome to join me."

Bob had other plans, but I accepted and told Frank

PICKING A MUZZLELOADER

Antique muzzleloading rifles are seldom used afield, because they are too valuable. Modern blackpowder rifles are presently offered by at least 25 companies, and some of them are more accurate than most antiques. Many have much-better sights. Muzzleloaders suitable for hunting include those listed below, but rifles made by individual craftsmen are available, too. These are usually custom-built to order and often sell for high prices. Smoothbore muskets and even muzzleloading shotguns can be loaded with a ball or conoid bullet for deer (where legal), but rifled arms are more accurate. The arms listed here are all rifled.

The Hawken, the Renegade, and the Seneca by Thompson/Center Arms Co., Dept. OL, Rochester, NH 03867. Available in .45, .50, and .54 calibers. Fully adjustable sights.

The Buffalo Hunter and the Hawken by Navy Arms Co., 687 Bergen Blvd., Dept. OL, Ridgefield, NJ 07657. Available in .45, .50, and .58 calibers. Sights adjustable for windage.

The Kentucky and the Pennsylvania Rifle by Dixie Gun Works, Dept. OL, Union City, TN 38261. Available in .36 and .45 calibers. Sights adjustable for windage. Sold also in kit form for assembly by the buyer.

The Zouave Rifle by Centennial Arms, 3318 West Devon, Dept. OL, Chicago, IL 60645. In .58 caliber. Adjustable sights.

The Springfield by Harrington & Richardson, Park Ave., Dept. OL, Worcester, MA 01610. In .45 and .58 calibers. Adjustable sights.

The Deer Stalker and the Minuteman Brush Rifle, Hopkins and Allen. From Numrich Arms, 209 Broadway, Dept. OL, West Hurley, NY 12491. Underhammer and standard models in .36, .45, .50, and .58 calibers. Adjustable sights.

The Texas Allen & Thurber by Mowrey Gun Works, Box 711, Dept. OL, Olney, Tx 76374. In .50 caliber with adjustable sights.

Muzzleloader prices vary from $165 to $450.

about all the buck sign I'd seen. We agreed to meet at the same place.

With the first streaks of dawn, I moved up the old logging road and took my stand overlooking one of the scrapes I'd found the previous afternoon. It was still early when the *ka-boom* of a muzzleloader echoed across the countryside. Maybe Frank has his buck, I thought.

I stayed put until after 9 a.m. but saw nothing. Then I decided to slip along the hogback trail and check out the deep hollows off to the sides. I had gone about a quarter of a mile when my eye caught a slight movement.

As I turned my head, the biggest whitetail buck I had ever laid eyes on stepped clear of an oak at 50 feet. His rack was tremendous and I was dumbfounded for an instant.

That split second was all the deer needed to make his move. Instantly, the hammer on my rifle was back. As the butt touched my shoulder I looked along the top of the barrel. I saw the big oak at the side of the trail and I tried to shoot before the buck ran behind the tree.

The big rifle bucked and bark on the side of the oak exploded into shreds just as the deer came out on the other side. An instant later, the buck was broadside to me—an easy shot. I watched helplessly as the huge deer loped down the logging road for 100 yards and then disappeared into a tangled hollow.

He was by far the finest buck I have ever seen in more than 20 years of hunting whitetails. His antlers were wide, massive, and deeply knurled with five points to the side.

I checked to be certain no part of my bullet had gotten through to him. I tried to continue hunting but my concentration was gone, so I returned to the main road and found Frank coming out with his eight-pointer.

"Son of a gun," Frank said with a grin, "I heard something just after I got settled. Two does came along and, a minute later, here comes this guy sniffing the trail where his girlfriends had run. When he got to 40 yards, I touched off. He ran but collapsed in full stride."

My partner's .45-caliber Dixie Arms Kentucky rifle had put the lubricated conoid bullet through the buck's lungs.

I hunted for that big deer whenever I could for the remainder of the muzzleloader season and on into the second half of the regular firearms season, but I didn't see him again.

In January, with two days of deer season left, my brother Tom came face to face with the same buck on the same trail. It was a cinch shot at little more than 30 yards. Incredibly, his .308 misfired and the deer was gone.

My brother's description of the antlers leaves no doubt that we both shot at the same buck. He, too, calls it the trophy of a lifetime.

That old boy may be living a charmed life, but there's one thing for sure: I'll hunt for him again.

PART 3

HUNTING MULE DEER AND BLACKTAILS

Formula For A Muley

By Jim Zumbo

The three hunters sat in camp, dejected and confused. The meat pole they'd set up between two trees was bare, even though the men had hunted for three days. It was their first trip West and they hadn't seen a decent buck yet.

We drank black coffee warmed on their campfire coals and discussed mule deer hunting. My buddy and I were invited to the camp because we'd tagged two nice bucks that morning. The nonresident hunters obviously wanted advice on what they were doing wrong.

It was immediately apparent that they had the wrong impression about mule deer. They believed bucks would be readily visible in the open country, so they spent much of their time driving roads and glassing from their vehicle.

My pal and I suggested they try walking ridges and trails away from busy roads and looking for deer in the early-morning and late-afternoon hours when bucks are on the move. We recommended that, during the day, the hunters try some drives or stillhunt in brushy timbered places where deer were apt to bed.

A few days later, the hunters called me at home and said they'd been successful, though they had to work long and hard for the three bucks they'd collected.

Mule deer hunting is often considered to be easy compared to hunting whitetails. While the bucks of the West generally inhabit more open landscape than whitetails do, they're far from pushovers, especially because they live in a variety of environments.

If you look at the West from an airplane, you'll see a mosaic of forests and brushlands. Each area is unique and mule deer must be hunted according to terrain, vegetation, and the climate in which they live.

The hunters we'd met, for example, were looking for deer on sagebrush hillsides across from dense, oak brush thickets. They might have spotted feeding deer just after daylight in little clearings adjacent to the dense oaks but, instead, they searched in vain over expansive slopes with little or no cover. Muleys probably fed on those open hillsides during the night but had moved into the oak brush as dawn started to break.

If there's a formula for mule deer, it's simply to

High brush may mean miserable stalking but, after glassing from above on an opposite slope, author collects a large reward.

match techniques to the country you're hunting. In the West, the different environments can be grouped into six categories: desert, pinyon-juniper forests, low brush, high brush, aspen, and evergreen forests. Let's look at each.

The desert is often misleading and is often considered a barren, lifeless area with sand dunes, lizards, and coyotes. Western deserts are more commonly vast areas that receive little precipitation but that have adequate forage and water for mule deer. Stockmen and government agencies have created water holes for cattle and sheep throughout much of the arid lowlands. Mule deer reap the benefits of that water, as well, and consequently thrive in many desert regions.

An obvious hunting technique in the desert is to watch water holes until a buck shows up for a drink. It's a good idea but seldom successful because muleys prefer to water at night. A more logical approach is to first determine mule deer presence by checking watering areas for fresh tracks. If you find some, start looking at the terrain for clues. Many desert areas have rocky formations, brushy arroyos, and inaccessible canyons. Stillhunt these spots and glass them thoroughly. Bucks might try to slip away long before you're close to them. Because cover is often sparse, muleys bed early in deserts and you'll need to be watching at first shooting light for moving animals. Get as far from roads as you can and seek little secluded spots where deer aren't disturbed. Greasewood patches and unusually brushy spots should be investigated thoroughly. Don't let your guard down while hunting the desert. It's easy to be distracted in the vast and monotonous region.

Pinyon-juniper forests occupy millions of acres in the Southwest and harbor unbelievable numbers of mule deer in many places. This forest grows at low elevations and is often accessible to vehicles. Because it grows in thick stands, hunting is extremely difficult.

In many forests, forage isn't adequate for deer, so they move out into adjacent valleys, clearings, or canyon bottoms to feed. Wary bucks are usually back in the forest at the first hint of daylight, though they might continue to feed in small openings within the forest.

Because foliage from pinyons and junipers usually grows down to the ground, visibility is hampered. Most deer will wind, see, or hear you before you can spot them. A workable strategy is to make a quiet drive with two or three companions. In this case, an organized effort isn't necessary because there are few places where standers have a good vantage spot. It's best to simply walk randomly through the trees in hopes a buck will show himself after being routed by a driver. There's an obvious need to be cautious when making a shot because you won't know exactly where your pals are. Before making the drive, determine the routes you'll walk and stick to them.

The low-brush environment is most often composed of sagebrush, bitterbrush, and other low-growing plants. In many regions, large expanses of sage stretch from one horizon to the other. Inexperienced hunters might view this habitat as an unworthy place to find deer but muleys indeed live in it, especially if no other cover is nearby. The first mule deer I ever killed, more than 20 years ago, showed up in a sagebrush valley. I was used to hunting whitetails in thick forests and was amazed that a deer would exist in sagebrush.

The key to hunting deer in low brush is constant glassing in the early morning. If you're vigilant, you might spot a herd of feeding deer and pinpoint where they bed down. The next step is to check wind direction and make a careful stalk. Sagebrush is often high enough to hide a bedded deer, particularly if there are small clumps of bushes such as serviceberry, which is called "buckbrush" in parts of the West.

Making a drive in low brush doesn't work well unless you're planning on a long walk covering several miles. In this high-visibility open country, deer aren't going to approach a stander. You'll need to spook them over a ridge or into a canyon where they can't see standers, who should be spaced several hundred yards apart to cover the big country you're hunting. The secret to hunting low brush is to cover a lot of ground and to glass constantly when deer are feeding and heading to bedding areas. You can do a lot of looking from a vehicle in some places but you should walk away from roads as much as possible. Deer often spook when a vehicle appears, especially in areas where there is little human disturbance.

High brush commonly includes oak, mountain mahogany, and serviceberry. Deer feed in high brush and often stay in it without traveling for food or water, if both are available. The toughest hunting I've done has been in dense thickets of oak brush that are almost impenetrable. Deer are hard to see; it's difficult to move along quietly; and some thickets practically defy human encroachment. Nonetheless, huge bucks live in high brush and it's worth the misery.

Where high brush grows on sidehills, I employ a strategy during early-morning hours. I climb above the brush on the opposite slope and carefully glass the thicket for moving deer. The high vantage point gives me enough elevation to see down into the oaks, not unlike sitting in a tree stand. I try to find an observation spot within reasonable shooting range of the brush because, once I leave the elevated position, I've lost the height advantage. If I knock down a buck, I carefully plan a route to him, otherwise it's easy to become confused in the brush, making the deer difficult to locate.

High brush lends itself nicely to drives, provided you have companions who won't balk at traveling afoot through the tangle. When driving, it's best to use more standers than drivers because it's tough to cover the thicket thoroughly. If a drive doesn't produce but you're confident bucks are still around, re-work the drive in a different direction. If the brush is close to a steep canyon, make sure a stander covers the area. Muley bucks are well known for seeking escape down a rugged canyon.

Aspen forests are common in much of the West and harbor plenty of deer. These trees usually grow in uniform stands at mid to high elevations, generally above 7,000 feet.

My favorite hunting technique in aspens is to slip quietly along on a game or stock trail on a sidehill just under a ridgetop. By moving slowly with the wind in my face, I look for signs of bedded deer in the daytime. The openness of the aspens allows me to see a long way, though some stands have thick underbrush beneath them in places. Most deer will bed within 200 yards of the ridgetop where they can see below. By walking as high as possible without being skylined, you have the advantage of spotting a buck in its bed—provided you see *him* first.

In the early morning, I find a stand where I can see several hundred yards in the aspens. Deer might feed in the trees or wander outside on an adjacent sidehill. They commonly use trails in the aspens, which allows for another method—a tree stand. I prefer a stand just under a ridge near a saddle where deer are apt to cross. Before selecting a tree, I determine the amount of use on a trail.

Stillhunting in aspens is difficult if leaves have just fallen and are dry. Walking is noisy and deer are alerted a long way off. If that's the case, look for a well-used trail made by cattle if any are in the area. Cows travel the trails and beat down the leaves. The trail often will lead to a water hole, which is another possibility. A tree stand or good vantage spot might be just the answer as deer come in for a drink in late afternoon.

If aspen stands are relatively open with little underbrush and hunters are plentiful, look for deer in thickets such as a blowdown, a copse of evergreens, or in a weedy area along a canyon bottom. Muleys won't stay in the open trees if they're disturbed by hunters, but will seek a secluded spot.

Evergreen forests grow everywhere in the West. They might be ponderosa pine forests, thick lodgepole pine forests, or high-country forests of fir and spruce. In most cases, food is scarce and deer must leave the safety of the forest to browse outside.

Access to the high country is often limited, depending on the amount of logging or mining in the area. National forests in every Western state have a network of road systems throughout, so it's usually not a problem getting into reasonably good deer country.

The biggest chore in evergreen forests is finding mule deer concentrations. Expansive timber stands often cover several mountain ranges, making it difficult to locate places being used by deer. There are two spots to look in these forests: logged-over areas and old burns. Both offer the same ingredient—areas rich in forage, due to the removal of timber and sub-sequent growth of brush, and succulent plants preferred by muleys.

You can find burned areas and timbered places by inquiring at forest offices or you can seek them yourself. Prime spots are those that have had enough time to regenerate forage—five years or more, in most cases.

Rimrock areas above forests are often the domain of very big bucks because few people expend the effort of getting to them. Bucks often live at the fringes of the forest or in the timber itself.

National forests offer public hunting, so you'll probably have plenty of competition from other hunters. Some roads are closed to vehicular traffic, however, and are perfect access trails to good mule deer country. You might need to walk several miles to get away from crowds, but most human activity will be gone the first half mile from accessible roads.

Muleys in evergreen forests often behave like elk—they leave the protection of the timber to feed in late afternoon and, by sunrise, they're back in the trees. You need to be alert during those periods, even if it means a walk out of the woods by flashlight or missing a few extra winks in the morning.

Wherever you hunt mule deer, whether in the desert or in the high country, you might find a big buck anywhere. To increase your chances, however, prepare to go where other hunters don't. Leave the roads as far behind as you can and seek out undisturbed areas that offer solitude to bucks. A good share of the hunters you'll see will hunt from their vehicles. Many others will make short forays near roads. If you're really enthusiastic about a big buck and your physical condition will allow it, don a daypack and spend the entire day in deer country. Better yet, take a backpack with grub, tent, and sleeping bag and spend several days where the deer live.

There's a common belief that the biggest bucks live in the high country. I believe that statement, though I've seen plenty of dandy deer in the desert. In fact, my biggest buck ever came from a lowland pinyon-juniper forest. But if I had to choose all the environments for a big buck, I'd head for the ridgetops and rimrock where few hunters go.

Before spending a lot of time in an area, I do some hard scouting to determine deer are around, no matter where I'm hunting. Sometimes I can't scout before the season, so I scout on the first day of the hunt if I'm in an unfamiliar area. I walk a great deal, looking for sign that spells deer—tracks, rubbed trees, fresh droppings, and browsed plants.

If I find what I'm looking for, I hunt hard where sign was most encouraging and I stay with it as long as possible. That's probably the best formula of all—to hunt as hard as you can as long as you can. If you don't score, tally one for the mule deer. At least you know you tried your best. Don't figure luck has a major role on a mule deer hunt. Luck is important but you can increase your chances by meeting the mule deer buck on his terms. That's all you can do and, if you score, you'll know you earned him. That's the nicest part of hunting.

The Heat's On The Early-Season Hunter

By V. Lee Oertle

It was a huge rack, broad as the reach of both your arms, that curled up into the wind above the cab. Following hunters stared at the back of the passing pickup with astonishment. Below that trophy head, a nice mule deer carcass was suspended on a pipe framework across the cargo box. It made an eerie sight in our headlights.

We followed the pickup through the Virgin River Gorge, out of Utah into Arizona, where passing trucks frequently buffeted the carcass with flying gravel, sand, and moisture from over-worked refrigeration units.

Ahead of us stretched a solid string of red taillights from trucks, campers, trailers, and 4×4 vehicles—mainly hunters returning to the West Coast from Wyoming, Utah, and Idaho. A freshening wind sent exhaust smoke straight back over us. It was probably just my imagination that the mule deer carcass seemed to change color as we passed Beaver Dam Lodge, Mesquite, and Valley of Fire National Monument. Then it became splotchy purple as we finally dropped off the desert plateau overlooking the greater Las Vegas valley. The flesh of the muley seemed to shrink and wrinkle right before our eyes in that desert heat. Behind us, the Utah nights had probably frosted the carcass. But, on the way down I15, temperatures now stood at 86°. That's not unusual for an October night in this part of the country.

By coincidence, we pulled alongside that same pickup in downtown Las Vegas. Gassing up, we watched a curious crowd gather to admire the animal. At first, the smell of gasoline blocked my senses. When I hung the nozzle and capped our own tank, though, it hit with a solid fist of unpleasantness.

Heat determines when to skin your deer. If you must transport it a long distance in hot weather, leave the hide on. If the locker's

Others around the pickup noticed it and began making comments. The driver climbed up into the cargo box and pulled open the brisket.

"Whew!" he said. "Sure be happy to get him into the freezer to quiet that odor."

I've often wondered how his wife reacted when she opened the first package of frozen venison. That is, if the processor accepted the carcass in the first place. Most meatcutters are fussy about what they allow into their plants because one spoiled carcass can taint a score of others. Freezing does not eliminate the original problem. If it was overripe when wrapped, it'll come out smelling the same or maybe worse.

nearby, skin the deer, but protect the carcass with a cheesecloth bag to prevent fouling the meat in transit.

With early small-game seasons, and early archery and primitive weapon seasons, many hunters are out in warm weather even in the East and in many parts of the Midwest, West, and South, it can be very hot. Hunting in such weather calls for special techniques to keep hunters and their kills from going bad. Here are some things to do that can make hot-weather hunting and camping a much pleasanter experience.

CONSERVING WATER

Carry as much water as you can. Allow at least two gallons a person per day for drinking, minimum washing, and cooking. Four hunters camped to-

gether will need eight to 10 gallons a day to be comfortable. Less water will be consumed if you use waterless hand cleaners.

A recreational vehicle shower will use from 15 to 35 gallons of water for one person if he dallies; seven to 11 gallons if he's reasonably quick. The best way is to take sponge baths outside if the area permits it. Half a bucket of water and a wash cloth will do.

Water need only be carried one way, remember. On the return trip, any excess can be given to other hunters or poured around trees.

Paper plates, plastic forks and spoons, and paper cups will eliminate much dish washing and conserve both water and fuel.

If outside pit toilets are available, use them instead of the RV bathroom.

CAMPING COOL

If the planned campsite has no shade at all, take along a 20×20 overhead fly. Pitch the tent underneath it. Preventing direct sunlight from striking tent walls will keep the tent livable by day and cool by night. Just make sure that the lowest part of the fly is at least a foot above the tent; two or three feet is better.

Leave all screened tent windows open day and night. Constant ventilation will prevent the interiors from getting stuffy.

On hot nights, particularly in the Southwest dove and quail country, many hunters prefer to sleep under the stars. That's fine but, before leaving camp in the morning, put sleeping bags under cover out of the sun. Otherwise, the padding will absorb so much heat that the bags will retain it all night.

If a windbreak is erected around the camp, suspend it a few inches above ground so that air can circulate under and around it to avoid a hot-box effect under the flycover.

RV PARKING

Few RV owners seem to be aware of the fact that the direction in which they park their units makes a great difference in how cool the rig will be. The ideal way is to point the tongue of a trailer east or west (or front bumper of any other RV). An awning will shade the south side of the RV, the north side will get no sun at all, and only the roof will collect heat. If the tongue is pointed either north or south, by contrast, both sides will heat up.

If there are any trees in the camping area, try to align the RV or tent for morning sun and afternoon shade. If rows of trees grow in an east-west direction, pitch on the north side of them. If trees are in a north-south line, park on the east side of them.

RV campers should open all sidewall and roof vents and leave them that way, even if it means collecting a bit of dust. In the mistaken belief that morning coolness can be trapped and held in the coach, most campers close the vents at dawn and don't open them again until noon. By that time, the roof and sidewall insulation will have absorbed so much heat that it will last all night and make sleeping miserable. Operating an air conditioner is not the answer, unless you have a built-in electric generator. Even so, it isn't advisable to leave a generator chugging away while you are out hunting. And, at night, nearby campers may object to all the noise and vibrations.

SLEEPING COMFORTABLY

Don't cook a hot meal inside the coach before retiring and then start the generator and run an air conditioner until everyone reaches for an extra blanket. It's far better to leave vents open, cook outside, or cook only briefly. Don't allow hot showers in the RV during the evening.

MAKE ICE LAST

Ice will last much longer if it is protected in this way: Dig a shallow pit, lid-deep, on the shady side of the camp (usually the north). Set the ice chest down into it. Cover the top of the chest with a couple of burlap sacks and pour a little water on them a few times each day. By doing this, I have frequently stretched four days out of a 50-pound ice block when air temperatures hovered at 114°.

COOKING

A portable barbecue brazier or small propane stove should be carried even in the most luxurious RV for outside cooking. If the hunting season is unusually dry, open campfires may not be permitted. Plan simple meals—one hot dish, if any, with pre-packaged or pre-cooked canned foods as side dishes. A small ice chest kept well stocked with cheese, bread, rolls, pickles, and a variety of lunch meats will eliminate a lot of cooking.

Stock your larder with canned tomatoes, peaches, grapefruit sections, beans, juices, and canned or bottled drinks. Keep a jug of ice water available. Taking a drink occasionally will replace body moisture and prevent nausea, weakness, or muscle cramps.

Carry a canteen and refuse to hunt with those who don't. They'll be nipping on yours all day. Dehydration prevents the kidneys from functioning normally. Take a drink if you feel heat exhaustion coming on. The symptoms are weakness, nausea, dizziness, fuzzy vision, splotchy skin, and difficulty in breathing.

Years spent hunting in areas such as the Salton Sea, the lower Colorado River, and the fringes of Death Valley have convinced me that salt tablets do more harm than good if adequate water is available. I don't take them.

Spoilage of food can be a serious problem during hot weather. Don't hesitate to throw away a few rolls or a salad now and then. Stomach cramps, nausea, and worse can occur from eating food left out in the heat too long. Replace lids on food containers promptly. Don't try to reuse frozen lemonade or orange juice leftover from meals. Discard it. Be particularly careful when handling potato salad. Keep it in the ice chest, even when dipping it out of the container. Some products such as milk, butter, and eggs will warn of impending trouble with foul odors. Salads and lemonades will not. The fewer perishables carried, the better.

CLOTHING

Hunting in hot weather calls for light, loose-fitting clothing. I prefer long-sleeved shirts because they prevent sunburn, repel insects, and prevent painful scratches in dense brush. A duckbill cap is almost useless. Wear a broad-brimmed hat; it will shade your head better.

Insulated boots should not be worn in hot weather, no matter how comfortable they may feel. Low-topped (ankle length) hiking shoes are best, unless you're worried about snakes.

STALKING

Warm weather creates extremely difficult stalking. Leaves, twigs, and grass are brittle. Everything pops, crackles, and snaps as the hunter tries to sneak along quietly. As a consequence, the type of footwear worn is important. Pliable Birdshooters are good. Some serious hunters wear moccasins or even tennis shoes.

Hanging around water holes may not be as productive as some hunters believe because the hotter it gets, the higher game such as deer and elk go—within reason. And they'll water at night, up among the seeps leaching out of last winter's snowfields. By day, they'll hole up in forests or bed down in thickets in ravine bottoms. Despite the fact that undergrowth sends a quick alarm every time a hunter takes a step, those dense stands of timber are a good bet. Deer and elk don't like walking in it either.

Almost the only time deer and elk will move during hot weather is early morning and at dusk—and then only briefly. Trail sitting won't be too productive at such times. The best approach, I've found, is to make a few drives or roll a few stones through dense canyon thickets.

Following stream beds—even dry ones—is a good bet. Drift along slowly, stopping at each bend of the trail to peek around it. I've jumped old bucks pawing sand in search of water. But one hop, skip, and jump and they're back in the forest. You've got to shoot fast.

Pick a spot on a hill overlooking stock watering tanks, above grassy meadows, and around ponds or springs. It can be a long wait. Probably the best tip of all is to go an extra mile. Pick any direction and start walking until you're well past your usual hunting grounds. Get as far from roads as possible.

A surprising number of big bucks are taken during hot weather just by crisscrossing a brushy hillside until every square yard of it has been covered. Northern slopes are best.

HANDLING KILLED GAME

The following comments apply where daytime air temperatures hover above 80°.

Immediately after the kill, drag the animal into the shade, if there is any. Quickly field-dress the carcass and then start looking around for brush. If camp is a long way off, cover the carcass with brush, grass, tumbleweeds, or anything that will keep the direct sun off it. If night is approaching, it's probably best to hang the animal in heavy brush or at least to drag it into a thicket and leave it overnight.

Prop the rib cage open with sticks and wipe out the body cavity thoroughly. Make sure no bits of lung, heart, liver, or other fast-ripening tissue are left inside. Then, slip a cheesecloth bag over the animal, taking care not to rip it. The idea is to keep insects away. Early the next morning, while it's still relatively cool, take the animal to camp.

If you leave game to cool, prop it open with sticks, suspended in the shade. Pull it up out of reach of predators.

If high temperatures persist, better think about taking the game to the nearest town for cooling. While many small towns will no longer process big game for nonresidents, some of them will cool it for a day or more for a small fee.

Whether or not to wash out the body cavity is the subject of hot argument among many hunters. Some say water spoils the meat, particularly during hot weather; others say it does no harm. My own opinion is that washing the body cavity can be good, particularly if there are any bits of bloodshot meat or body organs in the cavity, or if dust has filtered into it. But it's important to dry the surfaces with cloth afterward. Sometimes, the outside of the animal should also be washed, particularly if the head is to be mounted or if the wounds are bloody. If you know that you will be hunting in a dusty, windy area, bring extra water for this purpose.

TO SKIN OR NOT TO SKIN

Arguments rage pro and con over this but, after running a hunting camp for seven years, I came to these conclusions:

1) Skinning in cold weather does not seem to affect the meat.

2) During hot weather, skinning allows the meat to dehydrate, especially so during a long transport back home. My suggestion would be not to skin big game unless the trip to the meat processor will take only a couple of hours. For those intending to cross two or three states, leave the hide intact until the processor is reached.

Removing the scent glands located on lower rear legs is said to improve the flavor of venison. Having tried it both ways, I no longer worry about that because I always remove lower rear legs in camp.

FACTORS AFFECTING FLAVOR

1) Failing to field-dress an animal quickly.

2) Allowing killed game to lie in the sun for several hours.

3) Forgetting to remove fatty tissue, bits of lung, heart, or esophagus from the body cavity.

4) Carelessness in removing entrails; allowing them to contact rear quarters.

5) Breaking the spleen or stomach bag. In a gut-shot animal, that may be unavoidable. In that case, clean the area thoroughly and slice off tainted meat.

6) Stuffing body cavity with sage brush, rabbit-brush, or other strong-smelling plants.

7) Hanging carcasses in the way of campfire smoke. Some hunters do this deliberately in the belief that smoke drives away insects. That may be true. But the smoke from some kinds of burning brush and driftwood can do more harm than the insects.

8) Storing a properly handled carcass adjacent to one that already has started to spoil.

9) Transporting game in a hot wind where dust, smoke, and automobile exhaust can pollute it.

Cheesecloth bags protect fresh-killed game from insects, dust, and surface contamination while the body cools.

10) Allowing a carcass to hang too long without proper cooling.

11) Skinning too long in advance of cooling.

12) Dragging a game animal through swampy areas, bitter-smelling thickets, turgid streams, and so on.

PROPER TRANSPORTATION

Perhaps the best way to discuss this is by type of vehicle, because improper handling is usually the result of inadequate storage space.

Passenger cars:

Car-top racks usually end up holding the extra gear. Four hunters should never use only one car unless they tow a trailer to bring the animals back in. But, if the carcasses must be carried in a car, then the best place is on the rear seat, wrapped loosely in a tarpaulin. The worst place is in a closed trunk where heat builds up rapidly. And, if the trunk lid is deliberately propped open to provide ventilation, exhaust fumes will be sucked in. The car-top rack should be a last resort in hot weather. If game must be transported in that location, wrap it loosely and place it crosswise so that wind does not blow directly onto it.

Pickup Trucks:

There's plenty of space in these, but observe these cautions: Exhaust pipes heat up the floor in a cargo box. It's a good idea to put down wood slats on the floor and to place a sheet of plywood or boards on them. Then put the game on top of it. Stretch a cover across the cargo box, allowing space of at least a foot above the animals so that direct sun will not overheat them. Or store camping gear and other equipment on the cargo box floor, put the game on top of a tarpaulin spread over the equipment, and cover it. Allow for plenty of ventilation.

RVs:

Big racks can damage the interior of the coach, so pad the antler tips with burlap or foam tape. Spread old carpet on the floor to prevent blood staining. Keep one roof vent and one side window partly open during the drive, but don't leave a rear window, vent, or door open while under way.

4 × 4 Vehicles:

The typical Bronco, Blazer, or Scout has such limited space that many hunters who drive them tow a small trailer. That's the place to tote camping and other gear. Carry big game in the cargo area of the main vehicle but provide plenty of ventilation. Because manufacturers refuse to install rear-seat windows in many offroad vehicles, that can be a problem. Insulate the floor with boards or carpets to prevent heat damage to the game.

Packing big game in ice or dry ice is risky. Unless expertly done, the meat may eventually spoil. Part of the carcass may overheat, creating zones of partly frozen and fully frozen meat that ruin the flavor or spoil the meat. Stuffing the body cavity with plastic bags filled with crushed ice that's heavily wrapped to prevent surface-freezing contact may help, though. But the best thing to do is to take the meat to a processor and have it thoroughly chilled before starting home with it. If that means spending an extra day or two, balance it against the value of the meat and the need to prevent waste.

In some areas, big game is no longer as plentiful as it once was. Give it the best protection you can, particularly in hot weather.

Hunt High
For Muleys

By Brian Kahn

I was half way up the steep, timbered slope when I heard the shot. It sounded far off in the thin Wyoming air, but I knew that either Dom or Bill had fired. I guessed it was Bill, who was working up the opposite slope beyond the open draw between us. Dom had been moving up the center.

A second shot interrupted my speculation. My eyes searched the open patches on Bill's side, hoping that the shots would move a buck into sight. Nothing. Then I moved toward the draw, guessing that whoever had done the shooting might need some help. This time I was right.

Emerging from the timber, I saw the Blaze Orange of Dom's coat as he bent over a gray form in the snow.

"You got one!" I called.

He looked up, smiling. The width of his grin was a better answer than any words could have been.

It was Dom's first mule deer and it was a fine animal. Four points sprouted from each side. The outside spread measured 28 inches. Back in camp, the field-dressed buck pushed the scale to 235 pounds.

That evening, while sitting in the big wall tent near the pulsing heat of the sheepherder's stove, Bill and I savored the success that Dom, as a novice, might well have taken for granted. Bill and I had been hunting mule deer for 15 years and we often had the feeling that we were chasing weather, rather than bucks.

We began hunting mule deer back in the 1960s, in the northeast corner of our native California, camping and hunting where Bill's father had in the '40s and '50s. But wildlife management policies had changed since the '50s and the seasons ended in early

October instead of lasting until winter storms. Although Bill's dad had done well, we drew blanks.

Convinced that California's deer population, rather than our hunting methods, were to blame, we began to hunt out of state. Montana, Oregon, Idaho, Colorado—we tried them all during the '70s. Relying on the advice of old-timers, we planned our hunts for season's end, to hit snow and catch the big bucks moving.

Our success improved but not by much. In eight years, I took six bucks. Three were small, the others average. I saw and shot at only one trophy buck, managing to miss him cleanly. Bill, on seven trips, bagged only two deer. As for snow, we hit it only once. Overall, we seemed plagued by warm, dry weather.

"Darn. You ought to be here when it snows," the locals would tell us. "Bucks everywhere."

Each year we would break camp and head home talking about *next* year.

One week's hunt with a bow and arrow changed everything. Egged on for years by a bowhunting friend, I finally gave archery a try in 1981. Following my friend's instructions, I hunted the bucks' summer range, high in Nevada's Ruby Mountains. He told me that my main problem would be trying to keep track of a single buck when there were so many others to distract me. I was certain he was stretching things a bit. He wasn't.

My biggest difficulty on that hunt was stumbling over small bucks while stalking trophy-size ones. I didn't get a deer, but it wasn't because they weren't there.

Bill and I discussed my Nevada experience while

preparing for our Wyoming hunt. By hunting high and early, I'd seen more bucks than in all my previous mule deer hunts combined. We decided to take the hint.

Wyoming was new country to us and we knew it would require some planning. I called the wildlife department headquarters for the area we planned to hunt and inquired into hunter success rates, access, campsites, and probable hunter competition. Finally, I got to the key question: "Would you recommend hunting early or late?"

At first, the answer was equivocal.

"Take your pick, they're both good. Hunting's tougher early because the bucks are way up high. Late, given the right weather, they come down into the sage draws. If you hit it right, it's great."

I didn't say anything but I knew all about "hitting the right weather." I pushed a little further, asking: "If it were you, when would you hunt?"

There was a pause, then, "If it was me, I'd hunt early and hunt high."

My volunteer advisor made it clear that the hunting would not be easy.

"Of course, you'll probably hit warm weather. And it's no place for a jeep hunter. You'll have to work for your bucks—both to get them and to pack them out. And in that high ridge country you've picked, you won't see too many. But what you see will be worth it."

As things turned out, he was right on all counts except the weather. The day we arrived in camp, October 13, it snowed. And I, a hunter who prides himself on coming prepared, had left my snow pacs at home.

Before dawn on opening day, we moved through virgin powder, heading toward the high ridge. As the sky lightened in the east, the snowy landscape turned from soft gray to blue to red. We moved in silence, then stood still as the sun poured into the high basin, bringing the light and life of another day.

Because we did not know the country well, we picked a difficult place to climb the ridgeline. With 18 inches of snow covering slippery boulders, we simply couldn't make it to the top. Our failure was all the more frustrating because we could see, threading through the snow just below the scantily timbered ridge, a meandering trail that ended in a patch of scrub pine. It simply had to be a big buck.

After breaking for lunch, we decided that, if we couldn't get to the top, we'd try the next best thing. We would hunt parallel to the ridgeline, working the high basins that sloped up toward the top.

The first two basins provided nothing, not even a track. And, having worked through deep snow into early afternoon, my suburban legs and snow-soaked feet let me know that they'd had enough.

Dom felt the same, but not Bill.

"Heck, the next basin's just beyond that timber. I'll go have a look, then meet you down at the Scout."

He headed off, leaving Dom and me envying his stonemason's legs and rubber pacs.

"He's younger than we are," I said.

"And crazier," replied Dom.

Forty minutes later, we heard Bill shoot. And shoot again and again.

"I'll be darned," said Dom. "There *are* bucks up here."

"That's what I've been telling you," I said, not wanting to admit that I'd been wondering since morning whether the early snow had driven the bucks down from their summer range.

A few minutes passed before Bill's dark figure appeared on the snowy slope above and gave us the clean miss sign.

Back at the jeep, Bill told us how he'd no more than crossed into the basin when he spotted two fine bucks on the far side.

He had shot from the sit, unable to see his bullets strike in the snow. He had disturbed the bucks just enough to prod them into walking out of the basin.

Bill pointed high on the slope to a faint thread in the snow. First it ran parallel to the top ridge, then it cut up the nearly sheer face and over the top.

"That's the trail," he said. "They're up on top."

We planned to follow the bucks the next morning but low snow clouds shrouded the mountaintop. So, we hunted as high as we could, working a lower range to the west.

Things looked good when we stepped from the Scout and jumped six fat does. Less than an hour later, sweating up the steep, timbered slope, I heard the two shots and found Dom with his trophy.

By the next morning, the clouds were gone and we were back in the high country. Dom, having filled his tag, had the luxury of sleeping in. Bill and I decided to work the basin where he'd missed his two bucks.

We hit the trail at first light but our plan was interrupted by a tiny dark spot a half mile distant. My 8X binoculars showed the "spot" to be a fine buck browsing. He fed on the north slope of an open basin. A timber-lined stream cut between us.

With the morning breeze coming from the east, we planned a stalk that formed three sides of a rectangle. We would sneak west along the stream until we were well downwind of the buck. Then we would cut up over the northern rim and head back east until, by cutting back into the basin, we would be directly above him.

The plan worked fine until the wind changed. The 180° shift gave us no choice but to backtrack and then reverse the plan in order to stay downwind.

To complicate things, the buck had disappeared. We assumed that he had bedded down in one of two small stands of fir on the slope, but we couldn't be certain.

It was slow going in the snow and we were three hours into the stalk when we finally hit the rim about 400 yards east of the nearest grove of firs.

I lay in the snow and glassed the grove, hoping for some sign of the deer's location. On the high side of the trees, I saw a patch of bare earth and an empty deer bed. Glassing under the trees, I strained

Photo by Erwin A. Bauer

to penetrate the shadows until the off-white patch took shape, then an eye and part of an antler. We had found our buck.

We had come too far to chance a long shot, so we moved behind the rim until we could cut to the top directly above the grove. After crawling the last 50 yards, I took sitting position on a rocky point 80 yards from the buck's bed. I couldn't see the deer from my position but I knew he was there.

Bill continued along the ridgeline in order to come at the grove from the west, thus covering the upper basin in case the buck jumped in that direction.

I had been calm during the hours of stalking but now I became a bundle of nerves, repeatedly checking my scope, safety, and shooting position.

Then I saw Bill, working around the slope's contour, rifle held high across his chest, approaching the grove as if he were walking up quail. First at 70 yards, then at 60, 50. With the wind at Bill's back, that buck had to smell him. But he held tight.

Suddenly the timber exploded with snapping limbs. Not one, but two bucks burst into the white light. One cut down and below Bill, out of my sight. The other plunged down the slope to my left.

I felt calm as I swung the crosshairs ahead of his heavy chest and touched off the .270. The shot felt good but there he was, bounding through the open snow. Just before my buck disappeared behind the contour of the slope, I heard Bill's rifle crack. I fired a second shot. Then Bill shot again.

In the eerie silence that followed, I sat shaking and wondering if my second shot had hit and if my buck was now down—fallen where I couldn't see him. His trotting form emerged from a shallow draw, dispelling that illusion.

"Get serious," I told myself as I picked him up in the scope at 350 yards. He was quartering away and my backline hold looked solid as I swung the vertical crosshair ahead. The rifle jumped against my shoulder and the buck stumbled and went down. Again, silence.

Following his tracks, I found that my second shot had hit, taking him high and a little back, leaving a heavy blood trail.

Coming on him lying gray and still in the snow, I felt satisfaction and regret. Satisfaction at having executed a good stalk and having secured the winter's meat, regret that a fine animal now lay dead.

Bill's shout broke the silence. I turned to see his victory wave and knew the time for work had come.

Both bucks were prime animals—four-pointers in the 180-pound class. That weight in venison, so fine hanging at the meat locker, pulled heavily as we worked them through the snow. An exhausting four hours later, we got to the jeep. It was twilight when we pulled into camp.

A few hours later, the three bucks hung in the cold night air while golden embers glowed in the belly of the stove. Bill and I slipped into our down sleeping bags with quiet satisfaction. After 15 years of trying, we were on the right track.

For the hunter who must plan his deer hunt well in advance or who has limited time in the field, hunting high makes sense. Dates for the trip can be set with confidence. Unless a rare, early-season storm dumps more than two feet of snow on the summer range, the bucks will be there when you arrive. And fall, rather than winter weather, tends to make camping and driving more enjoyable. Physically, the hunting may be tougher than at lower elevations, but the thrill of sighting and stalking high-country mule deer is a unique wilderness experience.

If you decide to give the high country a try, here are some tips which may prove helpful:

- Get good information on the summer range in the region you intend to hunt. Game officials, once they understand you are willing to work hard for your deer, are likely to help. If possible, get information from more than one source.

- Get good maps. The country is big and easy to misjudge. Fine topographical maps are available from the U.S. Geological Survey, Branch of Distribution, Box 25286, Federal Center, Denver, CO 80225 (303-234-3832). U.S. Forest Service maps are excellent, too, especially for help in locating roads and trails and in identifying public land. The headquarters of the national forest in the area you intend to hunt will have them.

- Get in shape. You won't be jeep hunting and the mountain air is thin. Regular jogging and climbing stairs will really pay off. And be well equipped. Good broken-in boots and quality binoculars are musts, as is a flat-shooting scoped rifle.

Finally, be prepared for the unexpected. Take along a nice warm pair of insulated snow pacs!

Muleys In Your Pocket

By Jack White

You'd think it would have been high adventure last fall when Birt Enterline collected the biggest mule deer of his life. Actually, the episode unraveled in the low foothills of Colorado's eastern slope, within clear view of Denver's bright city lights.

"The economic crunch hit me hard last year," Birt recalled, "and I just couldn't afford my usual 10-day timberline hunt. Cash and time were short, but there was no way I was going to entirely forego my annual hunt for a nice muley buck."

Luckily, a brainstorm was in the offing when Enterline recalled seeing a small band of deer in a particular alfalfa meadow that he passed while driving to work every morning. The 10 or 12 muleys were all does. But, with the rutting season rapidly approaching, it seemed inconceivable the deer wouldn't have any male suitors hanging around. There just had to be at least one buck in the vicinity keeping tabs on them.

What happened shortly after that proved to be a revelation for Birt. Hunting permission was easily gained and, after only a few hours of scouting, he found a stand location not far from the meadow in a willow-choked stream bottom. Later, on opening morning, he couldn't believe his eyes when he saw two bucks—both of which were bigger than the buck he had finally settled for during the previous season's high-country hunt. A few moments after that, he was filling out his tag and attaching it to the antlers of one of those deer.

The entire notion that bucks of such caliber should be in the lower elevations so early in the season completely violated a cardinal rule of mule deer hunting that had been drummed into Birt at an early age. That tenet, which most other hunters still subscribe to, is that mature mule deer bucks always migrate to the high country in early spring and stay there until deep snows and bitter winter storms force them back down much later. And those small pockets of cover in the low elevations are home to only a few does with their current fawns, plus the occasional spike buck or forkhorn.

Enterline's firsthand experience greatly contradicts that theory. Biologists who have studied the migratory patterns of the species are beginning to offer many plausible explanations.

From a historical perspective, many scientists believe that mule deer, like elk, actually evolved as low-elevation creatures that thrived on open plains and prairies. Their eventual seeking of high-country refuges came only as a direct result of man's encroachment upon their habitat.

Simple examination of the muley's habits and body features bears out this theory. For example, mammals that live in open areas typically have large ears, keen eyesight, and an ability to run at high speed for long distances. Pronghorn antelope, still plains creatures, reveal these very traits . . . and so do mule deer. Even the way mule deer run when alarmed, with high, pogo-stick bounds, is a characteristic of species originally adapted to thin cover and open ground, animals that need to make so-called "observation jumps" during their escape maneuvers to keep tabs on trailing predators.

With muleys possessing the genes and physical features conducive to low-elevation and thin-cover habitat, increasing numbers of the deer are reverting to the former lifestyles of their predecessors.

89

"There is probably a combination of factors that can account for this," explains Jim Warthau, a biologist based in Boulder, Colorado, who acts as an environmental consultant to many companies pioneering oil shale development. "An unusually cold spring followed by a mild summer often causes a disruption in the migratory patterns of mule deer. Many of the animals simply elect to remain in the lower elevations throughout that particular year, and those deer that do head for higher ground may not travel as far or go as high as in previous years. But, even more significant is the influence of this kind of weather upon any given year's new fawn crop."

If, during its first year of life, a fawn does not follow its mother and other deer in a massive migration to the high country, the usual behavioral chain of events is broken and a low-elevation pattern of life is imprinted upon that young deer. Moreover, as those particular nonmigratory fawns eventually grow to adulthood and in turn begin reproducing, they will tend to perpetuate the cycle by passing on to their offspring the very same inclinations toward living year-round in the lower elevations.

One advantageous result of this behavior is that a small percentage of hunters are now succeeding in taking some very impressive bucks from low-elevation regions—areas normally scoffed at by legions of other hunters in their annual treks to the peaks.

"In addition to unusual weather," Jim Warthau continued, "the activities of humans can also have a disruptive effect upon mule deer behavior. Vast mining operations sprawling over miles of terrain, superhighways bordered on both sides by high deer-proof fences, and other man-made 'blockades' across traditional migration routes may all play a role. But, whatever the exact cause, many succeeding generations of deer are now living secret lives in the foothills of the Rockies."

Wyoming game biologist Norris Wolcott goes even as far as to estimate that perhaps as many as one-third of that state's mule deer herd can be classified as permanent low-country residents.

Yet none of this news surprises Mickey Thompson, an enterprising hunter who has long known that his chances of collecting a nice muley buck are as good, if not better, in the low country than they are in the high elevations.

"My brother and I are custom combiners," the affable farmer recently told me. "We travel a three-state area—Colorado, Wyoming, and Montana—transporting our heavy equipment from farm to farm to harvest grain. We can usually combine about 1,200 acres a day and you just wouldn't believe the number of muleys we see on foothill farms. They're not in the open fields, of course—except during the hours of dawn and dusk—but in adjacent swales, brushy culverts, and especially stream and river bottoms containing a lot of tag adlers and jumbled rock formations."

The Thompson brothers often put in 16-hour workdays during fall and early winter, so they long ago had to give up high-country hunting vacations. But they dismiss that loss with a shrug because it hasn't diminished their success one bit. Now they hunt one day at a time, whenever the opportunity arises, concentrating exclusively upon low-elevation pockets of cover. Both of them have taken handsome muley bucks for the past dozen years in a row.

The real beauty of hunting pocket muleys is three-fold: Seldom does the weather become severe enough to hamper hunting efforts, as it frequently does in the high country; one does not generally need packhorses, four-wheel-drives, wall tents, sheepherder stoves, and an extensive entourage of other gear to hunt the lower elevations; and, because a network of highway arteries course through the lowlands, it's easy to arrange one-day, two-day, or weekend hunts in prime regions that few others hunt.

I once hunted out of a camp on a tract of Bureau of Land Management land on Colorado's western slope where our base of operations was merely a pickup camper parked in a shady glen. We were hunting after spending only two hours getting our gear in order and, by lunchtime, a four-by-four muley buck was hanging from a nearby tree limb. At dusk that same day, I collected an extra-large forkhorn and, the following morning, the third member of our party shot another very nice four-by-four.

"I can't believe we had such an enjoyable and successful hunt in only two days," Jim Bielchek mused in the truck on the way home. "On our last high-country hunt, it took two days just to get the damn camp set up!"

Pocket muleys are taken within rather close proximity to where humans live and work, so one might incorrectly think there would be little chance of taking deer of trophy proportions. Whitetail hunters have long known that their quarry easily adapts to living in close quarters with man. Each year, countless buster bucks are taken just beyond the city limits in clear view of farmhouses, highways, and the skylines of major metropolitan regions. Nonmigratory muleys behave much the same way, learning to coexist with man by skulking, sneaking, and hiding in the checkerboard swatches of cover separating meadows, pastures, and croplands.

Some scientists are even speculating that a higher percentage of year-round, low-elevation muleys may actually grow larger racks than their counterparts that spend most of their time in wilderness high country, although the latter usually live longer.

The reason is simple: Pocket muleys have access to larger quantities of much higher quality food than do high-country mule deer. As with all antlered game animals, food and mineral intake always goes first into body growth and maintenance. Only after those requirements have been satisfied are excess nutrients channeled into antler growth and development. In the lower elevations, mule deer have not only native grasses and foods to choose from but also a wide variety of agricultural crops such as alfalfa and corn. Furthermore, they're likely to ingest much higher concentrations of trace elements such as calcium, phosphorus, and potassium—all of which are conducive to rapid antler growth—than those deer living far from intensive farming operations.

Hunting muleys in low elevations is not entirely unlike hunting whitetails, but there are a few similarities worth mentioning. In those pockets where cover is virtually impenetrable and the approach of a stillhunter would only send the deer running, finding a good stand location and playing the waiting game is the best bet. Here's where scouting for feeding areas can pay off because, when the deer decide to move, it will invariably be in the direction of food.

I like to first find dense junglelike cover and then hike the perimeters of adjacent grassy meadows and croplands looking for tracks and other signs indicating where the animals are entering and exiting the feeding area. Then I select the best vantage point for a stand, sometimes using a portable tree stand. Early and late in the day are the best times for stand hunting because muleys, like whitetails, may be up and around at almost any time during the night or day, but their activities are greatly amplified during the low-light hours of early morning and late afternoon.

During the midday hours, when the deer are usually bedded, two partners can execute a stillhunting maneuver that sometimes yields incredible dividends. The game plan involves locating long, narrow, fingerlike cuts and ravines that are filled to the brim with deadfalls, brush, and tall grass. The hunters walk parallel to each other along the upper rims on either side. By periodically throwing rocks down into the cover, hunters can often roust muleys from their beds, but only *one* of the hunters should do the rock throwing. Often, a buck will rivet his attention on the rock-throwing hunter and, in planning his sneaking-away escape, be entirely oblivious to the other hunter on the opposite hillside, offering a clear shot.

Yet sometimes, even the best laid plans go awry. Once, Bill Matthews and I were staging this kind of hunt in deep arroyos that wound their way downhill toward Colorado's South Platte River. This was the year we learned from hard experience that mule deer do not always run a short distance and then stop to look back, as we had heard so many times. During our two-day hunt, the two biggest bucks we jumped—both absolute monsters—just kept right on running without breaking stride once. So there we stood, waiting so long for them to slam on the brakes and give us easy standing shots that eventually they were long gone without a single round fired.

Perhaps in the high country, where muleys are unaccustomed to seeing man, their fabled habit of stopping to curiously look back may still ring quite true. But when it comes to lowland muleys living close to human activity, don't bank on it.

Another opportunity for lowland hunters is working pockets of aspens and stands of pines. The very best possibilities exist with those timbered tracts less than 20 acres in size and situated on sloping hillsides. One hunter hikes the long way around to station himself above the trees, then his partner enters on the low side and begins slowly stillhunting through the cover. Unlike whitetails that may spurt out of cover almost anywhere, one trait of muleys is that they always seem to travel uphill. This ruse puts one of the hunters in an excellent location to have a shot.

But the very best way to collect a lowland muley buck is to home in upon stream and river bottom regions. The flatlands bordering river bottoms usually harbor the most fertile soil, so farmers typically maintain grassy meadows or croplands right up to where the edges of such ravines suddenly pitch off sharply downhill. This condition gives local deer the best possible combination of food, water, and ample security cover within a several-hundred-square-yard area.

When working river bottoms, we post stand hunters during early morning and late afternoon on rimrocks and similar vantage points where they can look down and into the dense cover. Such locations also allow them to occasionally pan the higher ground to their right or left to spot previously unseen deer that have suddenly popped into view on an adjacent meadow.

During midday, we enact drives, concentrating upon those particular stream and river bottoms that are bordered by sheer walls. The deer are then encouraged to travel the length of the bottomland rather than to attempt to climb up and over one of the sides. And the best possible place to have one or more stand hunters is on a high outcropping overlooking a narrow neck or funnel in the bottomland, through which the deer must travel to gain access to parts elsewhere.

Pocket muley hunters must travel around a good deal. By their very nature, pockets of lowland cover are small. Once a given cover has been worked by any of the aforementioned techniques, the hunters will then want to move on to the next likely looking thicket, bottomland, or woodlot. Often, in a day's time, we'll hunt as many as a dozen different pockets, then return the following day and hit them all again.

Hunting the largest ranches is the most practical undertaking because it minimizes having to gain trespass permission from many different landowners. Hunting pressure is light, so trespass permission isn't overly difficult to obtain, although in some instances a modest daily fee may be required.

In addition to private lands, there are extensive BLM and national forest holdings on both the eastern and western slopes of the Rockies, where public hunting access is allowed without having to seek trespass permission.

But maybe my friend Birt Enterline summed it up best of all when he first discovered this new approach toward mule deer hunting.

"I'm not about to entirely give up my high-country hunts because wilderness timberline regions offer a special alluring attraction no other type of hunting can compare with. But it sure is nice to occasionally go after pocket muleys in the lowlands where you can enjoy balmy 50° to 60° temperatures while walking on flat ground for a change, not to mention seeing almost as many deer in a day's time."

The only thing I can add to that appraisal of hunting pocket muleys is that hunters who overlook this untapped deer hunting bonanza are missing out on plenty of exciting, affordable action.

Eastern Way
For Mule Deer

By John Weiss

orning's first light was incredibly crimson, as though the sky were on fire. Irregular swatches of snow littered the landscape, providing an almost eerie contrast to the ground. Perched in a tree stand, I felt like a sentinel at his post, rigid as if at attention.

An impressive buck I desperately wanted, after two long days of trying to dope out his movement patterns, had just climbed out of a brushy swale. He was threading his way through tangled undergrowth in search of a secluded bedding site. My pulse began to hammer as I flipped off the safety and, in slow motion, tucked the butt of the .270 rifle into my shoulder pocket. When a coyote howled in the distance a few seconds later, the old gentleman turned his head, pointing his ears toward the sound, and that is when I collected both the rack I wanted and my winter's supply of venison.

As I was climbing down from my tree, another rifle roared. One of my partners, Mike Wolter, had likewise been waiting in a portable Baker stand about 500 yards away. Mike is a first-class marksman and I was confident he had just filled his tag.

"Two down and three to go!" I yelped when I reached Wolter and saw the respectable buck he already was beginning to drag out. I slapped him on the back.

"We'll give Whitey, Frank, and Al another hour on stand," Mike said. "Then we'll spend the rest of the day working drives. All of us should have good bucks in camp by sundown or by noon tomorrow at the latest."

Mike is a mechanic from St. Paul, Minnesota. His brother Al, a recent transplant from Ohio, lives near Duluth, where he works for the U.S. Forest Service. Frank Stocke, a building contractor, also lives near Duluth. Whitey Ellard is a restaurant chef in St. Paul and I'm a writer from Chesterhill, Ohio.

The five of us hunt together every year and we've all spent our adult lives as serious students of whitetail behavior and biology. That amounts to more than 125 years of combined deer hunting education that we're sure makes us far more effective hunters than if we were loners. It's not unusual for us all to fill our tags on the very first day of the season, or shortly thereafter.

What might seem unusual, however, is that on this particular outing, strictly stand hunting and driving, we were hunting mule deer. Eventually, we took all five bucks in less than 18 hours of hunting. All were legitimate trophies and one just missed qualifying for the record book!

The place was White River National Forest, just an hour north of Glenwood Springs, Colorado. But this was not the first time we found stand hunting and drives effective on muleys. Regardless of the state, every time we embark upon our annual Western hunt we hunt mule deer the way most others go after whitetails back home. We're firmly convinced that other Eastern and Midwestern hunters who make at least occasional treks to various Western states can do no better than play the same game.

Eastern and Midwestern hunters who go westward but once a year are, for all practical purposes, strangers in paradise. Their limited familiarity with the terrain and the behavior of the animals cannot begin to compare to the intimate know-how of hunters who live in the West year-round.

Furthermore, the great majority of visiting sportsmen cannot afford backcountry hunts. Instead, small groups of hunters plan their outings around tight budgets. They are not able to enjoy professional guide service, the use of horses, or all the other personnel and equipment necessary to establish a remote camp in the high country. Consequently, most do-it-yourself nonresidents often hunt crowded areas near roads.

This should not discourage any hunter from traveling to the state of his choice for a try at mule deer. Any enterprising nonresident hunter can more than double his chances of success merely by disregarding the standard rules of mule deer hunting and pursuing the critters the way he knows best. That means relying upon proven whitetail hunting methods. I've learned that a hunter can take a muley by using two whitetail strategies.

What's more, the old saw that you have to hunt the wilderness high country for big bucks is not entirely true. The growing consensus among knowing hunters is that trophy bucks are where you find them. During my last Colorado hunt, my partners and I actually saw as many big bucks in 6,000-foot ranges as did other hunters working from 8,000 feet to timberline. We know because we talked with these hunters as they passed our camp. That wasn't surprising to us because, time and again, the same scenario has been played in recent years.

The game plan we typically follow goes like this. In the morning, we climb out of our sleeping bags about an hour before first light and head for our chosen tree stands. Usually, we wait on stand no longer than 2½ hours because that's when muley bucks are on the move. Then it's back to camp for breakfast.

After breakfast, we fill our pockets with sandwiches for lunch and leave camp to execute carefully planned drives. Depending on the terrain or the time it takes to drag out a buck, ordinarily we make about four drives between 10 a.m. and 4 p.m. Then, those who still have not killed a deer hustle back to their stands for a 2½ hour evening watch while the others return to camp.

The ritual is efficient and effective, yet does not differ one bit from the strategy we work on whitetails back home.

After Mike and I had hung our bucks and after breakfast, we made our first drive. The action was so frantic we almost could not believe what happened.

We had selected a steep draw saturated with aspen and junipers. In places, the cover was as impenetrable as a tropical jungle. Because sage flats nearby

seemed an excellent place for deer to feed at night, we reasoned that any bucks would retreat to the draw during the day.

"John, you and Mike, of course, are the drivers," Al instructed as he scratched out a blueprint of the maneuver in the dirt. "About 500 yards away, this draw forks. A small split goes to the right, and that's where we'll station Whitey. A large arm goes to the left, and Frank and I will cover that."

After giving our partners half an hour to position themselves, Mike and I entered the opposite end of the ravine and began slowly hiking toward them. We've learned from hunting whitetails that any drive comes off better when the drivers are quiet. Shouting and making other noises spooks the deer and, when that happens, they may stampede and go almost anywhere. But when hunters are silent, the deer are more likely to sneak out using predictable escape routes. Therefore, Mike and I were not driving, in the customary sense, but simply stillhunting (with cameras, not rifles) toward our partners' locations.

Twenty minutes into the drive, I heard a single shot from Frank's direction. A moment later, another shot came from Al's position. I began thinking everything was going routinely when suddenly there were three more shots. Then two more. Then a volley of three more after that! When I eventually made it through a dense stand of junipers, I could see Frank close ahead. He was already dressing out a nice buck. On the opposite hillside, Al was kneeling over a buck so big that, at first glance, I thought it was an elk.

"All I can say is wow!" Frank exclaimed, trying to catch his breath from the excitement. "The first buck that came along was good enough for me, but I missed him at only 100 yards. About the same time, Al saw a buck he wanted, and he missed. We couldn't believe it when six more bucks came right behind! When we began shooting, they all took off. I shot three times at the biggest buck I've ever seen but my slugs kicked up dirt far behind him. Just when that buck disappeared, another big one dashed right in front of me and I dropped him on the spot with my second shot. Right after that, an even bigger buck almost ran over Al and, on his third try, he got him."

I've seen big deer before, but Al's buck was mindboggling. Later, field-dressed, it weighed 260 pounds. Its antlers were even more impressive, spreading more than 30 inches, and the rack was just as high as it was wide.

For some reason we still do not clearly understand, when Mike and I moved the deer on that drive, they had decided to part company. The bucks, eight in all, took the left fork toward Frank and Al, while more than a dozen does went to the right and bounced past Whitey.

This seems to be a common characteristic of mule deer when driven. The crafty and elusive bucks seem to seek companionship with other bucks rather than

Eastern and Midwestern hunters who hunt only rarely out West should rely on proven whitetail hunting methods. Use tree stands in the early morning and conduct drives during the mid-day hours. Photo by Erwin A. Bauer.

to consort with does. So, when waiting on stand during a drive, don't pay much heed to does in the hopes that a buck or two is following. Instead, scan adjacent thick cover for a buck slinking along his own escape route. Whitetail bucks usually do the opposite. They seem to follow close behind does.

Mule deer bucks behave differently than whitetails in a few other ways. When sandwiched between drivers and standers, for instance, whitetails often sneak back through the line of drivers. But mule deer usually don't attempt to filter back between the drivers. This means a party of mule deer hunters can get by with fewer drivers than ordinarily would be required to move whitetails.

If the cover is relatively flat, however, muley bucks may just as well pop out somewhere along one of the sides. In fact, on flat land, their most common behavior is to travel perpendicular to the drivers. To take full advantage of this, many times we do not even post hunters on stand. We make what we call a line drive.

In this maneuver, all five of us line up along the edge of thick cover, spaced perhaps 100 yards apart so that, as we move parallel to each other, each hunter can occasionally see his orange-clad partners to his right and left. We try to make no noise. Each man is a stillhunter but, simultaneously, a driver for his partners.

When we jump a buck from his bed in this kind of level terrain, he generally moves a short distance straightaway and then cuts sharply to the right or left. A hunter may or may not have a shot at a buck he jumps himself, depending upon how far away the deer is when it sees the driver and decides to move out. But a hunter is very likely to have a shot

when a buck is jumped by another hunter to his left or right. In most cases, the hunter will get a broadside shot at a slow-moving animal.

Later that evening, Whitey resumed his vigil on stand but saw no bucks. The following morning, the rest of us had the luxury of sleeping late while Whitey again made pre-dawn tracks across crunchy snow to his station. He saw two bucks but they were only three-pointers (Western count) that he elected to pass up. During midday, we pushed two other bucks by Whitey. He had no clean shot at the first, and the other he missed. That evening, from a stand, Whitey got still another chance—this time at a handsome buck—and, finally, he scored.

"I knew deer were coming out of dense juniper and scrub oak to feed on a buffalo grass flat," Whitey recounted. "But they weren't coming all the way out into the open until after full dark. So, instead of continuing to watch the outside edge as I had done the previous night, I moved my stand about 75 yards back in the cover. Sure enough, after only one hour of waiting, three does and two bucks came poking along, and they stopped just before they reached the edge of the junipers. They hesitated and milled around, not wanting to go any farther until it was dark. I picked out the largest buck, had all the time in the world to plan my shot, and dropped him where he stood."

Stand-hunting tactics for whitetails also are ideal for mule deer for several reasons. Both species are secretive, have keen noses for testing prevailing breezes, and are acutely aware of movement. This means the hunter who watches and waits from an elevated vantage point has the odds in his favor. He can look down and through surrounding dense cover from high above more easily than he can see around the same cover from ground level. The hunter's scent is more likely to rise and dissipate from a tree stand than from the ground. And, when it comes time for him to raise his rifle, a deer is not likely to detect the motion in a tree stand.

My pals and I like to use portable, climbing-type stands because they can be installed quickly, don't harm trees, and can be relocated easily if a better stand site is found. Yet, a tree stand is not even necessary many times because a hunter can wait from a steep hillside or rock outcropping to watch terrain that is significantly lower.

Like whitetails, which habitually use familiar trails between feeding and bedding areas, mule deer are often just as specific in their behavior. And, it is this trait that underpins the effectiveness of stands.

"If you take a panoramic view of a mountainside," Al Wolter once taught me, "you'll note that most of the high country, all the way up to timberline, is thick with cover. In that type of terrain muleys tend to wander and hunters usually have their best success using popular Western methods such as hunting on horseback or with four-wheel-drive vehicles. They use binoculars a lot, until they see a nice buck, and then stalk within shooting range.

"But, in the lower elevations, many patches of aspens and pines are separated by open meadows, sagebrush flats, draws, and narrow fingers of cover. There are many more edges; the deer have well-defined travel options; and muleys living in those elevations, therefore, behave much like whitetails. At a quick glance, you can look at various places on a mountainside and see where bucks are most likely to bed and where they feed early and late in the day. Because of the broken-up designs of the cover and resulting edges, you can also see the routes they most likely use in traveling back and forth."

Although a single stand may suffice for a whitetail hunter, a mule deer hunter often must have a morning stand and a second, evening stand.

In the morning, bucks travel from open feeding areas to heavy cover or higher ground, whichever is closest or predominates. Yet, quietly getting into a morning stand can be more difficult than securing yourself in an evening stand because you usually have to navigate upside-down terrain and heavy cover during darkness.

If mule deer are feeding upon pinyon nuts, for example, and the nearest likely bedding site is just below the crest of a nearby canyon rim, that's where Wolter will be come daylight. Mule deer bucks, just like whitetails, spend most of their travel time concentrating upon their backtrails and often seem oblivious to what lies ahead. As a result, more than a few trophy muleys have been surprised, upon reaching their nearly inaccessible bedding site, to find Al there waiting for them.

Just the opposite procedure applies when selecting an evening stand. About an hour before dusk, the animals begin moving from heavy cover to open browsing areas, so the best point to waylay them is at a slightly lower elevation yet inside the leading edge of their dense security cover. This latter point cannot be emphasized too strongly because, as Whitey Ellard learned, bucks that have been bedded all day are extremely cautious when they leave their hideouts to begin feeding. If your evening stand is too far from their bedding sites, by the time the deer reach your position, it may well be dark.

Although the prime times for waiting on stand are near dawn and dusk, longer vigils sometimes pay off. Virtually every hunter who goes after mule deer has long been conditioned—i.e., brainwashed—to believe that he must cover many miles of ground every day. What happens, then, is the same thing that regularly occurs in whitetail territory. Numerous hunters prowl about, especially in public hunting areas in the lower elevations, and they keep the deer circulating. The man with his pants glued to a wooden board is therefore likely to be the one who dines upon fresh liver later that night.

During the rut, whitetail hunters scout not only for well-used trails but also for rubs and scrapes that bucks have made. This is useless in mule deer country because the bucks do not make scrapes and their rubs are not well pronounced.

During the rut, which usually occurs in late November, hunters should watch for small bands of does. Unlike whitetails, mule deer bucks gather harems of four or five females. A hunter may not see a buck with does but, if he can locate small groups of does here and there, at least one mature, dominant buck is almost surely keeping tabs on them. Couple this presence of does with nearby dense stands of security cover and adjacent open zones for feeding, and a savvy party of hunters should not have much difficulty determining suitable stand locations and chunks of landscape worth driving during midday.

As we began striking camp only four days after our arrival and after only two days of hunting, other hunters were still arriving in the vicinity. Colorado offers two separate deer seasons, so sportsmen can be flexible in scheduling their hunts.

Many of the incoming hunters were driving four-wheel-drives with Colorado license plates. Passing our tent camp, they easily wound up the steep, rocky trail that led to the high country. Other groups of hunters were nonresidents in the company of professional guides who were towing horse trailers. From convenient parking locations along the trail head, they methodically unloaded gear and looked eagerly toward the nearby mountain passes where they soon would be leading their packtrains.

Perhaps right then and there we had a mixture of bittersweet feelings. We greatly envied the local men in their four-wheel-drives and the well-heeled nonresidents who could afford high-class outfitting services. Yet, we had five handsome bucks of our own to take home and no one could complain about that.

Call For Blacktails

By Will Troyer

The large alder stand below us looked like a good spot for deer, so I suggested to John and Cal that we attempt to lure one out. I sat down next to a willow bush and clenched my deer call between my teeth. A shrill sound rang through the air as I blew three times in quick succession. A light breeze was blowing parallel along the hillside, and the possibilities of a deer hearing the call were quite good. We watched the alders intently for a few minutes but didn't spot any movements.

I called again, but all was silent except for the squawk of a raven overhead.

Then, John pointed toward the bottom of the alder stand and whispered, "Here comes one!"

For a moment, I couldn't see anything. Then, suddenly, I spotted it.

"Great Scott," I hissed, "it's a bear!"

And there was no doubt of its intentions.

The large brownie was moving rapidly through the alders in our direction. It had heard the predatorlike squeak and was coming to investigate a possible meal.

"Don't blow that call again," John pleaded.

He didn't need to speak. I had no intention of becoming the bear's meal. In unison, the three of us leaped to our feet and quickly moved along the hill away from the alder stand. A large grassy opening gave us some elbow room, in case the bear came busting out of the alders.

"Let's move down the hill so the wind will carry our scent to the bear," I suggested.

We hurried down the slope and stood on a knoll to watch the bear's reactions. We could see the large boar moving through the brush, heading toward the spot where we had called. He was a beautiful, dark brown bear with long fur that glistened in the morning light. Now and then, he would stop to listen, then quickly resume his climb.

In a few minutes, the bear reached our elevation and stopped some 200 yards away. He stood up on his hind legs, peering toward the top. His powerful front legs hung at his sides as he sniffed the air. Suddenly, he dropped to all fours, whirled, and ran. We watched him plunge through the alder stand. At its edge, he broke into a wild gallop and quickly disappeared over the next ridge.

"I'm glad he was the running kind," Cal said.

"Are you sure that's a deer call?" John asked.

Most people know Kodiak Island as the home of the giant Kodiak bear, but Kodiak also has a good population of the small Sitka blacktail deer. These deer are native to the coastal islands of southeastern Alaska and were introduced to Kodiak Island between 1924 and 1930. They were slow in getting established and, when 60,000 troops were stationed on Kodiak during World War II, the deer were nearly wiped out. They gradually increased after the war.

I first hunted them on Kodiak in 1955 when the limit was one buck in a one-month season. Back then, the hunting was confined to the northern part of Kodiak Island and only 30 to 60 deer were taken by hunters. But the deer spread rapidly and are now abundant over most of Kodiak and other nearby islands.

As in some other areas of Alaska, seasons are liberal on Kodiak. For deer of either sex, the season usually runs from September 15 to January 31 with a bag limit of five or seven deer per hunter. The

Most people know Kodiak Island as the home of the Kodiak bear, but it also has a good population of the small Sitka blacktail deer.

coastal deer make excellent eating, and I—like many Alaskans—depend on them as a main source of meat.

It was the last week in October when John Kobalartz, Cal Fair, and I flew to Kodiak for our hunt. We chartered a 206 Cessna from Flirite Air Service and it dropped us on a freshwater lake on the south end of Kodiak Island. We pitched camp in a grove of cottonwood trees. It was one of the area's few patches of trees. Most of the cover was low alder and willow patches interspersed with open grass and fireweed meadows. The leaves had already fallen so visibility was good. Deer, however, hang out in thick alders and sometimes come out only in the early morning and late evening. So even with the leaves gone, deer are hard to spot. That's why I hunt with a call. I can usually entice them out, even in the middle of the day.

Cal and I had hunted this area for several years but this was John's first trip with us. The three of us have hunted big game all over Alaska; John, however, had never used a call or seen one used to hunt deer. He was skeptical of its ability to lure deer.

By the time we had set up camp, it was late; we decided not to hunt that evening. In late October, daylight on Kodiak lasts from about 7:30 a.m. to 5:30 p.m., which makes a rather short hunting day.

About dark, the wind started blowing—a common phenomenon on Kodiak. It picked up speed as the night wore on. I dozed off to the sound of a flapping tent and awoke to a howling gale at about 2:30. Soon, a pelting rain added to the storm. I hoped the tent would hold.

At about 5 a.m., the wind abated somewhat, slowing to a tolerable 30 knots. But the rain continued, and no one was in a hurry to get out of a snug

It is a simple matter to make the call used by the author of this article. Take two pieces of soft wood, each about 3½ inches long and as thick as the rubber band you will use.

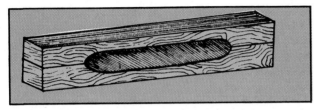

With a knife, hollow out facing sides of the two halves to make an opening. Its size is exaggerated here for illustration. It is actually one-eighth of an inch.

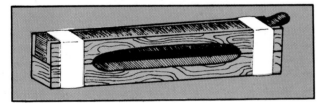

Finally, a rubber band is passed around one of the sides and stretched until it produces the right tone, which is a falling note from E to B. Tape call together. Illustrations by Stephen Fadden.

sleeping bag. It was nearly daylight when the rain stopped and we were eager to hunt. An hour later and a mile from camp, we had the episode with the bear.

After the bear departed, we crossed a tundralike ridge to the far side of the valley. A creek made an S-turn across the end of the ridge. About 300 yards to the south, the base of a mountain angled steeply upward and a dense patch of alder covered the foot of the mountain. Separating the alders from the creek was a grassy meadow that looked like an ideal site for deer. We were again in the lee of the wind so we sat on the ridge above the creek.

"OK," John said, "try your squeaker again, but for God's sake don't call up another bear."

Cal looked at me and grinned as I drew the call from my pocket.

I checked the call carefully, then clenched it between my teeth and blew. I waited about three minutes. Everything was quiet. As I prepared to call once more, a deer came bursting out of the bottom of the alders on a dead run. It was a young spike buck and he sure was looking for whatever was making the sound. He stopped in the middle of the meadow

and looked intently, but he never spotted us on the hillside about 125 yards away.

Because we were hunting primarily for meat, we decided to take the little buck. A young deer provides some choice eating. We had not agreed, however, on who should fire the first shot. As we whispered back and forth to decide who would shoot, the young buck continued to stand very alert. Cal and John insisted that I take the deer because I had called it. Feeling a little cocky and wanting to impress John with my calling ability, I cupped a hand over the call and gave another short muffled blast. The deer immediately bounced over to the edge of the creek and stopped. He was now only 50 yards away. I drew a bead on his neck with my .270 and he never knew what hit him.

"I'll have to admit you called up that one," John said reluctantly.

"I've seen him call a lot *more* like that," Cal told John as we walked to the deer.

Deer calling doesn't always work, of course. But when it does, the caller feels especially satisfied. In Alaska, deer calling is as traditional as hunting with a rifle. Natives of southeastern Alaska call deer in the rain forest by placing a leaf on their tongues and blowing to produce a sound similar to the high-pitched squawk many of us used to make as youngsters by blowing on a blade of grass held between our thumbs. Most Alaskan hunters, however, use homemade calls that they fashion by stretching a rubber band between two pieces of wood.

The whole trick in making this call is to get the right tone. I prefer a high-pitched tone that I create by clenching my teeth on the top and bottom of the call and then blowing. Try different tones until you find one that deer will respond to. Perhaps you can tune your call to the same pitch as a call that's been successful for another hunter.

I don't call all the deer I take, but calling sure improves my chances. I'd no more think of going deer hunting without a call than of going without a rifle. Calls are especially productive in a mixture of heavy cover and small openings. If you hide at the edge of an open meadow or muskeg, you often can call deer out of the heavy timber or brush and into the open.

Deer react differently to the call. Does often come running in great bounds while bucks, particularly large ones, tend to sneak slowly toward the caller. Yet I've called many bucks that bounded out of dense cover in great leaps. This usually happens during the rut, when deer seem to respond better to calls than they do at other times.

Two years ago, Cal Fair and I were hunting a series of draws on Kodiak Island early one morning. Cal was walking a ridge above me while I covered a fairly steep hillside about 100 yards below. The hillside was interlaced with alder and willow thickets and dotted with fireweed meadows. I came to the edge of a brush-covered draw that looked good. A trickling stream ran through the bottom and a tundra-covered knoll lay at the head of the draw slightly above Cal's ridge. There was no wind, and the sun still had not broken over the mountains.

I knew the call would carry far in such conditions. As usual, I blew two long blasts and a short one. About 15 seconds after my last call, I heard the *thump, thump, thump* of a deer bounding down the slope above me, but I couldn't see it. Then, suddenly, a huge buck appeared on the knoll at the top of the draw and stopped. He stood silhouetted against the sky with his head high. He was a magnificent animal with four points on each side. I was watching the buck through my binoculars, wishing he were a little closer, when a shot rang out and he dropped from view. I rushed up the hill and found Cal bent over the animal.

"A beautiful buck!" I said excitedly.

Cal was elated and said he'd seen the buck burst through the alders and come bounding down the ridge. The buck had stopped on the knoll, giving Cal an excellent 100-yard shot.

I've found that does are easy to call throughout the year. Sometimes the sound seems to literally drive them crazy. I once sat on a stump in the middle of a muskeg in southeastern Alaska and called three does to within 20 feet. When I stood up, they ran, but they immediately returned when I blew again. This time they came to within a few feet of me. The stump was in the open so they obviously saw me sitting there.

I don't really know why deer answer calls, but I suspect it may sound like a distress call to them. Once, I found a doe near Petersburg, Alaska, that had been hit by a car and had a broken back. As I approached, the doe struggled to stand and she let out a distress cry that sounded like a hunter's call.

I find calls less effective in the sparse cover of high alpine country. Quite often, deer detect you there and don't respond to the call. Often, they'll even run away at the sound. But, in the right hands and under the right conditions, a call is very effective and increases your chances of success.

John, Cal, and I hung our young buck in a cottonwood when we got back to camp. As we ate lunch, we debated where to hunt in what remained of the afternoon. The winds had picked up and calling was going to be impossible, so we decided to hunt close to camp along the ridges to the southwest.

We hunted hard but failed to spot any deer until late evening when a small buck and a doe stepped out beside an alder patch. John and Cal made a stalk and were successful in getting both, so we had three deer in camp. That evening, we feasted on fresh deer liver smothered in onions and deer gravy.

During the night, the winds died down. The next day was one of those fall rarities on Kodiak with calm winds, clear skies, and a touch of frost on the willows.

We left camp at first light and headed south toward a ridge that separated our camp from the saltwater bay below. John circled far to the left while Cal and I hunted the ridge. We stayed about 100 yards apart, winding in and out of willow and alder patches. This technique often enables us to jump deer to each other.

I stopped to call several times but had no success. Then, about 45 minutes from camp, Cal and I heard the crack of John's rifle. We walked up the ridge toward the shot and found him dressing a nice three-

Blowing through the sides of the call, the author produces a diminishing two-note sound like the bleat of a young deer.

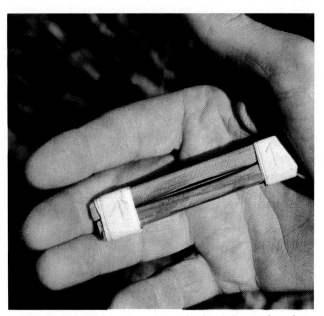

The call is made from two pieces of soft wood carved so that a strip of rubber band stretched between them can vibrate.

Calling from uphill, the hunters were able to draw bucks out of the cover.

a young buck and a doe standing together on a distant ridge. They were too far away to have heard the call and well out of shooting range. I called twice more and waited.

Suddenly a large doe came over the ridge and stepped into the meadow, followed by a nice fork-horn buck. They were alert and looking for the caller. The shot would be more than 200 yards, but I thought Cal could handle it. He took off his pack and got a good rest. At the crack of his rifle, the buck dropped, shot through the head. We cleaned the deer, laid it on a knoll and tied a white cloth nearby so we could find it when we returned.

By now, the sun was shining on the mountain above us. We used binoculars to study the ridges. Deer seemed to be popping out all over, apparently enjoying the morning sunshine after several days of wind and rain. We counted eight. Two bucks were grazing far up the mountainside. John decided to try for the biggest one. Cal and I continued across the mountain, hunting the low ridges and meadows. A few hundred yards farther along, we saw a young spike buck move out of the alders into some scattered willows. He was feeding toward us while two does stood on a ridge just above the buck.

It was a beautiful setting—deer stood here and there on the surrounding mountainsides. Far below us shone the blue waters of Shelikof Strait. It seemed like deer paradise. I brought the buck down with one clean shot.

As Cal and I dressed the small buck and tied him on a pack, we watched John stalk a deer on the mountain above. He walked over a rise and a large buck that was bedded down leaped to its feet and trotted off. We watched John raise his rifle and we saw the deer go down before we heard the shot.

"Well, I think we'd better do some packing," Cal said. "We're a long way from camp and we have four deer down."

I agreed. "By the time we get those four deer to camp, it will be dark," I said.

Cal and I picked up his deer on the way back and took our time packing down the hill. We stopped often to rest and glass the area. Seven deer stood on another ridge far across the valley. Cal kept a record of all the deer and said that 19 had been sighted.

Because the Sitka blacktail is a small deer, you can easily pack one back to camp in a single load. Most mature bucks don't weigh more than 125 pounds dressed, while spikes and does rarely weigh 100 pounds.

Cal and I rested a few minutes at camp, then we hiked back to John's three-point buck. We split the animal in two and reached camp for the second time just before dusk. John followed with the big buck we'd seen him take on the mountain.

The weather changed again that night. Cal and I left camp at daylight in a misty rain and were both back in camp by noon with a deer apiece. We then had nine deer in camp—that was the quota we had set. And nine deer made quite a load for the 206 Cessna that came for us the following morning.

point buck. He had spotted the animal standing on a knoll above a mineral lick that the deer regularly use.

It was such a beautiful day that John decided to cache his deer in a tree and continue to hunt up the ridge with us. About 300 yards farther along, a large meadow lay in a swale surrounded by alders and willows. Deer trails crisscrossed the frost-covered grass and, to the left, a buck had polished his antlers on a willow bush. We stopped to call.

On such a quiet morning, the tone of the high-pitched call seemed to roll across the ridges and meadows in all directions. As we waited, I spotted

High Climb For Blacktails

By Jim Martin

A glittering satellite streaking through the heavens was my signal for the opening of California's late deer season on September 20. Snuggled warmly in my down sleeping bag, I watched the man-made star as it cut a path through constellations in the dark sky above the majestic Trinity Alps.

Dawn was still an hour away and the temperature was well below freezing. Someone stirred. I remained silent, savoring the last few moments before the call I knew would soon come. A flickering light followed by the sharp crackle of burning branches told me that reveille was near.

"OK, you sack rats, let's get up."

I recognized Scott Carter's voice. He spoke softly, careful not to alert the game we knew was near. Two trophy bucks had been spotted browsing on an open slope about 500 yards away when we first arrived to set up camp the day before.

Camp came to life immediately. We had all been playing possum, hoping someone else would brave the cold, kindle a fire, and put the coffeepot on to boil.

There were five of us. Scott Carter, 30, led the party because we were hunting in his home territory. Nearly 20 years before, he had dropped his first Columbia blacktail buck in the rugged high country of the Trinity Alps in northern California. Ed Thomas, a 28-year-old attorney from Portland, Oregon, was also a veteran at stalking bucks in the Alps. His first attempt at taking a trophy was more than 10 years before, when he and Scott were college buddies. Ed, by the way, is the only out-of-stater I have ever met who travels to California to hunt deer. That's quite

a switch. In the normal pattern, thousands of Golden State deer hunters travel to other states in search of game. Ed's preference is a real tribute to the Trinities.

Rounding out the group were Dave Niles, a 37-year-old San Francisco radio personality, who was back after successfully bagging a buck during the 1968 season; veteran Army Maj. Gen. Len (Dunk) Dunkel, now retired; and myself. Dunk, at 70, had the stamina of a man half his age. I'm 45. As a writer for OUTDOOR LIFE, I was hoping for a good story and a blacktail trophy.

We had started from the Trinity Alps Lodge near the headwaters of the South Fork of the Salmon River. The main lodge building, situated within the 286,000-acre Salmon-Trinity Alps Primitive Area, was constructed in the 1930s by Scott's grandfather, Jesse W. Carter, who was a California supreme-court justice. For years, the lodge was the secluded wilderness retreat of Judge Carter, his family, and friends. Today, it is a guest resort operated during the summer months by Scott and his mother. It's a perfect jumping-off point for the primitive area.

Our strategy called for a packtrip to the upper reaches of the primitive area—rough country full of sawtooth granite ridges, V-shape valleys, and heavy timber. This primordial splendor is easy to explain. Regulations prohibit the use of motor vehicles within the primitive area and the only commercial use allowed is cattle grazing. The big bucks range unmolested throughout the summer and leave the high country only when deep snows drive them down.

California deer hunters are no different from those in many other parts of the nation. If a fellow is forced to explain why he failed to connect, it's easy to say that the big bucks didn't come down from the high country and won't until a storm forces them out. We didn't plan to use that excuse. We were going to hunt as high in the Alps as a deer can range.

Friday morning, shortly after breakfast, we delivered our sleeping bags, food, and camp gear to a packer who would take them to our campsite. We would follow along on foot, carrying our rifles and light backpacks. Riding horses were available, but the hike into the beautiful high country was so appealing that we elected to make the climb on foot.

After leaving our gear with the packer, Dave Niles and I sighted-in our rifles. Scott and the others had done so on Thursday. A grassy meadow near the lodge serves as a range. After a few rounds, Dave and I were both making respectable groups at 100 yards. I shoot 150-grain factory loads in a Model 70 Winchester .270 fitted with a Leupold 3X-to-9X scope. Dave uses a scoped Model 70 in .270, too. As he puts it, "It takes a flat-shooting rifle to get your buck in the high country."

Dave, Scott, Ed, and I left the lodge during mid-afternoon. Dunk had gone ahead with the packer, planning to exercise his dog on the way. Scott had advised him against taking a dog into the area we were to hunt because it would spook the deer, so Dunk had decided to give the animal a workout along the trail and then return and leave the animal at the lodge.

Ascent into the Alps is via foot trails used by gold miners more than 100 years ago. The restrictions against motorized vehicles inside the primitive area keep out everyone except hikers and horsemen. One look at the steep, winding grades that rise from the valley floor to the 7,000-foot saddlebacks discourages most would-be visitors. The high country isn't overrun by hunters.

Only one other party would be hunting anywhere near us that weekend, Scott told us. That group was guided by his brother Kent. They had used our packer, too. Other packers operate in the primitive area but, by gentlemen's agreement, each one tries to confine his party to certain zones.

Our talk along the trail brought forth memories of other successful hunts in the Alps. Scott told about the morning he dropped a dandy buck in a canyon on the far side of a towering ridge. He was 13 years old at the time, and his brother Kent was 14½. It took the two boys more than 12 hours to wrestle the deer to the top of the ridge, and they didn't get it down to the lodge until the following day.

Their 1965 season opener was also recalled. Nine members in the party took 18 bucks during the two-day hunt. Trinity County is in a two-buck district. Those fellows worked overtime bringing in venison that weekend.

Dunk failed to meet us with his dog at the appointed place and we were worried about him. We finally met him near the crest.

"My dog's gone and I'm afraid he fell over the edge," he told us as he motioned toward the cliff. "I just can't find him."

We offered to search for the dog, but Dunk insisted that we go on. We had been huffing up the trail for nearly three hours and still had a long way to go. The sun had already dropped behind a sawtooth ridge, and a chill was in the air. Common sense told us to set up camp as soon as possible.

Scott was camp cook and dished up thick steaks with gourmet trimmings for our first night's feast. He carries a transistorized walkie-talkie for communication with the lodge. Shortly before bedtime, he radioed below and got the good news that the missing dog had turned up at the lodge in good shape. Dunk was very relieved.

Breakfast went down in quick gulps as we all hurried to be in shooting position before sunrise on opening morning. Dave and Ed each had secret locations they planned to prospect. Scott suggested that I accompany him to work a series of brushy ravines that had always produced big bucks in the past. When searching for his dog, Dunk had left his Model 110 Savage in .270 with scope leaning against a tree, so now he had to retrieve it before he could hunt.

"Walk quietly," Scott whispered, as we picked our way through a dense stand of small firs. "We'll jump them close and hope they break into the open."

The sharp report of a rifle interrupted him. Then there was another shot.

"That's Dave," Scott said. "He can't be far from camp."

My wristwatch said 6:55; only five minutes earlier, we had been talking to Dave in camp.

"That buck must have been waiting for his breakfast near camp," I whispered.

Then we saw a big-eared deer standing motionless at the edge of a fir thicket about 150 yards below us. Scott took a good look and then cupped his hands over the sides of his head to show that the deer had no antlers and wasn't legal. Then I caught a glimpse of brown in the brush a short distance to the right of the doe. Bucks often let the ladies take exposed positions first while they themselves wait in hiding.

I glassed carefully, hoping to pick up antlers, but the bark of Scott's sporterized .30/06 Springfield interrupted me. I whirled around and saw a big buck crashing into a brushy draw.

"I missed," Scott yelled, working his bolt. "I jumped him out of his bed."

Suddenly the buck broke into the open, traveling fast. Scott's rifle went off again, but the buck continued to bounce.

"Shoot, shoot! He's getting away!" Scott yelled and fired once more.

The buck made a midair turn and then highballed down the ridge.

I finally found hair in my scope and touched off. A solid *plop* told me that my bullet had hit home, but the deer plunged into a dense clump of manzanita. There was one moment of suspense, and then he emerged in a series of end-over-end tumbles.

"He's down," Scott said.

I checked my watch again—7:15, less than half an hour after leaving camp.

We scrambled down the rocky hillside. As I clambered over the loose shale, I thought of the many seasons I have hunted for weeks before seeing a buck and of the times when the season ended with deer tags still unused.

We found the buck at the lower end of a talus slope, where his momentum had carried him. No follow-up shot was needed. He was a prime animal with four points on each side.

"Man, I'd like to see this one hanging back in camp with about four other big bucks," I remarked.

"I've got news for you, Jim," Scott said with a grin. "This buck isn't going to hang in camp."

Scott explained that he and his brother had learned their lesson years before when they carried Scott's buck out of the canyon. Now, they dress and quarter a deer where it falls, in order to eliminate manhandling the bulky carcass. California law requires that the tagged antlers and hide be retained until after the end of the deer season, so those are kept. Unless a hunter wishes to save the head for mounting, however, it's legal to discard it along with the lower legs and any other unusable portions. Occasionally, in that area, it is possible to drag a buck downhill to a trail where a packhorse can navigate, but most times the quartered carcass is carried out on someone's back.

Dressing the deer was easy. Scott's hunting pack contained a folding meat saw and a heavy-duty cloth bag for the trimmed meat. I had a handy pulley rig. We each carried a keen knife and a sharpening stone.

We found two bullets in the deer's boiler room— one .30/06 from Scott's rifle and one .270 from mine. Either one would have killed the buck. Because Scott had fired before I could find the four-pointer in my scope, the buck was Scott's and he used one of his tags.

During the excitement the weather had changed drastically. Low clouds drifted up through the canyons and blotted out the sun. Then came a chilling drizzle sprinkled with a few flakes of snow. After

Scott Carter validates one of his tags in the Trinity Alps, northern California.

we were soaked, we suddenly remembered our camp gear. Anxious to start hunting, we had left our food and bedrolls out in the open. I took both rifles and made a beeline for camp, leaving Scott to bring up the rear.

I was stowing the last of our gear under cover when Ed showed up in camp with his .300 Weatherby Magnum still clean. Dave arrived shortly after him. Both reported seeing plenty of sign before the clouds closed in. After that, they had heard deer moving out but couldn't spot them. Dave also confessed that he had missed a good buck shortly after leaving camp.

"I'm not the first guy to miss a buck," he remarked, "and I'm sure not going to be the last."

Poor visibility throughout the rest of the day hampered our hunting. Deer were all around us. We found fresh beds and droppings, and we heard animals moving out ahead of us. But spotting them was almost impossible.

During a break in the weather just before dark, Dave and Scott did see two large bucks feeding in an open meadow, but the deer escaped unscathed. Our campfire bull session that evening was sparked with more deer stories and hopes for better weather.

Dawn broke clear and cold. Visibility was perfect, but we had new trouble. Moisture from the rain had frozen during the night, and the ground was covered with an icy crust. Pussyfooting on that surface was impossible. Every step made a loud crunch guaranteed to alert any deer.

Ed got the first chance. He fired a volley of three shots at a four-pointer larruping across a distant hillside, but couldn't connect. I spent a fascinating 30 minutes watching a young buck browsing on a sunny slope but passed him up, hoping for a more presentable trophy. Yet, if a blue-ribbon had been awarded for the top tale of the morning, Scott would have won it.

He and Dave, moving as a team, were working the timber along the rim of a granite basin. Bucks frequently bed down in that kind of terrain in the middle of the day. Scott came over a ridge and spotted a big buck feeding along the edge of a meadow. Then Scott dropped low and signaled Dave that a buck was in sight. They met to plan a stalk.

The deer was feeding near the open end of the granite basin. High cliffs ringed the entire bowl except for one end of the meadow. The hunters planned to take up stations on the rimrock on opposite sides of the meadow, where they would have the buck in a crossfire.

Scott and Dave separated and crept slowly along the rim. Scott arrived first at his appointed place. The buck had vanished. The big deer had not crossed the open meadow. Scott concluded that the animal had bedded down in the brush at the base of the rimrock. He signaled Dave to cover the meadow while he moved closer. Then Scott inched his way to the brink of the cliff overlooking the last-known

Scott glasses for an alpine buck, left. Above, I use a pulley rig to hoist the deer for gutting.

position of the deer and peered over the rim. The big buck was lying down less than 10 yards below him.

"Do you think he charged out the obvious way?" Scott asked. "Hell, no! That smart old devil took one look and then charged uphill, almost straight at me. He was over the rim and gone before I could even raise my rifle."

Scott's version of The Great Escape was a lot of fun, but time was running out for me. Not expecting foul weather, I had planned to hunt only two days. Because of a previous commitment, I couldn't stay any longer. I decided to work my way back to the lodge, hunting as I went. Dunk was concerned about his dog and went along, so we said our goodbyes on the mountain to the rest of the crew.

Evening shadows covered the lower valley when Dunk and I finally put our rifles away. We didn't spot a buck on the way down, but we left the high country with some memorable experiences to think over.

Every tale has an epilogue. In this case, it came in a small package I received about a week after I'd returned home. It contained a selection of color transparencies and a short note.

"Dave got a buck Sunday night," it read. "Ed got two bucks Monday. I got a five-pointer the same day. Sorry you had to leave." The note was from Scott.

As a P.S., he added, "Kent's party brought in nine bucks."

Four Ways For Muleys

By Bruce Brady

In the late 1960s, Charlie Elliott and I hunted for 10 days in Colorado's Book Cliffs adjacent to the Utah line. It was a perfect fall. The aspens and cottonwoods were aflame with color, and the days were crisp and clear. Our hunting area had a two-buck limit, and the high meadows above camp teemed with deer. We saw 10 to 20 bucks every day. We hunted selectively and collected exceptional bucks late in the hunt.

Ten years passed and I got the itch to take another big mule deer buck. I could think of nothing better than to return to the same camp Charlie and I had shared. The mountains were the same, the weather just as glorious. And, though the limit was reduced to one buck, the deer were still there. The hunting, however, had changed.

Instead of seeing numerous bucks from which to choose a trophy, I had to hunt hard to find any buck.

The deer I found were not browsing in open parks and sage flats. They were lurking in the thickest cover. I refused two shots at decent bucks. Then, on the last afternoon, I had to settle for a "freezer" forkhorn.

Times have changed, and so, too, have mule deer in the West. Bucks have adapted to reduced habitat and greatly increased hunting pressure. First-time mule deer hunters are often misinformed about their chances to take good bucks, and come home disappointed. No longer can hunters amble through high country and collect the buck of their dreams. Hard hunting is required, new techniques must be learned, and productive strategies must be applied.

To help you bag a trophy buck, I consulted four mule deer guides, each of whom has vast experience. Here are the techniques and strategies they use to outsmart these modern muleys.

COVER THE COUNTRY

Russ Reid

Russ Reid, 47, guides for mule deer out of Cody, Wyoming. He has vast experience as a professional guide and hunter.

"The days of easy hunts are over," Reid says. "It takes effort and some luck to bag trophy bucks now.

The more selective you are, the tougher it is to fill your tag. I've given up on on areas that are easy to hunt and turned to rugged, tough country to find good bucks. We usually have to cover a lot of mountain to find the quality of buck I want my hunters to take."

For this reason, Reid considers the use of horses just about essential.

"I don't ride the high country much anymore," he says. "Instead, I comb areas that contain rough and dirty little canyons, rocky coulees, and pockets of heavy brush. These are the spots to find heavy-horned bucks today. With horses, I can get my hunter across lots of country. We can check out more rough cover in one day than a man on foot can see in a week."

Reid suggests that hunters, before coming West, spend some time on horseback. Muscles are used in riding that aren't exercised in any other way. Horseback rides prior to the hunt tone muscles and build confidence.

This Wyoming guide explains that he doesn't simply ride the rims and wait for a good buck to reveal himself.

"When I approach a canyon where I have previously located a good buck," says Reid, "I tie my horse some distance away and ease up to the rim on foot. I pick out a good vantage point, get out my binoculars, and glass every inch below. Bucks lay up most of the day and they have learned to stick tight when they spot a hunter. I guess half the bucks I spot are in their beds when I see them.

"Once I locate a good buck, I try not to alarm him. The idea is to check the surrounding terrain, then make a stalk to provide the hunter with an open shot at reasonable rifle range. Sometimes, long shots are required and being able to handle a rifle well is far more important than it was in the old days. Because of the thickets that muleys have come to like, it's often hard to move up for short-range shots. Besides, stalking heavy cover is chancy and the buck is apt to spook. Most hunters can't handle running shots.

"Any hunter who puts out the dough to make a mule deer hunt will be smart to master his rifle before he leaves home. Most guys sight-in their rifles at 100 yards and then head West. They have no idea what to do with a 200 to 300-yard shot. A little practice on the range goes a long way on the mountain."

START EARLY— STAY LATE

Lee (Cougar) Bridges

Lee Bridges, 44, lives in Pocatello, Idaho, but he's a licensed guide in Utah where he hunts mule deer. He's a big buck specialist and prefers to guide his hunters one at a time. He has taken five bucks that qualify for inclusion in the record book of the Boone and Crockett Club.

"Hunting has changed greatly in recent years," says Bridges. "Big bucks still browse open hillsides, but not during daylight as they once did. For my money, the first 15 minutes of dawn and the last 15 minutes of daylight are worth all the rest of the day combined when it comes to taking big bucks."

Bridges explains that bucks begin moving from feeding areas to bedding areas even before dawn breaks. He says that, by the time the sun touches the mountain, the best hunting is over. For this reason, he starts early.

"Bucks generally move up the mountain to bed down. So, if you wait for daylight, you'll never see the best deer on the mountain. I begin my climbs in the dark and use a flashlight to find my way. I get to a high spot and into position so I can spot the old busters when they start up to their bedding grounds."

He picks a vantage point that lets him see a broad sweep of country. Then he sits down with 10×40 glasses and a spotting scope to comb every inch of terrain.

"Deer hunting, nowadays, is about the same as hunting bighorn sheep," says Bridges. "The idea is to locate a buck to hunt. I see hunters every fall pounding the mountains, hoping to jump a buck that most of them couldn't hit anyway. They scare the deer silly and wonder why they can't see a buck. It's far better to spend a minimum of time on the move and a lot of time glassing for deer. It's hard for the average guy to do this. He doesn't think he's hunting unless he's puffing up and down the hills."

Bridges prefers to glass open areas that are adjacent to heavy cover. He spots most of his bucks either when they come out to feed just at dark, or when they return to bed down at the first hint of dawn.

"Old bucks are strongly territorial," he says. "They have a relatively small area they call home. Pressure can push them out for a few days, of course, but they drift back home when things get quiet. Once I locate a trophy buck, I usually stay after him until my hunter scores."

Bridges says old bucks often emerge from cover at virtually the same time and place each day, and he says it's not unusual for one to return to cover on a set routine. Once he observes a buck's habits, it's all a matter of being in the right spot at the right time.

A buck that is jumped in his bedding area will usually travel a specific escape route, says Bridges. This bit of knowledge has accounted for a number of big bucks for his hunters.

DRIVING PAYS OFF

Jerry Hughes

Jerry Hughes, 48, of Las Vegas, guides for mule deer in both Nevada and Utah. Because he also guides for cougar and bear, he spends time in mule deer range almost year-round.

"Every year, I hear hunters complain that all the big bucks are shot out in the areas they hunt," Hughes remarks. "Because they don't see deer, they assume none are around. That's the wrong conclusion. When I begin my cougar hunts, after deer season, I observe lots of big bucks on the move. There's usually plenty of snow, which forces them to lower elevations where it takes less work for them to find their grub."

Hughes says that snows are seldom deep enough during deer season to push old bucks out of the high country.

"Weather is often warm and sunny during the open season," he notes, "and bucks find a rugged, shady hole to bed in during daylight hours. They wait until after sundown to feed and move about. So, when the weather is fair and warm, I like to make

"Last fall, a hunter and I observed an old buck entering his bedding thicket across a canyon. Except for this thicket, the mountainside was open sage. I stayed put to watch. Then I had my hunter walk up through that thicket. I saw where this old buck emerged at the upper end and slipped over the rim.

"The next morning, I stationed my hunter where I'd seen the buck leave the thicket. Then I made the drive up through the timber. The buck moved out well ahead of me and left the brush in exactly the same spot as the morning before. Only this time my hunter was waiting and laid him down. That buck had a 31-inch spread."

drives to put these bedded bucks on the move."

If he's using horses, he positions his hunters in a line 100 or so yards apart and has them ride slowly across the ridges and canyons on the side of a mountain.

"When making a drive on horseback," says Hughes, "you'll seldom see the bucks that you jump. Most of them will slip out before you get very close. Once they jump, they normally move either up or down the slope, away from the line of your approach. Any buck you spot was probably jumped by one of the other drivers."

He also has his hunters make what he calls "still-hunting drives."

"The stillhunting drive works like this," he explains. "The hunters ride or climb to the top of a long ridge. Once on top, I spread them out and have each hunter stillhunt down a separate finger ridge that falls away from the rim of the mountain. I instruct them to move along slowly, pausing often to glass the slope below as well as the canyons on both sides. Some fellas think of this as a race to the bottom, but the guy who takes his time and stops often is the one who usually scores."

Hughes says that using this technique gives each hunter two chances to spot a buck. He may locate a buck on his own, or another hunter may jump one and push it into his range of fire.

"I have used this tactic for years," he says, "and it's consistently productive. Incidentally, it's something any group of hunters can use to mutual benefit when hunting strange country."

Hughes enjoys guiding hunters one at a time and on foot.

"When it's cold and cloudy," he says, "I like to ease along just under the rims. Bucks seem to lose some of their caution when the light level is low. They're more inclined to move about during daylight hours. I go slow and use my binoculars a great deal. If the country I'm hunting has rocky ravines and brushy, steep-sided canyons, I kick a few rocks off the rim now and then. The commotion gets up bucks I failed to spot and starts them on the move. One rock is seldom enough to make an old buck leave his bed. He's accustomed to falling rocks and won't move unless he's convinced there's danger above."

USING THE WEATHER TO ADVANTAGE

Emmett Burroughs

Emmett Burroughs, 38, along with his brother Boyd, guides for mule deer out of Norwood, Colorado. Emmett has a passion for big bucks and has hunted them steadily since he bagged his first one at age 12.

"Mule deer populations are good," Burroughs says. "Plenty of big bucks are still available, if you know how to hunt them."

Over the years, this veteran has learned that weather conditions have great effect on where bucks are. So, he has learned to match his tactics to the weather.

"For example," he says, "when it's a clear, cold morning, I hunt about three-quarters up the mountain on the south side or on the sunny side, as the case may be. In the evening, I maintain the same elevation, but I move to the shady side of the mountain. That's usually on the north slope."

Through experience, Burroughs has learned that, when a cold front is approaching, he should hunt on top of the mountain. If winds accompany the in-

Hunter climbed high in the pre-dawn hours to get this buck.

coming front, he stays on top but concentrates on the downwind side.

"If the mountain is covered with snow," he adds, "I hunt on the sunny side all day long. Most deer will concentrate at an elevation of one-half to three-quarters up the slopes."

On dark and cloudy days, he watches for bucks near the bottom of brushy, protected ravines and close to a source of water. If snow is falling at dawn, he spends the morning stalking low saddles along the easiest routes between two ridges. From noon until dark, he moves to the north side of the mountain and locates protected pockets of cover that offer bedding areas out of direct wind and drifting snow.

"With experience," says Burroughs, "you can look at a mountain and pretty well know where the best bucks will be. A mountain that has a cap of rimrock is a natural for big bucks. The old mossyhorns bed up in the shade just under the rim, and they prefer to lie just off a finger ridge above a steep draw. This bed provides good visibility on three sides and the natural protection of the rims above."

Burroughs says that bucks will browse open hillsides early in the season. As pressure mounts, mature bucks become more nocturnal. Major feeding periods are after dark. Before dawn, bucks begin moving back to their bedding grounds, which may be several miles from feeding areas. By late season, old bucks have moved into remote areas and are bedding in heavy timber, in blowdowns, and under very rugged rims.

"Two tactics work well for me during the late season," says Burroughs. "For one thing, I study tracks to determine which trails the good bucks use as they move in and out of feeding areas. Then, I position myself well back up the trail so as to intercept the buck while shooting light is still good. The other tactic is to get on top of the mountain before dawn. Then I slip downward on foot, watching for bucks that move up the slope enroute to the bedding areas. These old bucks are wise and they seldom amble up the point of open ridges. You can expect to spot these bucks moving through aspen thickets, sparse stands of timber, oak brush, rimrock, and other types of cover."

Burroughs points out that the rut alters behavior patterns.

"During the rut, a monster buck may be around the next hill in the wide open at any time of day. When the rut is on, I hunt hard all day long. I try to be as quiet as possible but I keep easing along with my eyes peeled from dawn till dark."

Because Burroughs prefers to hunt remote and rugged country, he usually takes a backpack to get the head and the meat off the mountain.

"Most hunters," he says, "ignore remote areas and won't hike beyond sight of the road. To dramatically increase your odds of scoring, simply make up your mind to hike way back into the hills. This is where the best bucks live. It takes more work but it is well worth the effort when you draw down on a real trophy buck."

PART 4

GUNS AND SHOOTING

Coast-To-Coast Deer Rifles

By Jim Carmichel

The first explorers and colonists on the Atlantic shores of North America discovered a deer that offered them succulent venison, supple hides, and unequaled hunting pleasure. For a while, the whitetail was a mainstay of colonial life and commerce.

While the English, French and Dutch settlers were reaching westward, a current of Spanish aristocrats and soldiers flowed north from Mexico into the fertile coastal valleys of California. They, too, found a shy deer that provided tasty venison, skins that were fashioned into ornate suits for Spanish grandees, and hunting that appealed to adventuresome spirits. The Spanish had loving names for these graceful deer but we call them blacktails.

The buckskin-clad adventurers who traveled beyond the awesome Mississippi found yet another deer. It was a lordly creature with such big ears that its resemblance to a mule was unmistakable. The nickname stuck and these animals have been known as mule deer ever since.

These three races of deer can be further divided into a host of subspecies and the sporting merits of each one debated until the crack of doom. The rifles and calibers deemed best for the taking of these deer have also been divided, subclassified, reclassified, debated, and redebated until you could easily believe a battery of some 20 rifles is needed to take each subspecies of deer in its respective haunt. Of course, the makers of firearms love that notion and some gun writers are enthusiastic, too. But, with a bit of logic, we come to the money-saving conclusion that we can hunt deer from the East Coast to the West Coast with only three or four rifles. With some compromises, a skilled hunter could actually do very well with only one rifle.

I'm trying for a blacktail on the opposite side of a canyon with a scoped, bolt-action .25/06. It's a fine rig for this kind of shooting. A friend is ready to spot the shot.

BLACKTAILS

The prim Pacific blacktail is almost unknown to most American hunters but, in Washington, Oregon, and northern California, they outnumber other deer by nearly two to one. In Oregon alone, the blacktail population is more than 500,000 and the annual harvest runs around 50,000. That's a lot of deer and it's not surprising that my hunting pals on the West Coast get excited when the season draws near. The August blacktail opening in California reminds me of the "Glorious Twelfth" grouse opener in Scotland.

I haven't hunted blacktails enough to claim any special expertise but, because I have bagged a few in California and Oregon and have talked with many successful blacktail hunters, I have a fair notion of what's required in the way of rifles.

Like other deer, blacktails have a tendency to shade up in cover during the middle of the day and to show themselves on grassy hillsides early and late. This is especially true during the early part of California's season when midday temperatures often sizzle into the 90s. Hardy souls can get some short-range jumpshooting by busting through brushy valleys where blacktails hide out during midday but,

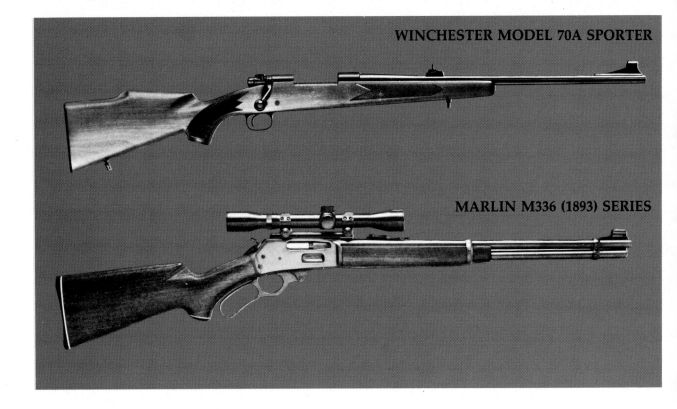

WINCHESTER MODEL 70A SPORTER

MARLIN M336 (1893) SERIES

the few times I've done it, I encountered more buzz-worms (rattlers) than deer.

The most productive technique is to walk ridges, and glass valleys and slopes. Because the coastal hills tend to be quite steep, slopes and ridgelines are often only a few hundred yards apart. This provides shots at deer that are interesting and productive if the hunter has the right rifle. Most of the shots I've had at blacktails remind me of woodchuck hunting in the Tennessee hills where hunters belly-down with a flat-shooting rifle steadied over a solid rest. The key to a good blacktail rifle is accuracy, rather than fast handling, high velocity, and a heavy bullet.

Because blacktails don't take a lot for killing, a .270 with 130-grain loads or a .30/06 with 150 grain represent the upper limit of the lethality you need. I like something lighter, such as the .257 Roberts or .25/06. These offer the most useful combinations of accuracy, flat trajectory, long range punch, and mild recoil for blacktail hunting. The .243 Winchester, 6mm Remington, and .240 Weatherby are also good choices for recoil-conscious hunters and, over the long haul, will put more blacktail venison in the freezer than a hard-thumping magnum. This is simply because they are "user friendly"—if I may borrow from computer jargon—and offer the average rifleman more precise bullet placement than is consistently possible with heavier, harder-kicking calibers.

Bolt-action rifles are favored, of course, and, for hillside-to-hillside shooting, lightweight rifles offer no advantage. Thus, standard-weight bolt guns with sturdy full-length barrels in the 24-inch category are preferred by many expert blacktail hunters.

Because shots are regularly taken out to 300 yards, it's a smart idea to use scopes with plenty of power. Variables with 9X or 10X magnification on the high end are an especially good choice in blacktail country.

If I were much inclined to beat the midday brush for these deer, I'd go for a carbine-length bolt rifle with a reasonable compromise of fast handling, portability, and long-range accuracy. For this purpose, the new bolt-action carbines are ideal.

By now, you've probably decided that a good blacktail rifle isn't all that different from what you'd use on pronghorns. As a matter of fact, the rifle I've used to best advantage on blacktails also happens to be my favorite antelope rifle. It's a Model 70 Winchester with a stylish stock by Bob Winter and a slender 25-inch Douglas barrel in .25/06 chambering. With a 100-grain spitzer bullet over 53 grains of IMR 4831, the muzzle velocity is about 3,400 fps. Adjust your scope so that bullet impact is about 2½ inches above point-of-aim at 100 yards. This will put you almost dead on at 300 yards and eliminate most excuses for missing. Because some .25-caliber bullets have thin jackets and are liable to fragment at close range when fired at this high-velocity level, it's a good idea to stay with tougher bullets such as the Speer Hot Core design and Nosler's solid-base or partition bullets.

MULE DEER

Moving eastward into mule deer country, there's not much need to change one's rifle, but it's arguable that heavier calibers may be in order. Over the years,

I've seen upwards of two score big-bodied mule deer shot with the .243 Winchester or the 6mm Remington by other hunters. With few exceptions, they went down as though zapped by a boulder from the slingshot of Zeus. A few didn't go down immediately but staggered around for a few moments before slumping to the ground. I don't remember any that got away, and I'm sure I would if any had. The people I hunt with are good shots, and a lost deer is loudly noted and long remembered. Of the 150 to 200 mule deer I've either shot myself or seen shot with all sorts of rifles and calibers, some went down in their tracks, some stumbled and fell, some ran off as if missed then piled up after a few steps, and some went considerable distances. The one certain thing I've learned from watching deer being shot is that it's impossible to judge what big-game caliber was used just by observing the immediate results. Specifically, I've seen deer shot with everything from a .243 to a .338 Magnum and, regardless of caliber, some deer drop, some stay on their feet for a few seconds, and some walk or run off. Yet, I periodically get mail from disgruntled hunters who tell woeful tales of how they busted a deer with a .243 only to have it run into the next county. I'm usually unsympathetic because these tales don't dovetail with my personal experiences and observations. The fact is that *missed*

deer do have a habit of hightailing it out of the country. And, a deer missed with a little .243 never seems to be all that much less injured than one missed with a blockbuster magnum. The only real difference is that, when a deer is missed with a raging magnum, the hunter can only blame himself. When a small-caliber bullet goes wide of the target, the hunter can soothe his tattered ego by blaming the cartridge, as if it were under a witch's curse that caused it to bounce off a deer's ribs.

If you like the idea of using one of the accurate, soft-kicking 6mms but fear it won't do the job on mule deer, by all means go to something bigger. Let's get that potential alibi out of the way before it has a chance to mess up your thinking. The next step up from a .243 or 6mm is a .25, and the .257 Roberts or .25/06 Remington are superb for mule deer. But, if you're afraid that the .243 isn't big enough, you probably won't get much consolation by increasing bullet diameter only 0.014 of an inch. So, play it safe and go all the way to a .270, 7mm, or a fast .30 caliber. The .270 with a 130-grain slug provides no excuses or apologies when used on mule deer, and the .280 Remington with a 150-grain bullet in a factory load is at least as good. Better yet is a good .280 or 7mm handload with any of the superb 139 or 140-grain bullets offered by component bullet makers. It

Photo by Bill McRae

goes without saying that the .30/06 is unbeatable for the purpose. The ever-faithful '06 with 150 or 165-grain bullets is accurate, fairly user friendly, and it is the standard by which I judge all mule deer loads.

A TEXAS VARIATION

In south-Texas whitetail country, a breed of gun is evolving that may become the most specialized of all deer rifles. This fascinating development is being brought about by some of the most awesome trophy deer ever hunted, combined with some of the most difficult terrain on which a hunter ever set foot. The high, dense chaparral and cactus limit visibility to a few scant yards, so hunting by traditional methods is out of the question. Therefore, south-Texas hunters have developed ingenious shooting towers that provide some visibility over thorny vegetation and some hunters have even mounted high seats on vehicles with which they patrol the fringes of deer thickets. Before you condemn this technique as unsportsmanlike, let me promise you that it is the most difficult and uncomfortable way to hunt deer yet devised. Because most shots are fired at running targets at almost impossible distances, the degree of difficulty is easily three or four times greater than that encountered in many of the usual forms of deer hunting. When a south-Texas hunter says he missed six or eight shots during a morning's hunt, his fellow hunters only nod in solemn understanding.

And it's not just the shooting that makes it so tough. Even when a deer is known to have dropped in its tracks, locating it can be frustrating. This often requires that the shooter remain in the high seat or tower with his eye on the spot where the deer was last seen so that he can direct a couple of his buddies through a maze of head-high cactus. Picking your way through a tangle of the prickly growth sometimes results in a circuitous, half-mile hike to find a spot only 200 yards away.

Naturally, if the deer manages to travel even a short distance after last being seen, the animal will be extremely difficult to find. It often takes hours to search a few acres. This problem has fostered appreciation for calibers that "wreck" a deer on the spot by doing such massive damage that the quarry is unable to move. In theory, this sounds great but, in practice, it doesn't always work well. Sometimes, the results are less than satisfactory because the rifleman can't stand the recoil of a real magnum and actually uses something that isn't a real immobilizer. Other times, results are poor because the hunter is afraid of the big magnum and shoots poorly. The bona fide class of game-paralyzing calibers is characterized by the .338 Magnum on the light end, and the .375 H&H and .378 Weatherby Magnum on the heavy side. Many hunters find that it's difficult to shoot these steamrollering calibers accurately, and some of them note a significant drop in the number of bullets that find targets. The solution, therefore, may very well be to select an ultrafast cartridge on the order of the .264 Winchester Magnum, or the

Weatherby magnums in .257, .270, or 7mm. The high velocity and flat trajectory of this kind of cartridge takes some of the guesswork out of distant shots, especially at moving targets. And the shock of the high-velocity bullet impact offers, to some extent, the desired "immobilizing" effect.

WHITETAILS EAST

Crossing the Mississippi and traveling east, the dedicated deer hunter encounters dense-pack deer habitat ranging from brushy river bottoms to thick woodlots. In the Atlantic Coast states, he enters thick stands of second-growth and third-growth timber interspersed with meadows and farmland. With this observation comes the realization that, when we talk about the rifles needed for the various North American deer, we aren't really matching the gun to the game. We are really selecting our firearms in terms of the terrain and the cover. If, for example, blacktails, mule deer, and whitetails all inhabited the Eastern forests, the best choice for all three would be a light, fast-handling carbine in an adequate .30 or .35 caliber.

If, on the other hand, whitetails inhabited the open plains and mountains, the perfect whitetail rifle would be a medium to medium-heavy bolt gun in some far-ranging, flat-shooting caliber. In fact, some savvy Southeastern hunters have found they get more and bigger bucks by abandoning the traditional Eastern "brush" rifle. These sportsmen shoot from tree stands and platforms situated around vast fields of soybeans and other deer-tempting crops. They snipe at big bucks that feed in the open fields. Sometimes, they can shoot at close range but, more often, the distance is 200 yards or better, and a flat-shooting rifle has a distinct edge over the lumbering projectiles often characterized as "brush cartridges."

For most deer hunting in the Eastern forest, however, the hunter needs a fast-handling quick-shooter, and I have little patience with bolt-action snobs who look down their noses at autoloaders, pumps, and lever-action rifles. These fast-shooting designs result from matching the rifle to the land and the cover. An experienced rifleman can get off three aimed shots at a bounding buck in some three to four seconds with a fast repeater. Given the unavoidable error factor inherent in shooting at running game but adding the "learning advantage" of multiple shots (with every miss we learn where *not* to aim), the deer hunter who frequently shoots at running deer is better off with a fast-firing repeater. But that is true only if he doesn't succumb to the notion that speed is a desirable substitute for careful aiming.

I once heard the argument for fast-firing repeaters summed up very neatly during a debate on the merits of brush rifles. One hunter was quite sure that if allotted only three cartridges for a day's hunting, he would rather have one shot each at three different deer than three shots at one deer. "But tell me, Sonny," asked a weathered veteran of the Maine woods, "how many days have you had shots at three?"

The Nonthinking Man's Trajectory Table

By Jim Carmichel

Ballistic tables are wonderful things. They provide us with all sorts of information about our rifles and cartridges and the way our bullets fly. The problem with many such tables, however, is that they presume we will remember the various trajectory figures and be able to recall them when a deer or elk or woodchuck presents itself. In the excitement of such moments, we are liable to forget if our rifle hits two inches high (or is it 10 inches low?) at 250 yards.

With these failings in mind, and thanks to computer wizardry, you can now use the nonthinking man's trajectory table. The table shows the three-inch (plus or minus) point-blank range of most American big-game calibers and gauges. By three-inch point-blank range, we mean that, within the recommended ranges, the bullet never rises above or falls below three inches of your line of sight. From the practical hunter's standpoint, this is more than adequate bullet placement because it is well within the vital-area size of all big-game animals and many varmint species.

The table is also the best-ever means of comparing the *useful* hunting ranges of various cartridges. All data are based on a line-of-sight 1½ inches above the bore line. This is typical of most scope-sighted rifles. The trajectory figures for shotgun slugs assume a sight line one inch above bore line, which is about standard for open-sighted slug barrels. To make use of the table, simply sight your rifle in at any of the ranges shown so that the bullet impact, in relation to point of aim, matches the impact point at that distance (assuming that you're using factory-loaded ammunition and a rifle that is in good condition).

For example, the table shows that the .270 Winchester with a 130-grain Bronze Point bullet is 2.5 inches high at 100 yards. Accordingly, simply adjust the sight on your .270 so that the bullet hits 2.5 inches above point-of-aim at 100 yards. From that point on, the bullet will hit within three inches (vertically) of where you aim out to more than 250 yards.

The last column of the table lists the range at which the bullet is three inches below line-of-sight. All the way out to that range, stated in yards, you can hold dead on and forget about trajectory when you're big-game hunting or when you're shooting most varmints. What could be simpler or more practical?

Caliber	Bullet weight (grains)	Bullet type*	Muzzle velocity (fps)	Trajectory (inches)							Range at which bullet is three inches low (yds.)
				50 yds.	100 yds.	150 yds.	200 yds.	250 yds.	300 yds.	350 yds.	
.243 Winchester	80	HPPL	3,350	0.9	2.5	3.0	2.4	0.5	−2.8	−7.9	302
.243 Winchester	100	PSPCL	2,960	1.1	2.6	3.0	2.0	−0.5	−4.5		284
6mm Remington	80	HPPL	3,470	0.9	2.4	3.0	2.6	0.9	−2.1	−6.7	311
6mm Remington	100	PSPCL	3,130	1.0	2.5	3.0	2.3	0.3	−3.1		299
.240 Weatherby Mag.	87	PT	3,500	0.8	2.3	3.0	2.7	1.3	−1.3	−5.2	324
.240 Weatherby Mag.	100	PT	3,395	0.8	2.4	3.0	2.6	1.2	−1.4	−5.3	322
.250 Savage	87	PSP	3,030	1.1	2.6	3.0	1.9	−0.8	−5.3		278
.250 Savage	100	PSP	2,820	1.2	2.7	2.9	1.4	−1.8	−7.1		263
.257 Roberts	87	PSP	3,170	1.0	2.6	3.0	2.2	−0.1	−4.0		289
.257 Roberts	117	SPCL	2,650	1.4	2.9	2.7	0.5	−3.8			242
.25-06 Remington	87	HPPL	3,440	0.9	2.4	3.0	2.5	0.6	−2.7	−7.9	303
.25-06 Remington	100	PSPCL	3,230	1.0	2.5	3.0	2.3	0.4	−3.1		299
.25-06 Remington	120	PSPCL	3,010	1.1	2.6	3.0	2.1	−0.2	−4.0		289
.257 Weatherby Mag.	87	PT	3,825	0.7	2.1	2.9	2.9	2.0	0.0	−3.0	351
.257 Weatherby Mag.	117	NP	3,300	0.9	2.4	3.0	2.5	0.9	−1.9	−6.1	315
6.5mm Remington Mag.	120	PSPCL	3,210	1.0	2.5	3.0	2.4	0.5	−2.9	−7.7	302
.264 Winchester Mag.	100	PSP	3,320	0.9	2.5	3.0	2.4	0.4	−3.1		299
.264 Winchester Mag.	140	PSPCL	3,030	1.1	2.6	3.0	2.2	0.0	−3.6		299
.270 Winchester	100	PSP	3,480	0.8	2.4	3.0	2.6	0.9	−2.1	−6.7	311
.270 Winchester	130	BP	3,110	1.0	2.5	3.0	2.3	0.3	−3.1		299
.270 Winchester	150	SPCL	2,900	1.2	2.7	2.9	1.6	−1.6	−6.7		266
.270 Weatherby Mag.	130	PT	3,375	0.8	2.4	3.0	2.6	1.2	−1.4	−5.3	323
.270 Weatherby Mag.	150	PT	3,245	0.9	2.4	3.0	2.5	0.9	−1.9	−6.0	316

HSP Hollow soft point
PSP Pointed soft point
HP Hollow point
SP Soft Point

JHP Jacketed hollow point
PP Power point
HPPL Hollow point power-lokt
PSPOL Point soft point core-lokt

BP Bronze point
SJHP Semi-jacketed hollow point
SPCL Soft point core-lokt
FMJ Full metal jacket

PP(SP) Power-point soft point
NP Nosler partition
HPBT Hollow point boattail
PT Pointed
ST Silvertip

Caliber	Bullet weight (grains)	Bullet type*	Muzzle velocity (fps)	Trajectory (inches)							Range at which bullet is three inches low (yds.)
				50 yds.	100 yds.	150 yds.	200 yds.	250 yds.	300 yds.	350 yds.	
284 Winchester	125	PP(SP)	3,140	1.0	2.5	3.0	2.2	0.1	−3.5		294
284 Winchester	150	PP(SP)	2,860	1.2	2.7	2.9	1.7	−1.1	−5.6		274
7mm Mauser	140	PSP	2,660	1.3	2.8	2.8	1.2	−2.1	−7.4		260
7mm/08 Remington	140	PSP	2,860	1.2	2.7	2.9	1.8	−0.8	−5.1		278
7mm Express Remington	150	PSPCL	2,970	1.1	2.6	3.0	2.0	−0.5	−4.5		284
.280 Remington	165	SPCL	2,820	1.2	2.7	2.9	1.4	−1.8	−7.0		264
7mm Remington Mag.	125	PP(SP)	3,310	0.9	2.4	3.0	2.5	0.7	−2.5	−7.1	307
7mm Remington Mag.	150	PSPCL	3,110	1.0	2.5	3.0	2.2	0.2	−3.4	−8.5	296
7mm Remington Mag.	175	PSPCL	2,860	1.2	2.7	2.9	1.9	−0.7	−4.8		281
7mm Weatherby Mag.	139	PT	3,300	0.9	2.4	3.0	2.5	1.0	−1.8	−6.0	316
7mm Weatherby Mag.	175	NP	3,070	1.0	2.5	3.0	2.3	0.3	−3.0	−7.8	300
.30 Carbine	110	SP	1,990	2.1	2.9	0.1	−7.1				176
.30 Remington	170	ST	2,120	1.9	3.0	1.5	−3.1				199
.30/30 Winchester	150	SPCL	2,390	1.7	3.0	2.1	−1.6	−8.7			212
.30/30 Winchester	170	SPCL	2,200	1.8	3.0	1.8	−2.3	−9.6			206
.300 Savage	150	SPCL	2,630	1.4	2.9	2.6	0.3	−4.4			238
.300 Savage	180	PSPCL	2,350	1.6	2.9	2.4	−0.2	−5.2			231
.30/40 Krag	180	PSPCL	2,430	1.5	2.9	2.5	0.2	−4.3			238
.30/40 Krag	220	ST	2,160	1.8	3.0	1.9	−1.7	−8.1			214
.30/06 Springfield	110	PSP	3,380	1.0	2.5	3.0	2.2	−0.2	−4.5		285
.30/06 Springfield	150	BP	2,910	1.1	2.7	2.9	1.9	−0.7	−4.9		280
.30/06 Springfield	165	PSPCL	2,800	1.2	2.7	2.9	1.5	−1.5	−6.4		268
.30/06 Springfield	180	PSPCL	2,700	1.3	2.8	2.8	1.3	−1.9	−7.0		263
.30/06 Springfield	220	SPCL	2,410	1.6	2.9	2.4	−0.3	−5.5			229
.300 Winchester Mag.	150	PSPCL	3,290	0.9	2.5	3.0	2.4	0.6	−2.7	−7.5	304
.300 Winchester Mag.	180	PSPCL	2,960	1.1	2.6	3.0	2.1	−0.1	−3.8		291
.300 Winchester Mag.	220	ST	2,680	1.3	2.8	2.8	1.3	−2.0	−7.3		261
.300 H&H Mag.	150	ST	3,130	1.0	2.6	3.0	2.2	0.1	−3.6		294
.300 H&H Mag.	180	PSPCL	2,880	1.2	2.7	2.9	1.8	−0.7	−5.0		279
.300 H&H Mag.	220	ST	2,580	1.4	2.9	2.7	0.8	−3.0	−9.0		250
.300 Weatherby Mag.	150	PT	3,545	0.8	2.3	3.0	2.7	1.5	−0.8	−4.3	334
.300 Weatherby Mag.	180	PT	3,245	0.9	2.4	3.0	2.5	0.9	−1.9	−6.0	315
.303 Savage	190	ST	1,940	2.1	2.9	0.6	−5.4				184
.303 British	180	SPCL	2,460	1.6	2.9	2.4	−0.4	−5.8			227
.308 Winchester	110	PSP	3,180	1.1	2.6	3.0	1.8	−1.1	−6.3		271
.308 Winchester	125	PSP	3,050	1.1	2.6	3.0	1.9	−0.6	−5.0		280
.308 Winchester	150	PSPCL	2,820	1.2	2.7	2.9	1.5	−1.5	−6.5		267
.308 Winchester	180	PSPCL	2,620	1.4	2.8	2.8	1.1	−2.5	−8.1		256
.32 Winchester Special	170	SPCL	2,250	1.8	3.0	1.9	−2.0	−9.2			209
8mm Mauser	170	SPCL	2,360	1.7	3.0	2.0	−1.6	−8.6			212
8mm Remington Mag.	185	PSPCL	3,080	1.1	2.6	3.0	2.1	−0.2	−4.1		287
8mm Remington Mag.	220	PSPCL	2,830	1.2	2.7	2.9	1.7	−1.1	−5.7		273
.338 Winchester Mag.	200	PP(SP)	2,960	1.1	2.7	3.0	1.9	−0.8	−5.1		278
.338 Winchester Mag.	225	SP	2,780	1.2	2.7	2.9	1.7	−1.1	−5.6		274
.338 Winchester Mag.	250	ST	2,660	1.3	2.8	2.8	1.0	−2.6	−8.3		255
.35 Remington	150	PSPCL	2,300	1.8	3.0	1.8	−2.6	−10.8			203
.35 Remington	200	SPCL	2,080	2.0	3.0	1.0	−4.8				188
.358 Winchester	200	ST	2,490	1.5	2.9	2.5	−0.1	−5.1			232
.358 Winchester	250	ST	2,230	1.7	3.0	2.1	−1.4	−7.6			216
.38/40 Winchester	180	SP	1,160	3.0	−0.2	−12.1					116
.38/55 Winchester	255	SP	1,320	2.8	1.5	−5.9					135
.44 Remington Mag.	240	SJHP	1,760	2.4	2.8	−1.7	−11.8				159
.444 Marlin	240	SP	2,350	1.8	3.0	1.6	−3.3				197
.444 Marlin	265	SP	2,120	1.9	3.0	1.1	−4.3				191
.45/70 Government	405	SP	1,330	2.8	1.4	−6.3					134

THE NONTHINKING MAN'S TRAJECTORY TABLE FOR RIFLED SHOTGUN SLUGS

Gauge	Slug weight (ozs.)	Muzzle velocity	Yards						Range at which bullet is three inches low (yds.)
			25	50	75	100	125	150	
10	1¾	1,280	1.8	3.0	2.3	−0.5	−5.6		114
12	1¼	1,490	1.5	2.8	2.8	1.0	−2.6	−8.3	127
12	1	1,560	1.5	2.9	2.6	0.5	−4.0		120
16	⅘	1,600	1.5	2.9	2.6	0.4	−4.1		120
20	¾	1,600	1.4	2.8	2.8	1.2	−2.4	−8.2	128
410	½	1,830	1.3	2.7	2.9	1.4	−2.0	−7.8	130

Optics For Shooting

By Jim Carmichel

It wasn't all that long ago when hunting glassware was a tiny, silk-lined fragment of the sporting world. It was an elitist market that catered almost exclusively to rich big-game hunters, professional guides, and a smattering of target shooters. In 1930, for example, the price of just about all hunting optics, including binoculars, telescopic sights, and spotting scopes, kept them out of the reach of nine out of every 10 hunters. By 1940, thanks to Bill Weaver, rifle scopes were an affordable item, but a good pair of binoculars by Bausch & Lomb or Zeiss, the brands best known to American sportsmen, still equaled the combined cost of a good rifle and a guided big-game hunt.

By the 1950s, the name brands were as remote from hunter's pocketbooks as ever. But, even then, a tidal wave was washing in from the Land of the Rising Sun that would swamp the American hunting scene with low-cost optics. At first, the "Made in Japan" label was considered to be synonymous with poor quality. But one doesn't have to look at a Nikon or other fine Japanese cameras very long to realize that they now know what they are doing when it comes to grinding glass. To be sure, some of the first Japanese binoculars and scopes weren't all that great, but their unbelievably low prices made up for a host of deficiencies. Useful and usable optics were at last available to any hunter who wanted a magnified look at his hunting world.

The second great piece of luck we hunters have had is the intense competition among the Japanese optical manufacturers. Unable to compete on low prices only, they have steadily improved the quality and variety of their products to the point that the best coming out of Japan today is truly excellent, even while prices are kept at bargain levels. Consider the new Japanese-made Bausch & Lomb Discoverer binoculars. In four sizes ranging from 7X to 10X power, this compact, center-focusing model is fog-proof and waterproof and backed by a 25-year limited warranty. The suggested retail price for Discoverer models runs from $350 to $380, depending on power. In 1950, the Bausch & Lomb center-focusing 9X binocular sold for $204, a bit more than half of today's binocular cost. When corrections are made for the differences in the value of the dollar in 1950 and 1983, today's Bausch & Lomb binoculars cost only about one-quarter as much as they did 33 years ago. Today's quality, though, is vastly superior—and that's what I call a bargain.

Big names such as Zeiss and Leitz, faced with the onslaught from Japan, have had to sharpen their acts in order to stay in the race. As a result, they also offer a huge variety of optics with ever-improving quality. Even though their prices seem steep, they are in fact a better buy than they were a generation or even a decade ago.

BINOCULARS

Old-time guides to binocular buying tended to recommend 6 × 35 glasses as the best for all-purpose hunting use. What they were really saying was that more powerful binoculars were considerably heavier and bulkier and tended to be prone to optical and mechanical problems. These problems have long since been solved, but traces of the stale advice seem to remain.

119

For the past several years, my standard binoculars have been lightweight 8Xs for all-around hunting, plus a pair of 10×42s for mountain and plains hunting. But even these habits are about to change. The subcompacts, weighing scant ounces and fitting in a shirt pocket, have progressed well beyond the novelty stage and represent an alternative that is well worth considering. I've used a pair of 8X Zeiss mini-binocs for the past couple of seasons for everything from woodchuck to elk, and see no handicap as compared to the bigger glasses.

Time was when optical experts felt that center-focusing binoculars, while convenient, represented some loss of precision. More recently, expert gossip had it that only individual-focusing models could be waterproof. These views no longer hold water (or keep water out). I always use center-focusing glasses because I am constantly changing focus and turning only one wheel makes it easier and faster—and there are good center-focusing waterproofs available.

Most binocular makers now offer rubber-covered models, and the idea is a good one. The semisoft covering is nice to the touch, reduces noise and glare, and offers some protection. However, not all rubber-

Miniature binoculars offer light weight, convenience, and optical quality equal to the finest binoculars of the past.

covered binoculars are waterproof so, before paying your money, make sure of what you're getting. Binoculars and other optical instruments that are indeed waterproof will say so on the package or in the brochure. Beware if the maker is silent on this point. But realize that being waterproof is only a nice bonus. Some superb glasses aren't waterproof, which is fine as long as you remember to remove them from your neck when taking a shower.

Gimmicks are no help. Zoom binoculars, for example, aren't worth the bother because what you gain in convenience is lost in clarity. That's why no top-of-the-line models have zoom power. Other doodads such as built-in cameras can be fun but, again, when you get away from the basic purpose of binoculars you begin losing optical precision. If you wear glasses or often wear sunglasses, be sure to get folding or retractable eyecups. Most of today's binoculars have them but check anyway, otherwise you may not see the full field.

A wide field of view is nice but don't get carried away. And just because the box says the binoculars contained therein have a big field doesn't mean they do. Some glasses that are advertised as having a big field may not, in fact, let you see any more than some standard models. Anyway, even though an extra-wide field may help you get oriented a bit faster, the truth is that we concentrate our attention on only a small area of the total field. You glass for game by searching under or behind every tree and bush. A wide field is generally bought at the cost of magnification so, given the choice, I'll go with more power every time.

SCOPES

When it comes to buying telescopic sights for rifles, a lot of the old rules need to be run through the shredder and forgotten. We used to spend a lot of

not enhance these three essentials, I'm inclined to consider them as superfluous, compromising, or downright undesirable.

When variable-power riflescopes started making headway at the marketplace, they got a black eye from some shooting experts because of their tendency to shift point of impact as the magnification was changed. For example, a scope might have been sighted-in at one power setting but, when the power was changed, the zero might shift a few inches. This was indeed cause for criticism and some writers had a field day condemning the zoom concept. But that day is largely past, with the best of today's variables tracking close and true across their power range. The Leupold 6.5X-to-20X variable, for example, will wander, at most, only a quarter minute between the two magnification extremes.

Though I can't resist mounting variable-power scopes on many of my big-game rifles, I also have to confess that I usually turn the power to the highest setting and leave it there. When it comes to fixed-magnification scopes, I tend to shout in the face of tradition and favor 2.5X for close-up brush shooting, 6X for plains and all-around hunting, and 10X or more for varmints and targets. Somehow, I've never been able to get all that worked up over the 4X and other compromises. If in doubt, get a variable.

Today's rush to lightweight rifles has precipitated a batch of compact scopes for which we should all be eternally grateful. A bit of brightness and field of view is lost with the compacts, as compared to a full-size scope of the same power, but the trade-off is well worth it in four out of five hunting situations.

time rattling our bridgework about such esoteric items as a scope's brightness index, the twilight factor, and relative luminosity (whatever the heck *that* means).

But when all the talk is over and we're down to the serious business of hunting, game hunters usually discover that other factors count a lot more.

To my notion, a riflescope needs to fulfill only three obligations: It should allow me to see and aim at the game precisely, should stay zeroed, and should remain usable under any weather and temperature conditions that a hunter is likely to encounter. Any additional features offered by a scope should augment its performance in any or all of these basic categories. If other features are offered that do

A comparison of a standard size scope, rear, and a compact. The compact is not only shorter and more compact, it also has a lower profile, thus increasing convenience and handling.

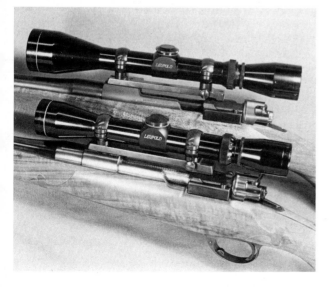

CONTACT LENSES

Contacts are not just for basketball players and movie stars. The small eye-fitting lens can be a terrific convenience to sportsmen who have been cursed with having to wear traditional spectacles. Sometimes, they even offer significantly improved vision.

Any hunter or shooter who wears glasses is well familiar with the aggravations of getting lenses splattered, streaked, fogged, or frosted when the weather is rainy, snowy, or hot and humid. Contact lenses bring these problems to an instant stop. Contacts often improve your visual acuity, as compared to corrective eyeglasses but, of at least equal importance to hunters is the tremendous increase in peripheral vision. The area outside the eyeglasses' corrective lens, plus the area blocked by the frames, is lost to your vision and accounts for a loss of up to 30 percent of your natural field of view. With contact lenses, you get all of this back, and the benefits are obvious.

I've been as nearsighted as a hedgehog since grammar school and know well the problems of wearing glasses in the field. Back when I was on an Army rifle team, I was fitted with contacts as a means of beating the sweat-fogging problem that affects all spectacle-wearing target shooters. The contacts solved the fogging problem and improved my visual acuity, as well, but they weren't all that comfortable back then and had a habit of popping out when a rifle slapped my cheek especially hard.

My next experience with contacts was in the early 1970s when Bausch & Lomb introduced their soft lenses. These offered excellent acuity and greatly improved comfort but had to be sterilized daily in boiling water. I've known several hunters who simply boiled their lenses over the campfire but, still, some hygenic problems remained. These and similar difficulties seem to be solved with the new extended-wear contacts that can be left in the eyes for a week or more. They are the most comfortable contacts yet and offer a bright new world of convenience to sportsmen.

Even though the price of contact lenses has dropped so that anyone who can rake up the cost of a case of shot shells can afford them, they still aren't for everyone. Certain health problems, such as diabetes, may rule out their safe use and some types of visual abnormalities can't be corrected with the soft lenses. Your eye specialist can fill you in on the details.

GLASSES

Whether you need corrective lenses or not, there's no getting around the absolute fact that you need eye protection when you are shooting. Visitors to Briarbank Ballistic Laboratory, OUTDOOR LIFE's test facility, are given protective glasses (as well as ear protectors). They must wear them while any shooting is in progress, even if they are only bystanders. My unflinching rule is that anyone who isn't smart enough to wear eye protection isn't smart enough to handle a gun. Some of my staunchest supporters are those who have lost or damaged their vision because they didn't wear shatterproof glasses.

Good shooting glasses offer a lot more than eye protection. Dig into a trap shooter's kit and you'll probably find a half dozen pairs of specially designed glasses in colors ranging from yellow to green to pink. Competitive shotgunners feel that the world does indeed look better through rose-colored glasses, especially when they're shooting at orange targets.

If a shooter or hunter allows himself only one pair of glasses, the choice should be yellow. This tint filters out some bothersome light rays and generally brightens up what you see, which is especially helpful on dark, cloudy days or late in the afternoon. The yellow tint seems to give a crisper visual definition to whatever you're shooting at, be it grouse, duck, quail, or targets. For all-purpose wear, glasses with photochromic lenses, which grow darker in bright sunlight and when exposed to snow glare, are very handy.

SPOTTING

A spotting scope is a rather clumsy, heavy-looking thing, certainly not the sort of extra weight you want when climbing mountains that seem to soar forever into the kingdom of the wild sheep. But don't consider a spotting scope in terms of how heavy it is to pack, consider how many miles of tough walking it can save.

Like every other optical accessory available to sportsmen, today's market offers such a terrific variety of makes, models, shapes, and magnifications that one can easily get confused. The first rule in

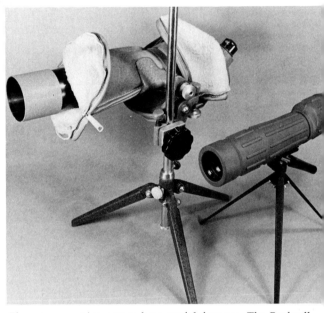

These two spotting scopes have useful features. The Bushnell Spacemaster, left, has a 45-degree angle eyepiece, convenient for target shooting. The Tasco spotting scope, with rubber armor, comes complete with tripod and camera-type mounting.

selecting a spotting scope is to stay away from gimmicks. Variable-magnification models seem like a great idea but, if you're tempted in this direction, stay with only the top brands. The optical complexity of the zoom system calls for extremely high-quality lenses and mechanics and, if the quality isn't there, you'll be disappointed. A quick test for a zoom lens is to simply turn the magnification to the high end and, while looking at distant objects, see if there is a tendency for the object to have a bluish or gold "halo." This can be a frustration when you are trying to judge a ram's curl or decide if a distant bull elk has six points.

I used to carry a big scope with a 60mm objective but, today's smaller scopes, those with 50mm objectives, are great. If I were buying a scope today, I'd probably go for one of the rubber-armored models, by a name-brand maker, with a simple 25X eyepiece. I'd also want it to have a camera-type tripod mount. This system is not only quick and simple, but it gives you double duty from your tripod. After the kill, you have a tripod at hand for your picture taking.

Muzzleloaders: A Practical Guide

By Jim Carmichel

Hunting with muzzleloading rifles and shotguns is one of the most exciting and satisfying shooting sports. Some states have special open seasons on big game in which only muzzleloading arms are permitted. Before taking part in these hunts, the blackpowder shooter should thoroughly acquaint himself with the state's hunting regulations in order to be sure his rifle meets the legal requirements. For example, some states specify certain minimum and maximum allowable calibers; some hunts are for flintlock rifles *only*; others are restricted to smoothbores firing solid projectiles. The most popular muzzleloading hunting arm is, however, a percussion-cap rifle.

Big-game hunters usually load their rifles with heavier powder charges than they use when shooting targets. The additional velocity increases the rifle's knockdown power, but you must be careful not to increase the charge so much that accuracy deteriorates.

When the charge is increased, the point of impact also changes in respect to point-of-aim, so be sure to test hunting loads on targets.

Experienced blackpowder hunters speed up their reloading time by using a homemade loading block. This is nothing more than a small block of wood with six or eight holes bored in it that hold pre-patched balls. To load, the block is aligned atop the muzzle, and the patched ball is pushed into the bore with the ramrod. Reloading time is cut in half.

Steps can also be taken to protect the gun in rainy or snowy conditions by sealing the capped nipple or the frizzen with waterproof wax.

Big-game hunting with a muzzleloader is a stalking sport because the effective range of even the more powerful rifles is 200 yards at the outside, with 100 yards as the practical maximum. Small-game hunting is a great sport, too. For instance, a well-made and carefully loaded squirrel rifle is accurate enough to hit a squirrel in the top of the tallest hickory tree, and it's twice as much fun to shoot as any modern rifle or shotgun. Before hunting with any muzzleloading rifle or shotgun, however, the hunter owes it to himself to work up a good load, and practice until he knows where the ball will hit at all hunting ranges.

POWDER

In 1781, the British standardized blackpowder at 75 parts, by weight, of saltpeter, 10 parts sulphur, and 10 parts charcoal. Charcoal black is the characteristic color of blackpowder but some brands range in hue from gray to brown to red.

Blackpowder used in small arms is made in different granulations: FFFFg, FFFg, FFg, and Fg. FFFFg is the finest and Fg is the coarsest. Because the finer granulations have more surface area per volume, they ignite easier and consume faster than the coarser grades. This makes them more suitable for pistols, small-bore rifles, and for flintlock priming. The coarser granulations are preferred for large-caliber rifles and muskets.

Because modern, smokeless powders may be as black in color as blackpowder, they are occasionally confused by uninformed shooters. That can be very dangerous. Blackpowder is always of irregular grain shape; smokeless powder consists of small tabular extrusions, uniform flakes, or smooth balls. Blackpowder produces a dense cloud of white, sulphurous-smelling smoke when it burns, while smokeless powder produces relatively little smoke.

Blackpowder burns at a constant rate and generates a specific volume of gas within a specific period of time. This is why long gun barrels are sometimes necessary to efficiently utilize heavy charges of blackpowder.

Smokeless (nitrocellulose) powder, on the other hand, burns faster and faster as the pressure inside a gun barrel increases. Thus, the pressures generated by smokeless powder may be several times that of an equal volume or weight of blackpowder. Because muzzleloading arms are not designed to withstand the high pressures generated by smokeless powders, it is essential that only blackpowder or a safe, modern substitute for it, such as Pyrodex, be used in muzzleloaders.

Modern smokeless powder, when not confined within a cartridge inside a firing chamber, burns rapidly with a hot flame, but it does not detonate. The same cannot be said of blackpowder, so it is important to store it in a safe place. Generally, it is best to keep it in the manufacturer's original container. It is also better to store many small quantities in several different places than it is to keep a large quantity all in one place. To be on the safe side, it's a good idea to check with your fire department for rules on legal blackpowder storage.

IGNITION

Early muzzleloaders employed several different kinds of locks but, in the United States today, almost everyone uses either a flintlock or a caplock (percussion) arm. For hunting, the caplock is favored because it is easier and faster to load and because ignition is more dependable than it is in a flintlock, especially when there is a great deal of moisture in the air.

In a flintlock, a small piece of sharp-edged flint is clamped between the jaws of the cock or hammer. When the sear is released, the spring-loaded hammer pivots downward. The sharp edge of the flint strikes the face or battery of an upright piece of steel called the frizzen. Struck by the flint, the frizzen pivots forward, uncovering the flash pan, which holds a priming charge of fine-grained powder. The harsh contact between the flint and the hardened steel of the battery produces white-hot sparks that shower into the pan and ignite the priming charge. The burning pan powder ignites the main charge inside the barrel through the flash-hole. Sometimes the priming charge burns without igniting the main charge, a mishap known as a flash-in-the-pan, an oft-used metaphor for something that didn't come off.

Despite hearsay, a properly loaded and primed flintlock can provide astonishingly fast ignition and a high degree of accuracy, often on a par with the accuracy of a caplock of similar quality. The biggest problem with flintlocks as hunting arms is keeping the priming charge free of moisture. The pan of a flintlock is primed after the main charge and the bullet are loaded. It's safer that way.

The percussion cap is a cup of thin metal that contains an explosive mixture. When fitted over the hollow, tubelike nipple of a caplock gun and struck sharply by the gun's hammer, the priming mix explodes and sends a flash of hot flame through the nipple to ignite the main charge. Cap your gun after you have loaded the main charge and the bullet.

Though percussion caps have been made in a variety of sizes, the average, modern blackpowder shooter is concerned only with two. The common size is No. 11; it fits all percussion pistols, sporting rifles and shotguns. The other is the so-called musket size, which fits the larger nipples of original military muskets and modern replicas of them.

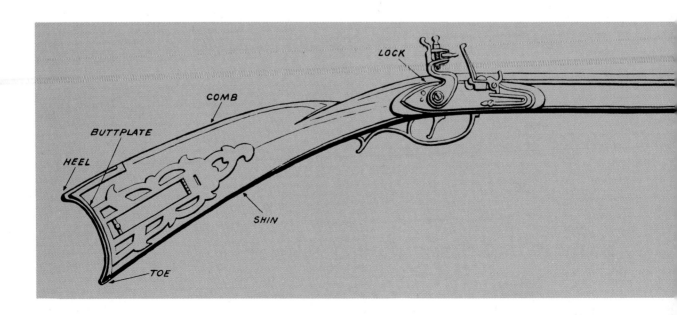

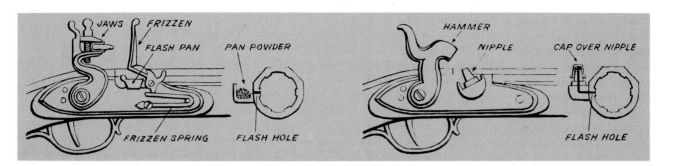

Until recently, percussion caps contained a priming mixture that deposited a corrosive agent in the interior of the barrel. This caused serious rusting unless it was promptly and thoroughly scrubbed out. Some modern caps contain noncorrosive priming chemicals that are less likely to cause serious rusting. They do not, however, eliminate the need for thorough cleaning because the residue of blackpowder can lead to serious rusting.

Sometimes, a percussion cap bursts. The hammers of most guns are made in shapes that usually shield the shooter from flying metal fragments, but don't depend on it. Wear good shooting glasses whenever you use a muzzleloader. Eye protection is important with a flintlock, too, because the flashpan powder burns outside the gun's chamber and can provide some surprises for the shooter in the way of hot gas.

BARRELS AND RIFLING

Modern muzzleloading barrels are made of high-quality steels by methods similar or identical to those employed in the manufacture of modern cartridge arms.

Cutting twisting grooves into the walls of a gun barrel causes the bullet to spin about its axis, and this gyroscopic effect causes the projectile to fly much straighter than a bullet from a smoothbore. Rifled barrels were known in central Europe as early as 1500. When using round balls in muzzleloading rifles, most modern hunters encase the ball in a cloth patch. When properly loaded, the lead ball never touches the rifling. Instead, the rifling engages the cloth patch, which imparts spin to the bullet. The rifling in most replica hunting arms is designed to work well with this kind of loading. But many other forms of rifling have been used. For instance, some early German rifled arms were used without patches. The lead ball was pounded into the rifling with an iron ramrod and a hammer. For that reason, the raised lands of these barrels have sharp triangular edges that cut into the unpatched lead ball.

Unlike modern, cartridge-firing arms, in which the caliber is determined by *groove* diameter (the widest measurement of the barrel's interior diameter), the caliber of muzzleloading rifles and some pistols (not including revolvers) is determined by the *bore* size (the distance between the raised lands).

The familiar gauge system used for shotguns is often used for muzzleloading smoothbore muskets intended for round balls. For instance, a 16-gauge musket takes a round ball that weighs $1/16$ of a pound;

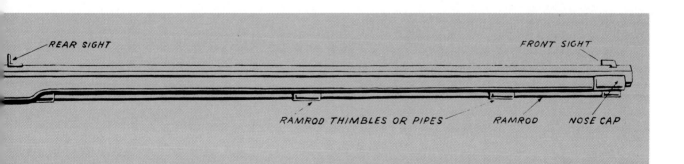

The flintlock (above and top left) depends on sparks struck from steel to ignite powder charge. A sharp piece of flint is clamped between the jaws of the cock in a patch of rawhide or a piece of sheet lead. With hammer at full cock, the shooter pulls trigger, the hammer falls and, when the flint hits the frizzen or steel, it strikes sparks. The frizzen flies upward to uncover the flash pan. The sparks ignite the fine powder in the pan. In turn, the main powder charge is ignited through the flash-hole. The simpler caplock or percussion lock (far right) employs a percussion cap containing explosive chemical. When hammer falls, metal cup is crushed, and flame ignites main charge through the mipple.

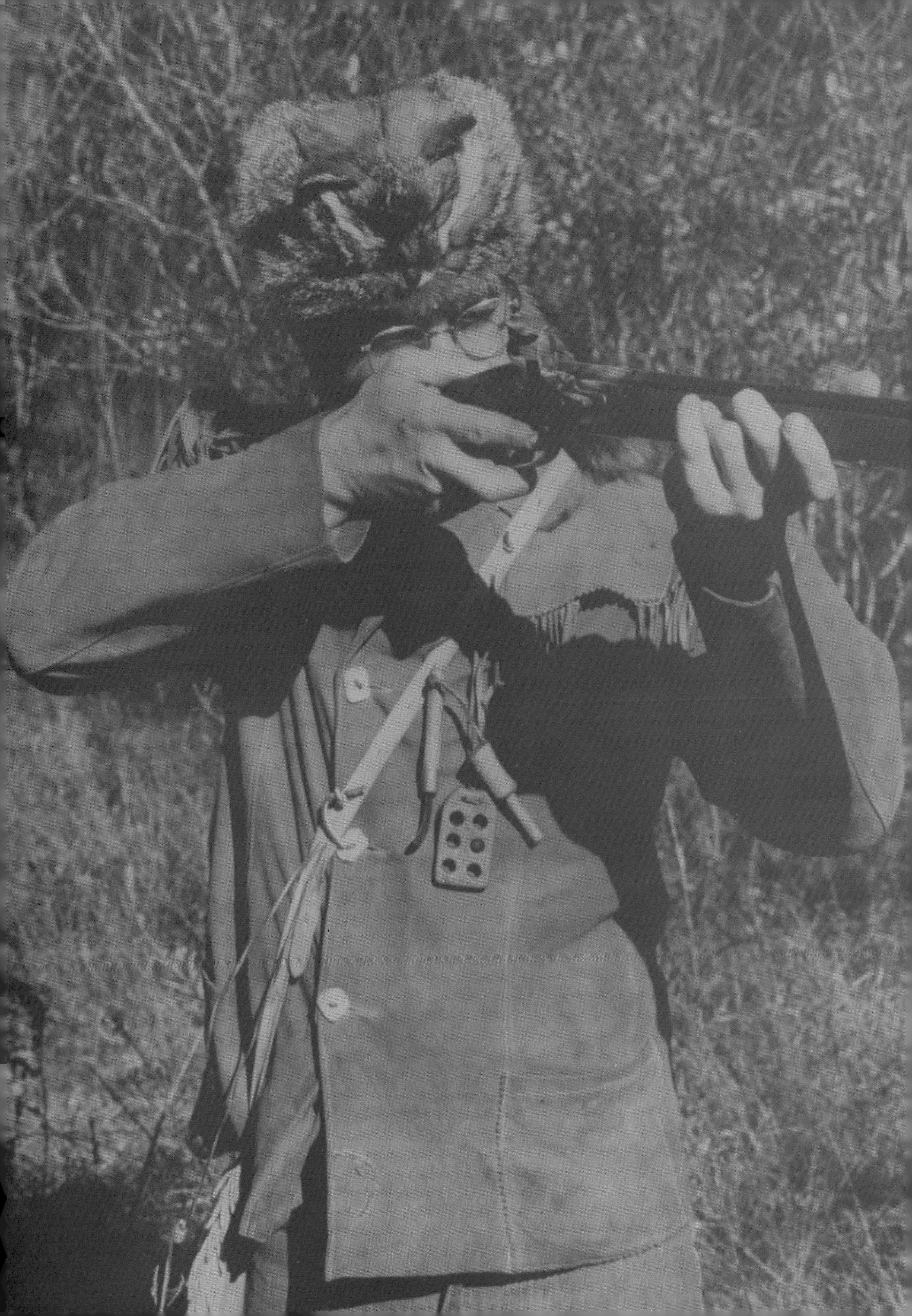

an eight-gauge gun takes a ball that weighs two ounces.

BULLETS

Though a properly patched and loaded ball is very accurate, it requires a relatively long time to load. Because of this, many attempts were made to develop a patchless projectile that could be speedily loaded and that would also engage the rifling well enough to impart a stabilizing spin. This meant that somehow the projectile had to be expanded into the rifling *after* it had been rammed down the barrel. These efforts resulted in the famous minie bullet used throughout the American Civil War. It was invented by a Frenchman named Minie. This conical bullet has a hollow base. The resulting thin skirt at the base of the bullet expands outward upon firing and engages the rifling. Because this expansion is minimal, muskets and rifles designed for minie balls usually have shallow rifling grooves of only .004 to .005 in depth. Likewise, they have fewer grooves.

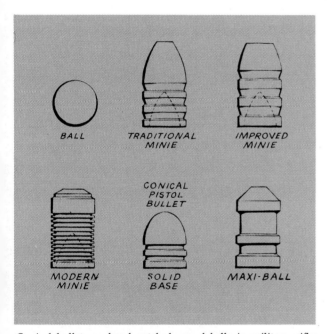

Conical bullets replaced patched round balls in military rifles because they are easier and faster to load. Minie balls (really conical) have hollow bases so that powder gas expands thin skirt and seals bore to prevent gas blow-by. Solid-base pistol bullets are swaged down to right size when they are levered into revolver's chambers. The Maxi-ball, far right, fits bore tightly and is also greased to prevent gas blow-by.

Minie-type bullets are widely used in skirmish marksmanship competitions, formal and informal target shooting, and hunting. In addition to the thousands of still-shootable muskets dating from the Civil War era, there are also several modern-made musket reproductions available that perform best with ''minny balls,'' as Civil War soldiers called

them. These easily loaded bullets killed thousands of soldiers on both sides in that war.

Though the original U.S. minie balls ranged from .54 to .69 caliber, they are now available in a wide assortment of calibers (from .44 up) and shapes. In addition to the traditional military shapes, there are several modern shapes for both target shooting and hunting. Though ready-made minie balls are available, most shooters prefer to cast their own in special molds. Many shooters fill the hollow bullet base with a stiff grease such as Crisco, which serves to soften the blackpowder fouling and also lubricates the bore. A lubricated bore generally improves accuracy with minie balls.

A projectile of more recent times is the so-called Maxi-Ball introduced by the Thompson/Center Arms Company. The Maxi-Ball, and copies of it, is a cylindrical, semi-pointed, solid-base projectile designed primarily for big-game hunting. The idea is to deliver a solid bullet of greater weight per bore size than is possible with a round ball or a hollow-base bullet. Maxi-Balls are made in a variety of bore sizes and can be bought ready cast, or you can make your own in Lyman molds. Maxi-Balls are loaded unpatched but with the grease rings filled with heavy grease or a commercial bullet lubricant.

In addition to the line of swaged, round lead balls offered by Speer and Hornady, American blackpowder shooters have available an extensive line of bullet molds manufactured by Lyman, RCBS, Lee, Shiloh, and others. With these high-quality molds, it is possible to cast an unending supply of low-cost bullets by utilizing scrap lead. Bullet casting should always be done in a well-ventilated area where the fumes from the molten lead are immediately carried away.

It is essential that only pure or nearly pure, soft lead be used for casting muzzleloading projectiles. Sometimes, slightly alloyed scrap lead can be used for round balls to be fired in rifles but, even so, nothing harder than common, automobile wheel-weight alloy should be used. If minie balls are cast of alloyed lead, they will be too hard to expand into the rifling, and performance will suffer. When in doubt about the composition of scrap lead, scratch it with your thumbnail. If it can be indented that way, the lead is soft enough for muzzleloading bullets, including minie balls.

All other factors being equal, the accuracy of a muzzleloading rifle loaded with a ball is determined by the ball's diameter. It is possible to shoot, say, a .30-caliber patched ball in a .50-caliber barrel, but accuracy will not be good unless the ball, in combination with a patch of proper thickness, tightly fits the bore. This is why makers of lead bullets and molds offer such a wide variety of seemingly odd sizes. The trick to selecting the proper ball size for a given barrel is to take into account the depth of the rifling and the patch thickness necessary to fill the rifling. Let's say your rifle has a bore diameter of .450. If the proposed patching cloth has a *compressed* thickness of .010, the proper bullet size should be .430 (.430 ball + .020 for two thicknesses of cloth,

LOADS FOR RIFLES AND REVOLVERS OF VARYING CALIBERS AND BARREL LENGTHS

The data in the following tables were developed by Lyman Products for Shooters. The information is printed here in abbreviated form with only a minimum and maximum load for each barrel length. In the *Lyman Black Powder Handbook,* many loads are given between the powder-charge minimum and the maximum. Lyman and this publisher accept no responsibility for use of the data. Only the shooter is responsible for the manner in which he loads a blackpowder arm. Maximum loads are intended only for arms that are in very good condition.

Barrel Length	Bullet Type & Diam.	Bullet Weight (grains)	Powder (grains)	Muzzle Velocity (fps)	Muzzle Energy (ft. lbs.)	100-yard Energy (ft. lbs.)
RIFLE .36 CAL. (.365 BORE DIAMETER)						
Min. 28"	.360 ball	71	25	1329	278	84
Max. 28"	.360 ball	71	60	2090	688	135
Min. 32"	.360 ball	71	25	1335	281	84
Max. 32"	.360 ball	71	60	2108	700	137
Min. 37"	.360 ball	71	25	1384	301	87
Max. 37"	.360 ball	71	60	2192	756	144
Min. 43"	.360 ball	71	25	1521	364	95
Max. 43"	.360 ball	71	60	2292	827	154
.45 CAL. (.453 BORE DIAMETER)						
Min. 28"	.445 ball	133	30	1089	349	N/A
Max. 28"	.445 ball	133	75	2025	1209	341
Min. 32"	.445 ball	133	30	1240	453	N/A
Max. 32"	.445 ball	133	75	2057	1248	352
Min. 36"	.445 ball	133	30	1294	493	N/A
Max. 36"	.445 ball	133	75	2055	1245	351
Min. 40"	.445 ball	133	30	1327	519	N/A
Max. 40"	.445 ball	133	75	2009	1190	338
Min. 28"	.454 minie	265	30	782	359	295
Max. 28"	.454 minie	265	65	1472	1273	789
Min. 32"	.454 minie	265	30	715	300	245
Max. 32"	.454 minie	265	65	1489	1303	805
Min. 36"	.454 minie	265	30	1041	636	477
Max. 36"	.454 minie	265	65	1506	1333	820
Min. 40"	.454 minie	265	30	825	399	327
Max. 40"	.454 minie	265	65	1547	1406	856
Min. 28"	.455 Maxi-B	230	30	939	449	292
Max. 28"	.455 Maxi-B	230	65	1588	1286	527
Min. 32"	.455 Maxi-B	230	30	1017	528	326
Max. 32"	.455 Maxi-B	230	80	1746	1554	598
Min. 36"	.455 Maxi-B	230	30	927	438	286
Max. 36"	.455 Maxi-B	230	80	1735	1535	592
Min. 40"	.455 Maxi-B	230	30	1065	578	344
Max. 40"	.455 Maxi-B	230	80	1803	1657	628
.50 CAL. (.503 BORE DIAMETER)						
Min. 26"	.498 ball	180	50	1348	725	304
Max. 26"	.498 ball	180	120	2041	1663	432
Min. 28"	.498 ball	180	50	1333	709	300
Max. 28"	.498 ball	180	120	2009	1611	515
Min. 32"	.498 ball	180	50	1445	833	327
Max. 32"	.498 ball	180	120	2101	1762	565
Min. 43"	.498 ball	180	50	1506	905	343
Max. 43"	.498 ball	180	120	2243	2008	657
Min. 26"	.503 Maxi-B	370	45	1033	875	559
Max. 26"	.503 Maxi-B	370	70	1286	1357	718
Min. 28"	.503 Maxi-B	370	50	1067	934	581
Max. 28"	.503 Maxi-B	370	85	1442	1706	819
Min. 32"	.503 Maxi-B	370	50	1116	1022	612
Max. 32"	.503 Maxi-B	370	85	1435	1689	814
Min. 43"	.503 Maxi-B	370	55	1212	1205	672
Max. 43"	.503 Maxi-B	370	90	1542	1951	895
.54 CAL. (.540 BORE DIAMETER)						
Min. 28"	.535 ball	220	80	1453	1030	436
Max. 28"	.535 ball	220	150	2008	1967	699
Min. 30"	.535 ball	220	80	1466	1048	440
Max. 30"	.535 ball	220	150	2024	1998	712
Min. 34"	.535 ball	220	70	1439	1010	431
Max. 34"	.535 ball	220	140	1973	1899	676
Min. 43"	.535 ball	220	70	1527	1137	462
Max. 43"	.535 ball	220	140	2113	2178	784
Min. 28"	.533 minie	410	50	739	497	N/A
Max. 28"	.533 minie	410	120	1505	2059	1192
Min. 30"	.533 minie	410	60	897	732	580
Max. 30"	.533 minie	410	130	1620	2386	1346
Min. 34"	.533 minie	410	50	941	805	627
Max. 34"	.533 minie	410	120	1614	2368	1337
Min. 43"	.533 minie	410	60	1089	1087	772
Max. 43"	.533 minie	410	130	1718	2683	1498
.58 CAL. (.575 BORE DIAMETER)						
Min. 22"	.560 ball	260	100	1249	899	440
Max. 22"	.560 ball	260	170	1648	1566	613
Min. 24"	.560 ball	260	110	1329	1018	469
Max. 24"	.560 ball	260	180	1783	1833	685
Min. 26"	.560 ball	260	120	1306	983	459
Max. 26"	.560 ball	260	190	1669	1606	623
Min. 32"	.560 ball	260	110	1352	1056	478
Max. 32"	.560 ball	260	180	1737	1739	659
Min. 22"	.575 minie	505	50	607	413	349
Max. 22"	.575 minie	505	120	1195	1599	1124
Min. 24"	.575 minie	505	60	791	701	587
Max. 24"	.575 minie	505	130	1253	1758	1198
Min. 26"	.575 minie	505	90	979	1073	852
Max. 26"	.575 minie	505	160	1340	2011	1317
Min. 32"	.575 minie	505	80	971	1056	841
Max. 32"	.575 minie	505	150	1393	2173	1393

Barrel Length	Bullet Type & Diam.	Bullet Weight (grains)	Powder (grains)	Muzzle Velocity (fps)	Muzzle Energy (ft. lbs.)
REVOLVER .44 CAL. (.440 BORE DIAMETER)					
Min. 8"	.451 ball	138	19	706	153
8"	.451 ball	138	22	752	173
8"	.451 ball	138	25	805	198
8"	.451 ball	138	28	885	240
8"	.451 ball	138	31	933	266
8"	.451 ball	138	33	979	293
Max. 8"	.451 ball	138	37	1032	326
Min. 8"	.450 conical	155	19	705	171
8"	.450 conical	155	22	768	203
Max. 8"	.450 conical	155	25	882	267
Max. 8"	.450 conical	155	28	861	255
REVOLVER .45 CAL. (RUGER OLD ARMY, .442 BORE DIAMETER)					
Min. 7"	.457 ball	185	30	858	301
Max. 7½"	.457 ball	185	40	917	344
Min. 7½"	.454 conical	185	26	860	303
Max. 7½"	.454 conical	185	35	905	335

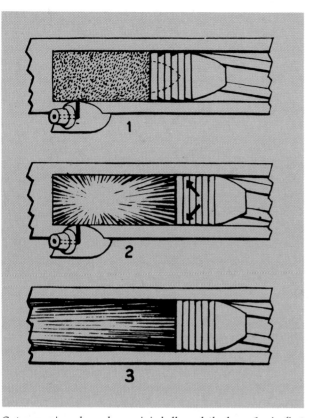

Cutaway view shows how minie balls seal the bore: 1. As first loaded, bullet rests on the powder but is not in firm contact with walls of the barrel or the rifling's spiralling lands and grooves. 2. When the main charge goes off, gas pressure expands base of the bullet so that the soft lead engages rifling and spins bullet. 3. Expanding gas moves spinning bullet down tube. It is now a bit shorter than before firing because of the expansion of the base. Grease in hollow base lubricates bore and softens fouling.

events for smoothbores only. The smoothbore was accurate enough when soldiers usually fired in massed volleys at large targets such as an enemy regiment in an open field.

LOADING AND SHOOTING

One of the chief stumbling blocks is determining how much and what type of powder to use.

As a general guide, FFg is the best granulation for rifles or muskets .50 caliber and over. This is by no means a hard-and-fast rule and some shooters prefer double F for somewhat smaller calibers. Double F is also a good choice for 12, 16, and 20-gauge shotguns. Larger-gauge shotguns may perform better with coarse-grained Fg powder.

Triple F (FFFg) powder is the most used granulation because it will work in just about any sort of rifle, shotgun, or pistol and it can even be used for flintlock priming. Generally, it is best for rifles and single-shot pistols up to .45 caliber and for all revolvers.

Four F (FFFFg) is mainly used for flintlock priming,

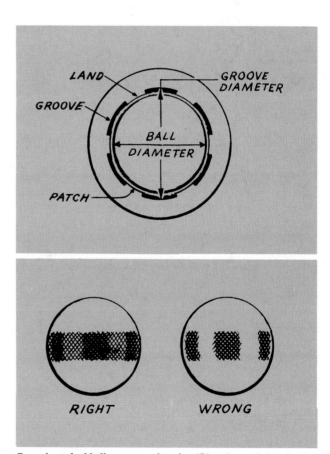

Round patched ball never touches the rifling. Instead, it is loaded encased in a cloth patch. Cloth engages rifling and spins the ball. Patch drops away a few yards from the muzzle. Patch should be thick enough to mark soft lead ball over the grooves of rifling as well as the lands. If impression of cloth shows only over lands when you pull a loaded ball, the patch is too thin or the ball you are using is too small. This permits gas to pass the ball and lowers power.

one on each "side" of the bore). If a thicker (or thinner) patch is needed to properly seal the grooves and prevent gas blow-by, the ball size should be chosen accordingly.

A patched ball should fit tightly in the bore but not so tight that it must be pounded down the barrel. With a properly fitted and patched ball, you should be able to push it home with one firm but smooth push of the ramrod. If the ball tends to stick in a clean bore, either a thinner patch or a smaller bullet is needed. As a rule of thumb, a properly fitted ball is so tight that the patch makes an imprint in the lead completely around the ball, not just where it is pressed by the lands.

Smoothbore muskets are usually used to fire round, unpatched balls. For instance, replicas of the British Brown Bess musket used in the Revolutionary War take a .715 ball that is 545 grains in weight. The shooter loads his powder charge and then drops in a paper wad. Then, the ball is tamped down on the wad with the ramrod. If the bore is heavily fouled, it may be necessary to ram the ball home forcefully. Accuracy with a smoothbore musket is never as good as it is with a properly loaded rifle, and these guns are used mostly in battle reenactments and target but it can also be used in the main charges for small pistols.

No particular load works best with any given caliber or bullet type. In fact, one of the great charms of shooting blackpowder guns is developing or "working up" the combination of powder charge, ball size, and patch thickness that gives the best accuracy in your rifle. Generally speaking, "hot" loads with heavy powder charges are not as accurate as milder charges. Loads in the 1,400 to 1,600-fps velocity range are usually the most accurate with patched balls. Minie bullets tend to be most accurate when loaded under 1,200 fps.

The manufacturers of replica muzzleloaders usually recommend bullet weights and powder charges for their products but, if you're in doubt for any reason, consult the *Lyman Black Powder Handbook*, provided by Lyman Products for Shooters. It is usually available wherever blackpowder arms and supplies are sold. Keep in mind that blackpowder arms are individualistic. Even guns of the same caliber and barrel length often do not shoot the same with the same loads. It takes experimentation to determine the right load for target shooting and for hunting.

With most rifles, the powder charge can be varied considerably. For instance, let's take the very popular .45-caliber rifle with a 36-inch barrel firing a patched round ball that weighs 133 grains. A practical load might be anywhere from 30 to 75 grains of FFFg powder. The resulting muzzle energy varies accordingly from 493 foot-pounds to 1,245. At 100 yards, the remaining energy of the heaviest load is only 351 foot-pounds. The Lyman manual gives these figures and many others for practically every kind of muzzleloading firearm.

The figures should tell you why a muzzleloading rifle is a short-range arm. Even the heaviest load listed for this very popular deer hunting arm produces only 351 foot-pounds of remaining energy at 100 yards. By comparison, the good old .30/30 rifle with 150-grain bullets, hits with 1,296 foot-pounds of energy at 100 yards. Bullet placement is very important with any muzzleloader.

Maximum loads should be used with great caution and then only in quality arms in very good condition. Lyman and the publisher of this yearbook accept no responsibility for the use of the data. It's all too easy for a shooter to load a blackpowder firearm incorrectly because he is the one who measures the powder charge and rams the ball home.

The name of the game is *consistency*. Once the best powder charge is determined, a reliable means of measuring must be used that assures uniform, shot-to-shot powder weight. There are several excellent, adjustable powder measures available, or you may make your own as the pioneers did. For safety's sake, do not pour powder into the barrel directly from the main container. Lingering sparks in the bore may cause a flash, which can be disastrous if it ignites the larger quantity of blackpowder in a flask, horn, or can. Use a separate measuring device.

The need for consistency carries over into the way

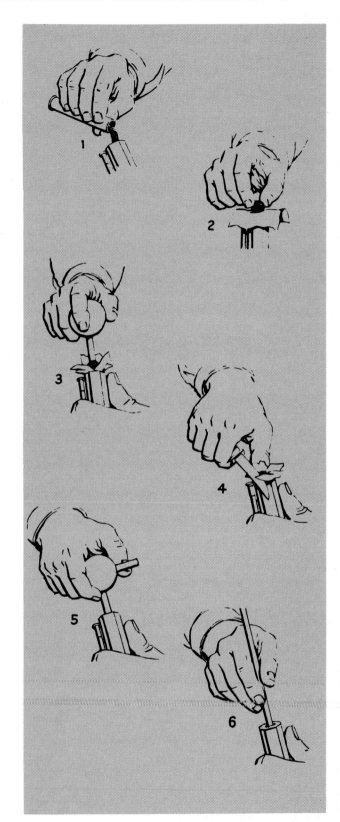

Here's one of the best ways to load rifle: 1. Pour measured charge of powder down the bore. 2. Cover muzzle with piece of patching cloth and place the ball in its center. 3. With short arm of two-prong bullet starter, push ball into bore so that it is flush with muzzle. 4. Cloth is cut off with patch knife. 5. Long arm of bullet starter is used to push ball six or seven inches down barrel. 6. Full-length ramrod seats the ball. The pan should not be primed or the nipple capped until after the ball has been seated.

you cut the patch and position the ball. Careful shooters position the sprue of their cast balls either straight up or straight down so that the ball will not be unbalanced as it spins through the air. The ball must be carefully centered in the patch when pre-cut patches are used, or the patch must be uniformly trimmed if it is cut after starting the ball in the barrel. If the patch is not centered, it may "slingshot" the ball or even come off while the ball is still in the bore, ruining accuracy.

Today's blackpowder shooter can select from a wide assortment of patch lubricants or he may choose, as do many expert shooters, to simply wet the patch with his tongue. Either way is usually better than dry patching because the grease or moisture both lubricates the bore and softens the powder fouling. Hunters tend to use pre-greased, pre-cut patches or pre-patched balls in a loading block while target shooters are more inclined to use spit-wet patches cut for each shot.

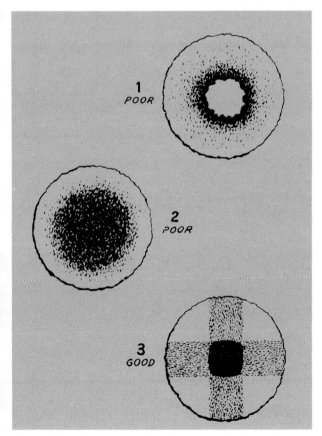

After a shot, the patch can often be recovered a few yards from muzzle. Examining these tells a lot about your loading: 1. If center has been burned away, the patch is much too thin to seal the bore. 2. If most of the patch has been charred and is covered with fouling, the patch is still too thin, though rifle may function fairly well. 3. Patch of the right thickness shows folded portions that weren't in contact with bore. They are clean, and patch will show a cross. If patching material seems to be thick enough, but gas still passes the ball, the ball itself may be too small for bore. Most shooters lubricate their patches with commercial patch lubricants or with saliva.

An examination of patches recovered after firing (usually a few yards from the muzzle) tells a lot about how the patch is performing and gives valuable clues to accuracy.

If the patch has a hole burned through it, for example, it is too thin or of poor material. If it tends to be soot blackened all over, it is too thin (or the ball is too small) and the patch is being burned by gas blow-by. If the patch seals properly, the creased or folded areas will still be clean. One of the best patching materials is cotton twill bed ticking. It is tough, uniform in thickness, and has sufficient density to effectively fill and seal the grooves of most barrels.

When the ball is driven home with the ramrod, it should be pressed down firmly and uniformly on the powder but not tamped. If the ball sticks in the bore with airspace above the powder, it should be removed with a ball puller. Do not attempt to shoot it out as it may be stuck fast enough to cause the barrel to burst.

SHOTGUNS

It can hardly be claimed that blackpowder shotguns place the hunter at a "sporting" disadvantage. Other than the increased loading time and the sometimes troublesome but romantic cloud of white smoke, blackpowder shotguns can be made to perform on a par with modern, breech-loading shotguns. In fact, the "dram equivalent" standard of rating the velocity of modern shotshells is nothing more than a system of comparing them to the blackpowder loads of a century ago.

Muzzleloading shotguns can be loaded in a number of ways. Perhaps the simplest is to use a wad of scrap paper between the powder and the shot with another wad of paper on top of the shot to hold it in place. That kind of loading is workable but it does not produce top performance. A far more efficient and faster loading system employs modern, one-piece, plastic wad columns and shot cups. They are easy to carry, very fast to load, and form an efficient gas seal, which results in higher velocity. A thin cardboard "over-shot" wad is used to hold the shot in position.

Another excellent system for muzzleloading shotguns utilizes felt or cork wads in combination with cardboard or plastic over-powder wads. Some competitive skeet and trap shooters soak their felt wads in water immediately before use as a means of softening blackpowder residue in the barrel to improve performance. Hunters fire fewer shots and few of them soak their wads. As with the one-piece plastic wad, a thin cardboard wad is placed over the shot to hold it in place.

The key to top shotgun performance is developing a good load and loading each barrel with care and consistency. The best way to test the performance of a muzzleloading shotgun is by shooting test patterns at a pattern board or a large sheet of paper. Patterns that are uneven, blown, or ragged are usually a sign of overcharging, careless loading, or a poor wad combination. A few small corrections will often result in a remarkable improvement.

For speedy loading in the field, a handy accessory is a leather shot pouch with built-in measure.

To convert original blackpowder shotgun loads rated in drams to grains, simply multiply the drams by 27.34 (one dram = 27.34 grains). For example, a 2¾-dram load is converted to grain-weight equivalent thus: 2.750 × 27.34 = 75.18 grains. Note that this conversion is for blackpowder *only*.

Finely made British muzzleloading shotguns were among the best firearms ever made. They had fast ignition time and were splendidly balanced—flintlocks and caplocks alike. But the average, modern blackpowder shooter will probably use a lesser arm. Usually, it is a percussion-cap gun because a flintlock double is a complicated affair, and most shooters find that they have slow ignition time and, therefore, require longer leads.

A percussion-cap shotgun can be about as fast as a modern gun, but the shooter who uses one for the first time is in for a surprise when the big cloud of dense, white smoke obscures his target. Usually, the only way you know that you have hit the bird is when it drops out below the powder smoke. Using Pyrodex is a good way to improve your shooting because the smoke is considerably reduced.

A muzzleloading double should be loaded with caution. It is all too easy to fire a shot and then reload the new charge right on top of the original one in the *other* barrel. The resulting pressures can burst the barrel.

With one barrel loaded, always be sure to keep your hand safely away from the loaded tube's muzzle.

PYRODEX

Pyrodex, a safe, blackpowder substitute, was designed to duplicate blackpowder loads on a volume-to-volume basis. This means that you can continue using the identical powder measure setting when switching from blackpowder to Pyrodex or vice ver-

sa. Do not attempt to duplicate charges by weight. If you customarily weigh your powder charges, use the following weight conversion chart:

Blackpowder	Pyrodex	Blackpowder	Pyrodex
10 Gr.	8 Gr.	110 Gr.	88 Gr.
20 Gr.	16 Gr.	120 Gr.	96 Gr.
30 Gr.	24 Gr.	130 Gr.	104 Gr.
40 Gr.	32 Gr.	140 Gr.	112 Gr.
50 Gr.	40 Gr.	150 Gr.	120 Gr.
60 Gr.	48 Gr.	160 Gr.	128 Gr.
70 Gr.	56 Gr.	170 Gr.	136 Gr.
80 Gr.	64 Gr.	180 Gr.	144 Gr.
90 Gr.	72 Gr.	190 Gr.	152 Gr.
100 Gr.	80 Gr.	200 Gr.	160 Gr.

Pyrodex produces relatively little smoke, barrel fouling is reduced, and it is much less likely to ignite by accident.

PISTOLS AND REVOLVERS

Blackpowder revolvers are a fascinating blend of the ancient muzzleloading art and modern firearms science. The percussion revolver ignition system is identical to any other cap-and-ball system, but the bullets aren't patched and they fill the grooves of the barrel. This makes the selection of a correctly sized ball or bullet somewhat more critical than it is with patched balls.

For example, the Ruger Old Army, one of the more popular and better-performing revolvers on today's market, has a groove diameter of .450. This means it is a true .45 caliber but, for proper loading, a somewhat oversize ball or bullet is required. Recommended bullet diameters are about .454 to .457 for round balls and .452 to .454 for conical bullets. When the bullets are levered into the chambers in

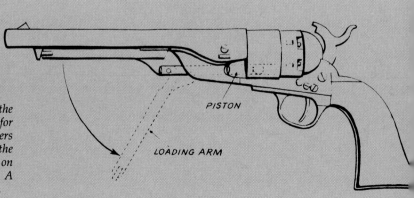

Cap-and-ball revolvers are called muzzle-loaders, but they are loaded through the front of the cylinder. After loading measured charge of powder in a chamber, a ball or conical bullet is forcefully levered into chamber. Ball or conical bullet must be slightly larger than cylinder diameter so that the soft lead is swaged down to right bore size for the barrel. Very tight fit also seals the chambers and prevents gas blow-by. After loading the powder and balls, percussion caps are placed on each of the nipples at the rear of the cylinder. A spring-loaded capping tool makes this easier.

the cylinders, they are swaged to a squeeze fit, which effectively seals the chamber. The sizing in the cylinder prepares the bullet for the barrel, and the tight fit helps eliminate "chain" or "jump" firing. This occurs when the flame from the chamber being fired enters the front of another chamber (or chambers), bypasses the bullet, and ignites the charge. Such multiple discharges can be dangerous. A further precaution against chain firing is to pack grease around the front of each bullet. This seals each chamber mouth and also lubricates the bullet and, in turn, the barrel, which improves accuracy.

Target shooters who customarily use only light to moderate powder charges for best accuracy in their revolvers have found that they can further enhance accuracy by using a cornmeal filler between the ball and the powder charge. Enough cornmeal is used to fill the chamber so that the ball is flush or nearly flush with the chamber mouth. This improves accuracy by reducing the distance the bullet must jump before contacting the rifling, and it is also believed that the cornmeal has a scrubbing action in the bore that reduces fouling. A properly loaded cap-and-ball revolver, careful experimenters have found, may be just as accurate as a good centerfire.

The following table lists the chamber size and recommended ball sizes for some of the more popular replica blackpowder revolvers. Tested loads for some blackpowder revolvers are given in the accompanying table.

Kentucky-style pistols of flintlock or percussion

cap persuasion are true muzzleloaders and are loaded in the same manner as ML rifles. And, as with rifles, top performance is the result of a proper combination of proper powder charge, patch, and the right-size ball.

Very few hunters use muzzleloading handguns, but hunting small game with them is a fine sport.

CLEANING

If properly cared for, a muzzleloading firearm will last several lifetimes. But, if it is neglected, any blackpowder arm soon deteriorates. Blackpowder fouling in or on a gun tends to absorb moisture and cause rust. Accuracy deteriorates very quickly. It is necessary to thoroughly clean any blackpowder arm as soon after use as possible. Most target shooters clean guns before leaving the range.

Fortunately, blackpowder fouling is soluable in water and in other cleaning agents such as detergents or special blackpowder solvents. The trick is to saturate the fouling with the cleaning agent and then wipe it away. With long-barreled muzzleloaders, however, this is easier said than done.

Some rifles, pistols, and shotguns, both original and current production, feature easy disassembly, which aids in cleaning. Most shotguns and some rifles have a hook-breech system that permits the barrel or barrels to be quickly removed from the stock simply by removing one or two pins or wedges that hold it in the forearm. The barrel then pivots rearward out of the stock. Free of the stock, it is easier to clean. Most revolvers feature easy cylinder removal, which considerably eases cleaning of the chambers as well as the barrel.

Attach a solvent-wetted patch to the cleaning rod (by means of a special patch-gripping jag), and pass the patch through the bore so that the fouling is removed bit by bit. This usually requires several wetted patches plus more drying patches and, finally, an oiled patch to protect the clean bore.

A faster way is to submerge the breech end of the barrel in a pail of soapy water or detergent, and pump water into the bore by means of a tightly patched cleaning rod or ramrod. As the rod is partially withdrawn, the vacuum created in the tube draws water into the bore through the nipple or touch hole. This in-and-out pumping action effectively washes away the residue. With barrels that cannot be easily removed from the stock, snug a rubber tube over the nipple, place the other end of the tube in the water pail, and scrub as described above. Cleaning kits of this type are available.

When the blackpowder residue has been thoroughly removed, the next step is to dry and oil the barrel and other metal parts. When flintlocks are used, it is a good idea to remove the lock and clean the mechanism from the inside, too. Some powder residue accumulates there. A coat of wax on the stock, and even on the metal exteriors, is good protection. Cleaning a muzzleloader isn't that much of a chore.

Revolver	Chamber Size	Ball Size
1860 Army, .44 cal. Centennial	.446	.450
1860 Army, .44 cal., Replica	.446	.450
Reb, .36 cal.	.375	.376
Model 60 Army, .44 cal.	.447	.451
Wells Fargo, .31 cal.	.315	.320
Paterson, .36 cal.	.378	.380
Yank, .36 cal.	.375	.376
Sheriff's Model, .36 cal.	.375	.376
1861 Navy Colt, .36 cal.	.375	.380
Baby Dragoon, .31 cal.	.316	.321
Leech & Rigdon, .36 cal.	.375	.376
Walker, .44 cal.	.440	.441
Dragoon, .44 cal.	.440	.441
Remington Revolving Carbine, .44 cal.	.450	.454
Remington Army, .44 cal.	.450	.454
Remington Navy, .36 cal.	.375	.376
Ruger Old Army, .45 cal.	.450	.454

Muzzleloaders: Making Them Go Off All The Time

By Rick Hacker

We had been sitting motionless behind a brush-covered blind for that past 2½ hours, waiting for that Big One to finally show before it got too dark to shoot. I had been lucky two days earlier and, using a .54-caliber, custom-built Hawken, had already filled my tag. Now, armed only with a 35mm camera, I was sitting with another muzzleloader hunter. I hoped to get some good black-and-white photos. It looked as if I was going to get my chance.

A few does and yearlings soon heedlessly wandered out of the brush and into the open. Then, a spike buck appeared and my hunting partner raised his Thompson/Center .54 Renegade to take aim, but he stopped when I placed my hand on his shoulder.

"Wait," I whispered. "There's a bigger one behind him."

A few minutes later, out walked a cautious but proud six-point muley—meat for the pot and a respectable wall-hanger. I heard the final "click" of the hammer being drawn to full cock but the big buck did not spook. Emerging slowly into full view, he was unknowingly offering the hunter a perfect broadside shot at less than 50 yards.

It seemed like an eternity as my partner took aim and finally pulled the trigger. The pop of the percussion cap broke the silence. Not the roar of the rifle—just the pop of the cap as it failed to ignite the powder. Although the rifle did not go off, the deer sure did: the six-pointer, the spike, and all the rest of the herd. The surrounding countryside was soon devoid of all wildlife and the only sound to be heard was the sudden tirade of well-chosen words emanating from a certain hunter's mouth.

"These old-time guns just don't cut it," he said, looking with disgust at his rifle, at me and, finally, at the silent world around him.

Back at camp, I carefully examined his Renegade to see what gremlin had marred a potentially successful hunt. The rifle itself was finely made and functioned perfectly. The problem, then, had to be with the charge. Trying a fresh cap and even trickling some powder down the nipple failed to fire the gun. However, upon pulling the Maxi-ball, we discovered that practically all of the FFg blackpowder was oil soaked.

"Didn't you run some dry patches down the bore of your rifle before loading it?" I asked.

"No," was the matter-of-fact reply. "You told me blackpowder was highly corrosive, so I left a coating of lube in the gun to keep it from rusting."

That incident points up an interesting phenomenon regarding today's blackpowder hunter. A little more than 100 years ago, when the cartridge arm was just starting to become accepted by our nation's shooters, outdoorsmen had to learn a whole new set of rules regarding loading and shooting. The advent of smokeless powder in 1895 only complicated things for hunters, but they gradually learned that it was not always necessary to clean their rifles with boiling water, or to drop to their knees immediately after shooting so they could see beneath the cloud of smoke, or to protect their weapons from rain and snow.

Today, however, with thousands of new muzzleloader hunters taking to the field each fall, firearms history has repeated itself. Sportsmen weaned on the self-contained, metallic, smokeless cartridge must

Sportsmen weaned on self-contained, metallic cartridges must learn completely new rules when shooting muzzleloaders. These rules are actually old gems of practical experience whose brilliance has been dulled by the simplicity of modern cartridge guns.

learn an entire new set of rules when shooting replica or original smokepoles. These rules are actually old gems of practical experience whose brilliance has been dulled by the simplicity of modern cartridge guns.

But anyone who agrees with the statement that "old-time guns just don't cut it" had better reread some early American history dealing with the Revolutionary War, the Lewis and Clark expedition, the mountain-man era, and the buffalo hunters. In the 500-year history of muzzleloader hunting, the front-loading sporting rifle has taken everything from field mice to elephants—cleanly, humanely, and reliably—just as it does today for thousands of black-powder hunters. The secret, of course, is learning the proper techniques of feeding and caring for your muzzleloader. Fortunately for today's big-game hunters, we have an easier availability and wider variety of blackpowder products than were ever dreamt of by the early frontiersmen. The basic principles of trouble-free muzzleloader hunting have never changed, though. It is a simple matter for America's reborn buckskinners to learn these techniques and put them back into practice.

Regarding the muzzleloading hunting rifle, there are three factors that can affect the success of the blackpowder hunter: the care he gives his muzzle-loading rifle, the method by which he loads it, and the weather. Realizing that we can at least have control over two-thirds of our potential problems, let's start with the rifle itself.

Unlike modern cartridge firearms, the igniting action of muzzleloaders—the hammer and cap or priming charges—takes place outside the lock area. Therefore, before taking any blackpowder rifle out on a hunt, the bore, breech, and touch-hole area must be thoroughly free of oil and moisture that could seep into your powder and render it inert, or clog up the all-important touch-hole that sends the igniting flame into your main charge. In the case of percussion guns, the nipple should be unscrewed and wiped dry, giving special attention to the threads and the base of the flash-hole—areas that come in direct contact with the powder. Use a paper clip or piece of wire to push out any foreign matter that might have become lodged inside the flash-hole.

With flintlocks, the frizzen (striking plate) and pan must be completely free of oil and the touch-hole should be clear. A new, fresh flint (wrapped in leather to prevent slippage) should be securely tightened in the jaws of the cock so that the flat edge of the flint's striking surface is perfectly parallel to the flat area of the frizzen, thus assuring the greatest concentration of sparks when the trigger is pulled. For caplocks, the hollowed-out, cap-strik-

Field essentials: speed loaders, caps, cleaning jag, ball puller, wire or paper clip, nipple cap, and small screwdriver.

Pinch the cap slightly before placing it on the nipple to ensure a snug, non-slip fit.

ing recess of the hammer should be checked for bits of fired caps because the soft bits of copper can build up and eventually deaden the blow of the hammer, which may cause a misfire.

New guns must be thoroughly cleaned of storage and shipping "gunk" if they are to fire at all. Even with the rifles I regularly use, I always run at least three, dry, tight-fitting patches up and down the bore, twisting them a bit in the breech area where oil can collect in guns that are stored muzzle-up. And, of course, all front-loaders should be checked to make sure that screws are tight, lock plates and hammers line up properly, and set triggers are adjusted. The blackpowder hunter only gets one shot and his rifle must be ready for it.

If there is any one factor that can affect the reliability of a muzzleloader at the moment of firing, it is the manner in which the rifle is loaded. It is just a matter of common sense, but all too many emulators of Davy Crockett and Jim Bridger have failed to learn this simple method.

First, a pre-measured charge of powder is poured down a clean, dry bore with the muzzle pointing up. Then, canting the rifle slightly so that the touch-

hole or flash-hole area is angling down toward the ground, slap the side of the forestock/barrel area two or three times to make sure that all of the powder settles into the breech and toward the nipple or pan on the outside of the lock.

Next, when loading either a patched round ball or greased conical bullet, make sure that the projectile is seated firmly down upon the powder charge. This is done by feel more than anything else but, to make sure, I always place the ramrod down an uncharged bore first, noting where the end of the rod is in relation to the muzzle. After pouring down my powder and seating the ball, I double-check the distance that the rod protrudes from the charged bore and match up that distance with the end of the breech, thereby determining whether or not the given measure of powder and lead projectile could occupy that particular space. I then give the ball a few extra taps down on the powder with the ramrod. This is especially useful in the case of Pyrodex, with which the powder must be compressed for best ignition. But the main reason for the tapping exercise is to prevent any air pockets between powder and ball that could harm the barrel—or you—when the

A cap cover will keep moisture out of nipple and breech area of percussion rifle.

When priming a flintlock, fill the pan up to—but not covering—the touch-hole.

rifle is fired. A tight-fitting ball also helps seal off the powder charge from moisture.

With the barrel properly loaded, the next step is to prime the gun. It is at this point that most mistakes occur. Understand that the best way to guarantee your front-loader will fire is to create the hottest flash possible and to make sure that it will reach your main powder charge. Therefore, I have equipped all of my percussion hunting guns with Uncle Mike's Hot Shot nipples, stainless-steel ventilated nipples that produce a hotter, more concentrated flash from the percussion cap when it goes off. I also use nothing but CCI or Remington Hot Caps for all my blackpowder hunting. There are less expensive caps on the market but these two are among the hottest I have found—besides being reliable and consistent.

As a final step before capping a percussion rifle, I always trickle a few grains of blackpowder down the nipple, filling it almost to the top. This assures me that the flash from the cap will ignite the powder. It is also a good practice to pinch the soft sides of the cap in slightly, so that it will fit snugly on the nipple without falling off when the hammer is cocked or the gun is carried over rough terrain.

Flintlocks require FFFFg blackpowder for their priming charge. Even with the frizzen closed down upon the pan, it is still possible for some of this finely grained priming powder to shift and spill out. You should check the lock from time to time on a hunt, repriming whenever necessary. To ensure that the main charge goes off, make sure that there is enough priming powder in the pan to fill it to a level where it meets the touch-hole—but is not covering it. I also make sure that a few grains are pushed into the touch-hole as an extra measure.

The greatest natural enemy to any blackpowder gun is moisture. The only two suitable and safe propellants in any muzzleloader are blackpowder or Pyrodex RS. (Unless preceded by a blackpowder priming charge, Pyrodex will not function reliably in flintlocks.) Both of these powders are extremely susceptible to moisture, hence the adage "keep your powder dry."

Try to load your first charge of the hunt while in a dry camp, rather than waiting until you get out into a wet field. Keep your extra charges in waterproof, pre-measured containers. The best that I have used are the Speed Loaders produced by Butler

Creek (1055 W. Broadway, Jackson, WY 83001) for hunters preferring conical bullets, and the Speed Shells by Blue & Gray Products (RD 6, Box 348, Wellsboro, PA 16901) for patch and ball. The Butler Creek container accommodates any caliber up to .58 and holds 200 grains of blackpowder (more than you'll need per shot) while the Blue & Gray tubes can be ordered by caliber and can hold well over 130 grains—again more than required. Hunters with flintlocks will find that by carrying their FFFFg priming powder in brass pan chargers, such as those sold by Dixie Gun Works (Gunpowder Ln., Union City, TN 38261) or Uncle Mike's, they will be able to re-prime quickly and waste less powder than with the traditional priming horn.

The early chronicles and diaries of our nation's frontiersmen are rampant with tales of guns misfiring in inclement weather. The traditional solution to this problem has been the old-fashioned "cow's knee," a piece of greased leather that was tied down over the lock of a rifle to protect it from rain and snow. There are some problems with this technique, though. First, by securely fastening the leather covering over his lock, the hunter cannot make a fast shot should he come upon game unexpectedly. Second, after a full day in heavy rain, even the heaviest-greased piece of leather will become soggy, thereby rendering itself useless as a protective covering. But, for short exposure to the elements, the cow's knee serves the purpose.

Although there are a number of "waterproof" lock covers now on the market, one of the newest and most efficient is the Weatherguard Powder Protector from Blue & Gray. This form-fitted piece of soft, molded plastic hugs the top and sides of your rifle's lockplate area, serving as a thick, protective shield against the elements. It also keeps the wind from blowing the priming charge out of the flintlock's pan. The Weatherguard can be quickly and quietly lifted off the lock. A dark cord tied to your trigger guard keeps the cover from falling noisily to the ground. This unique item is available for either flintlocks or percussion Thompson/Center, CVA, or Lyman rifles, but it can be placed in boiling water and remolded to fit practically any gun.

Another relatively new item for waterproofing the cap and nipple of percussion rifles is the Safe N Dry cap cover by K&M Industries (Box 151, Elk River, ID 83827). This two-part device consists of a neoprene "O" ring fastened to an Uncle Mike's Hot Shot nipple and a brass cap that fits over the nipple, providing a waterproof seal.

Butler Creek makes a handy, tight-fitting, plastic Nipple Cover that I have successfully used on more than one snow-soaked big-game hunt in the Rockies. Unlike the K&M product, the Butler Creek cover is used on a nipple that is not capped. It makes such an effective seal that I have also used it to plug up the breech end of the barrel when filling it with hot soapy water for cleaning.

One of the biggest problems for flintlock shooters

in the rain is the danger of little trickles of water leaking into the priming charge. A safeguard to this problem is Raincoat, a light, airy powder produced by Mountain State Muzzleloading (Box 154-1, Rte. 14, Williamston, WV 26187). When mixed in a one-to-six ratio with FFFFg, Raincoat covers the powder and keeps it dry, although it will slightly slow down the burning properties of your priming charge. Still, it is better than not having your flintlock go off just when you have settled your front and rear sights on the vitals of some potential venison steaks.

Many of the old-timers' tricks, such as covering the closed and primed pan or capped nipple with candle wax or animal fat, are still effective. However, these techniques are only good for one shot and are not as convenient for field use as some of the products mentioned above.

Although many round-ball shooters use a saliva-moistened spit patch on the target range, it has no place in a hunter's rifle. If the same charge is carried for days, the moistened patch will dry out and cause a ring of rust in your bore—a potential accuracy destroyer. Some of the more porous lubes also have a tendency to soak into your powder and should therefore be avoided. The thicker, cream-type patch lubes, such as those put out by Dixie, Blue & Gray, and Hodgdon's (7710 W. 63rd, Shawnee Mission, KS 66202) are far more practical, as they will neither dry out nor turn into powder-soaking liquid.

For those knowledgeable hunters using the highly efficient, conical, mini or maxi-style bullet for big-game hunting, commercial lubes put out by Dixie, Hodgdon's, and Blue & Gray can be used, but one of the best I have found for extended stays in the field is another substance marketed under the name of 300-Plus and sold by Winchester Sutler (Siler Rte. Box 393-E, Winchester, VA 22501). It comes packed in a Civil War-era tin cup.

Unless under attack or pursuing wounded quarry, the old-time hunters and mountain men made it a habit to thoroughly clean their smokepoles immediately after shooting and before putting in a fresh charge. Today's experienced muzzleloader hunter follows this practice, for he knows that fouling in the breech, whether it be from blackpowder or Pyrodex, is highly corrosive and attracts moisture. A new charge poured into a fouled bore and allowed to sit for any length of time has a better-than-average chance of becoming inert, losing half of its energy upon ignition, causing rust, or all of the above.

Whether we decide to carry a muzzleloading rifle into the woods for reasons of nostalgia, economy of shooting, or for the greater challenge demanded of the one-shot open-sighted front-stuffer, the end result is the same: Our rifles must be ready to shoot when we are. Otherwise, you might as well carry a nine-pound club because that is what a non-firing muzzleloader becomes. By following these simple steps of preventive maintenance, you will be continuing a legacy that helped form the basic rules of big-game hunting success today.

How To Hit Running Game

By Jack O'Connor

There are two extreme views on shooting running game with a rifle. There are those who blaze away at any game they can see as long as they can see it in the hope that, if they can throw enough bullets, they can kill it or at least slow it down. I have seen members of this school stand on their hind legs and pump bullets at running animals from 400 to 800 yards away.

Extremists of the opposite school say no one is ever justified, under any circumstances or at any distance, in taking a shot at a running animal. I was once taken to task by a reader because I related in a story how I took a crack at a running ram at about 150 yards. He told me that I was setting a bad example for the youth of America.

Members of the bang-away-as-long-as-you-can-see-it school wound a lot of game, cause needless suffering, and give hunters a bad name. Members of the never-shoot-unless-you-have-them-cold school must necessarily pass up a lot of fine trophies and some species they can hardly hunt at all.

My own beliefs incline more toward the conservative, one-shot-in-the-right-place school than they do toward the hail-of-lead school, but we must face the fact that, in some cases, we must shoot at running animals or not shoot. We must also face the fact that one of the hunter's most useful pieces of equipment is judgment.

Before a hunter takes a running shot he should consider a good many things. Is he skillful enough that he has an excellent chance of hitting the animal in a vital spot? If he misses or wounds with his first shot, will the animal be in sight long enough for him to try a second and third time? If he does not shoot and spook the animal, will he have a good chance for a shot later? If he wounds the animal, will following it up be dangerous?

Let's take a couple of examples—the ram my reader felt I should not have shot at, for instance. Was I justified in shooting or wasn't I?

This ram was a very good one, the best I had an opportunity to take a shot at, and the hunt was nearing the end. The ram was running broadside in the open at a moderate range. I had killed much game under similar circumstances and was quite sure I could hit the ram solidly. Actually, I did hit the ram, though a bit far back. It ran 100 to 150 yards, fell, and rolled over a little cliff 10 or 15 feet high. It was dead when we got to it.

I felt then, and still do now, that, under the circumstances, I was justified in taking that shot.

Another example: I was hunting lions in Tanganyika in 1959 when a big male popped his head out of the grass at what later proved to be 140 paces. I had an expensive lion license. Lions were not plentiful. If I did not get this lion, I probably would not get another shot and, in fact, in the next two weeks until the trip was over, I did not see another lion. The shot was much like the one I took at the ram, except that the lion was quartering somewhat. I swung the .375 with the horizontal wire traveling along his yellow body. When the intersection of the crosswires was well ahead of his chest (about two feet, as I remember it), the sight picture looked so pretty I couldn't keep from squeezing the trigger. The lion let out the half-growl, half-roar that signifies a hit on any of the great cats. Then he disappeared into high grass.

Luckily, I had put a 300-grain .375 Silvertip right through the lion's heart. It had run perhaps 35 or 40 yards into the tall grass and had died. Was I justified in taking that shot? I doubt it. I was quite certain of hitting the lion somewhere, but I certainly wouldn't have bet any money that I would shoot it through the heart. A mountain ram is a harmless animal. If I had wounded that ram and we had followed it up, he would not have turned on me. On the other hand, if I had gut-shot that lion, he might have killed me, the white hunter, or one of the gun-bearers if we had followed him up in tall grass where all the advantage was on the side of the lion.

My white hunter on this trip was John Kingsley-Heath who, a year or so later, was badly mauled and almost killed by a wounded lion. Would I take the same shot again if it were offered? I don't know. I'll be perfectly honest and say that it would depend on the state of my blood pressure. Even the most experienced hunters get excited when hunting and will sometimes take shots that the cold light of reason later tells them are unjustified. As I think about it, I think I should have let the lion run off. The money I had in a lion license and the satisfaction of owning another lion trophy did not balance the very grave risk I ran.

Traditionally, tigers are shot standing still and at a few yards. I have killed two and both have been running like the devil. One had been pushed out of a reed bed by elephants. He was bounding through high grass that grew among scattered trees. He was 150 to 175 yards away, as I now remember it. The other came tearing out of the brush, straight for my machan, roaring like a fiend. I was in a position to take several shots at the first tiger and was certain I could kill him. I was likewise certain I could roll the second. Anytime I can't hit a running tiger at 15 yards, I'll quit.

Many years ago, a great and experienced hunter wrote that any hit on a running animal at any distance is a first-class shot. I wouldn't say a first-class shot under all circumstances, but I'd say it was not too bad a shot. I have missed fast-jumping deer in heavy brush almost within spitting range, and I think most hunters who are honest and who have done much brush hunting will admit that they have done the same.

Hitting running big game, particularly hitting it in the right place, is by no means easy, but it is not as difficult as it might seem. I am all for taking the best shot possible and placing the bullet just right. Yet, in some cases, the hunter has to shoot at game on the run or never fire a shot.

A running animal at 100 yards, or whatever distance he is shot at, offers just as big a target as if he were standing. He generally isn't moving very fast. He looks as if he is going fast because our excitement makes us think he is. Probably the average running deer, elk, or caribou isn't going more than 15 mph. A thoroughly frightened deer chased by an automobile can probably go 25 mph, possibly 30. A

scared coyote can travel about 35 mph, but I don't think a fat, old bighorn ram can run as fast over level ground as a reasonably frisky man. The antelope is the real speedster and has been clocked by automobile at 55 and 60 mph.

If I have any small skill at shooting running game, I owe it to two wonderful animals—the Arizona whitetail deer and the jackrabbit. Most of the time I lived in Tucson, Arizona, blacktail and antelope jackrabbits were very plentiful. If I couldn't get a jackrabbit less than 100 yards away to run, I'd shoot at him offhand. My favorite target was the big antelope or "whiteside" jackrabbit. He ran more smoothly and was generally found in more open country than the smaller blacktail. My hunting partner most of the time was a fine shot and gun nut named Carroll Lemon. For 12 or 14 years, we must have averaged one jackrabbit hunt a week and, in the course of a year, we would blunder into and bump off quite a few running coyotes. I often left the car with 50 rounds of ammunition and returned without a single cartridge.

The Arizona whitetail, which is also called the fantail and the Sonora whitetail, is, for my money, the most beautiful of all American deer. In much of its range, it is found in semiopen country where the draws are full of trees and brush. But the grassy hillsides spotted with evergreen oaks are open enough for good running shooting. The mule deer buck can generally be depended on to stop for a backward look before he gets out of sight, even if he has been shot at. But not the Arizona whitetail. Once he has located and identified the hunter, he blasts off like a scared cottontail and keeps picking them up and laying them down until he is on the other side of the ridge or in the depths of a canyon.

It is entirely feasible, in many areas, to hunt these little deer from horseback. The hunter rides along the side of a canyon watching for a deer to move below him or on the other side. If he sees a buck, he bounces off his horse, yanks his rifle out of the scabbard, and starts shooting. The deer like to bed down in the heavy brush at the foot of a cliff where the talus slope of soil and rocks broken off the cliff begins. In such brushy, rocky country, conventional stillhunting is impossible. The country is so noisy that a caterpillar couldn't go across it without sounding like a bulldozer. Southwestern whitetail hunters get deer out of that country by getting on a cliff above a likely looking place and throwing stones into the brush. Even the smartest buck can take this only so long before his nerves are shot. Then he comes tearing out, and it is up to the hunter to cut him down on the run.

Another good method of getting a crack at these elusive little creatures is for one hunter to ride or walk on one side of a canyon and another hunter to take the other. Then each hunter will get a shot at the bucks the other hunter across the canyon has moved.

A good stillhunter who gets out early enough and finds the deer are still feeding and moving around

Before a hunter takes a running shot he should consider many things. Is he skilled enough to have an excellent chance of hitting a vital spot? If he misses or wounds with his first shot, will the animal be in sight long enough for a second or third try? If he does not shoot, and spooks the animal, will he have a good chance for a shot later? Photo by Leonard Lee Rue III.

can often get standing shots at bucks. The year my son Bradford was 13, he was pretty small and too inexperienced in riding and shooting to leap off a horse and belt a running buck. I acted as his guide and we stillhunted for the little deer. He got two—one in Arizona and one in Sonora. He got the Sonora buck in its bed, something that almost never happens with this wary whitetail.

The same principles apply to shooting running game as apply to shooting flying game with a shotgun. The chief differences are that big game shot with a rifle are generally shot at greater distances and the hunter must pin his faith on one bullet instead of a cloud of shot. He has to be more precise but, otherwise, the techniques are the same.

Depending on circumstances, the man who shoots running game will spot shoot, employ the fast swing, or use the sustained lead—a technique also called pointing out—just as he will employ these methods in wingshooting.

By spot shooting or snap shooting, I mean throwing up the rifle, aiming at a spot where the target (the vital part of the animal) will be when the bullet gets there, then shooting with a stationary rifle. This is exactly the technique used for some types of shotgun shooting. Most gunners kill quartering birds by aiming at the spot ahead where the bird will be when

the shot gets there. I do not swing down on the No. 1 high-house target at skeet. Instead, I shoot at a spot about 1½ to two feet below it.

If a deer is climbing out of a canyon going directly away, I hold above it or, if it is angling as it climbs, I hold above and to one side so he'll run into the bullet. In other words, I spot shoot it. If the animal is on the same level and going directly away from me, I shoot right at it (trying to break the spine at the root of the tail or to drive the bullet between the hams) as no lead is required. If a charging animal, such as a lion, tiger, or grizzly bear is coming directly toward the hunter, the aim should be low so the animal will be led. I once shot over a large British hare running directly toward me because I forgot this elementary fact and shot right at it with a shotgun. The graveyard in Nairobi is dotted with the graves of promising young Englishmen who forgot to hold low on charging lions.

The great majority of running shots that the hunter in heavy brush and forest must take will be of the spot-shooting variety. The distance will be short, the angle gentle as the animal runs away. The hunter should put his aiming point where he thinks the part of the animal he wants to hit will be and touch off a shot. As in shotgun shooting, he should fire the *instant* the sight looks right. If he hesitates, he'll be behind.

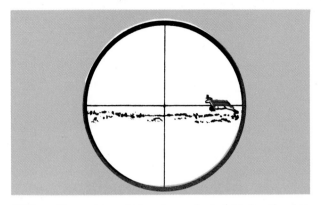

With a rifle moving as fast as deer, a lead of 1½ lengths of the deer should register a good hit at 200 yards.

Author once killed running deer with exactly this lead at 100 yards. Firing with wire at nose, the bullet struck X.

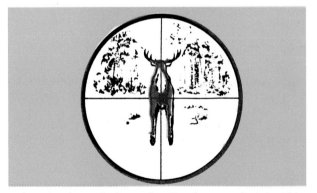

When shooting at buck running directly away, don't lead him. Hold dead on, shoot fast. Drive bullet between hams.

When shooting at deer climbing out of a canyon, hold to one side and high, so the buck will run into the bullet.

If the game is moving at anything but a gentle angle, the shot must be taken with a moving rifle, just as a crossing bird must be shot with a moving shotgun. At any distance, the aim must be well ahead of the target. If the hunter swings faster and has a slow reaction time and if the distance is short (50 yards or so), he may be able to aim for the spot he wants to hit and not be far from it. However, even under those circumstances, he will generally hit behind. Every year, tens of thousands of deer and antelope are gut-shot by hunters who did not get far enough in front.

When the 7mm Remington Magnum cartridge first came out, a gun nut at a luncheon party announced to one and all that the sustained velocity of the 7mm Magnum cartridge with the 150-grain bullet was so great that it was not necessary to lead running game with it up to 300 yards. In my usual tactful way, I told him he was full of prunes. I added that I had shot hundreds of running jackrabbits with .270s using the 100-grain bullet, .22/250s, and .220 Swifts using the 50 and 55-grain bullets (all of which would get to 100 yards faster than the 150-grain 7mm Magnum bullet), and that even at 100 yards and with a moving rifle, if you shot right at a running jack, you'd miss it every time. Depending, of course, how fast the jack is running, the bullet will be from one to two feet behind the jack at 100 yards, even if the sights are right on the jack and moving apparently as fast as the jack. If the shot is taken with a stationary rifle at a jack running broadside at 100 yards, the bullet will land at least three feet behind.

In the years when I lived in southern Arizona and hunted jackrabbits regularly, I developed a fair degree of skill in shooting running game with a rifle. Carroll Lemon and I got so that, if a running jack was tearing along an open hillside, we never missed it far and, a fair percentage of the time, we could roll a jackrabbit over if it were not more than 200 yards away and we could fire four or five shots as it ran along. I suppose we could keep our shots within about a two to 2½-foot radius around the jack. We'd have unlucky streaks where four or five running jacks in succession might get away and lucky streaks where we'd knock over three or four in succession.

Practice on running jacks is the best I know of for shooting running big game. Lemon and I got so sharp with all this practice that running deer and coyotes in the open were generally cold turkey. Before the Fish & Wildlife Service went on a poisoning rampage, there were a good many coyotes in the deserts around Tucson. They occasionally killed fawns but, for the most part, they lived on jackrabbits, cottontails, and pack rats. In the course of a year, I'd get nine or 10, sometimes more. Generally, they would be moving slowly but I shot at some going flat out. I remember one, so help me, that must have been at least 300 and maybe 350 yards away. I killed it on the second shot and I must have led it around 25 or 30 feet. A shot like that is not entirely luck, but it has a lot of luck in it.

In the same period, I hunted deer a lot in Mexico and shot a whitetail every year in Arizona. I remember one stretch of four seasons where I hunted every year on the Siebold ranch near Patagonia. I fired six shots and killed four bucks, all running at from 150 to perhaps 250 yards.

Fred Huntington, the R.C.B.S. tycoon, will remember this shot. We were hunting in Wyoming and Fred had already nailed an antelope. As we headed back home, a bunch of antelope circled around and cut across in front of the car. I sat down and swung the .275 H. & H. Magnum I was using with the horizontal crosswire moving along the middle of the buck's body. When the vertical wire looked to be about three to 3½ lengths ahead, I touched off the shot. A moment later, we heard the sound of a striking bullet and, an instant later, the buck slid on his nose. We paced the distance off over absolutely level ground and got 285 paces. I got an assist from luck on that one.

Those who do not live in jackrabbit country but who want to acquire a fair degree of skill in shooting at running game are in luck if they have access to a rifle club that has a running deer target. If it does nothing else, such a target will show the shooter that he has to get well out in front with a moving rifle if he is going to hit anything. I have seen a lot of persons shooting at running deer targets and I have yet to see anyone miss by shooting in front.

In 1964, I went with a friend out to a rifle club near Mexico City. The boys were practicing on a moving target at 300 meters (well over 300 yards). Beginners were often missing the target by 40 or 50 yards. Some of the old-timers were surprisingly good, hitting on or near the target with each shot. I asked one very good shot how much he was leading the target and he said about 30 meters. I asked another and he said he shot right at it. So much for having others tell you how much to lead.

If there are no running jacks and no running deer

Hitting running big game, particularly hitting it in the right place, is by no means easy, but it is not as difficult as it might seem. O'Connor advocates taking the best shot possible and plac- *ing the bullet just right. Yet, in some cases, the hunter has to shoot at game on the run or never fire a shot. Photo by Leonard Lee Rue III.*

targets, it helps the hunter to shoot cottontails with a .22 rimfire rifle and the same type of sights he uses for big game.

For woods hunting, most shots will be fast snaps at deer going directly away or at gentle angles. But, even in the woods, you will occasionally get a broadside running shot that requires swing and lead. On such shots, remember to get ahead and keep the rifle moving.

For open-country running shooting, such as is often done on antelope, Arizona whitetail, and mule deer, the rifleman should sit because sitting is a much steadier position than offhand and much more flexible than prone. Some hunters who are excellent running shots tell me that they use the fast swing. As with the shotgun, that means they start behind the running animal, swing faster than the animal, then touch off the shot when the lead looks right.

I use that method only at short ranges. If an animal is in open or fairly open country, I have more luck with the sustained lead. I swing the rifle along ahead of the animal with the aiming point traveling apparently as fast as the animal. Keeping the rifle swinging, I squeeze off.

How far should the running target be led? That depends on several factors. About the least of these is the speed of the bullet. I think it makes very little difference if the bullet leaves the muzzle at 2,500 or 3,500 fps. I have shot running jacks on alternate days with a .257 and a bullet traveling at 2,900 fps at the muzzle and a Swift with a bullet that left the muzzle at 4,100 fps. So far as I could tell, there wasn't a dime's worth of difference in necessary lead.

The important factors are how fast the rifleman swings, how fast the animal is moving, and how far away the animal is. I have seen tables of necessary lead. I think they are interesting but not very practical. They are based on bullets fired from a stationary rifle at animals at known speeds and distances. This is theoretical lead. As is the case with shotgun shooting, practical lead with a swinging rifle is about half of theoretical lead. Like the shotgunner, the rifleman thinks he shoots instantly, but he does not. While his rifle is swinging, the firing pin falls, the primer goes off, and the powder ignites. Powder gas pushes the bullet up the barrel and out after the game. All that time the rifle is moving.

The rifleman should remember to shoot as quickly as possible and not to dawdle, and to keep his rifle moving and never to slow or stop his swing. He should remember to sit and never to try anything but a short, running shot from unsteady offhand. He should watch for the dust thrown by his bullets and correct his lead. To do this, he must know exactly where his sights were when the rifle went off.

People miss running shots because they are excited. They don't really aim. They just poke their rifles in the general direction of the game and shoot. They also miss running shots because they shoot right at a crossing animal. Those who do that gut shoot the animals or miss them. They also miss because overanxiety makes them stop or slow their swings. As is the case with flying game, running animals are most often missed by shooting behind.

How much to lead? Here are some leads that work for me. If a deer is running across in front of me at about 100 yards, I'd swing along with it and let off the shot perhaps a foot ahead of the brisket. If it were an antelope at 100 yards and making knots, I'd swing about two or three feet ahead.

If the deer were out about 150 yards and running broadside, I'd try to be three or four feet in front of its brisket. At 200 yards, I'd try to be six or eight feet ahead.

Every individual must find out his own leads by shooting, by watching the spurts of dust, by missing, and by hitting. As with the shotgun, one man's lead is another man's poison.

I think by far the best sight for running shooting is the scope—a 2½ or 3X for the woods and a 4X for open country. I do not think anything is gained by higher power, even for antelope. Of the various reticles, I much prefer the crosshair, as the horizontal wire aids in maintaining the correct elevation.

A commodity that anyone attempting the running shot needs is judgment. He should do his best never to shoot at a running animal unless he is quite certain that he can knock it off before it gets out of sight. He should hold his fire if he thinks the animal will stop for one last look if it is not shot at. Generally, a mule deer or an elk will. A whitetail almost never will and a frightened antelope generally will not. Sheep that have never been hunted will often stand around and stare when someone opens up on them but, when they have been smoked up a few times, they are among the spookiest of animals.

The ideal of the skillful hunter of big game is to fire one shot, put the bullet in exactly the right place, and collect a trophy. But, alas, things don't always work out that way. The game may see you first and take off, or the stalk may go sour. Then, you may have to gamble on hitting your trophy on the run. The whole success of your trip may depend on your coolness, skill, and judgment for a few critical moments.

The great majority of rams I have shot have been standing or slowly moving and at no great distance but, as I write this, my two last rams were both going flat out. In one case, which I have already mentioned, the stalk went sour when we bumped into an urial ewe in Iran. The rams I was after took off. I picked out what looked like the largest, got ahead of him, and shot from offhand. He ran perhaps 150 yards and fell over a little cliff dead. This was the best urial I have ever shot. The other ram, a 40¼-inch Yukon Dall, was spooked by two companions and he came by me at somewhere around 250 yards. I whittled the big fellow down. For those fine ram trophies, I say thanks to the humble jackrabbit and the frisky Arizona whitetail. I learned everything I know about hitting running game from them.

Shotguns And Loads For Deer

By Jim Carmichel

Shooting writers are notorious for hedging their bets and skirting every direct question. For example, if you were to ask me point-blank what I consider the *one* best deer cartridge or rifle, I'd paw the ground for a while, try to move the conversation in five different directions at once and, finally, backed to the wall, I'd wind up naming at least a dozen "best" rifle-and-round combinations.

That's why I've even astonished myself by coming right out with my opinion that improvements in shotguns, rifled slugs, and buckshot loads have, for the past 10 years, outraced all other developments in deer hunting weaponry. Of course, it might be argued that, a decade ago, the smoothbore situation was so stagnated that there was vast room for improvement, but this is only partially true. Thinking back over the past quarter-century, shotgun deer hunters have had their lives brightened by some genuinely significant improvements in their equipment.

RIFLE SIGHTS

The most important of these, of course, is the availability of shotguns with rifle-type sights. At first, the offering was tentative because manufacturers refused to believe that hunters would shell out for a top-of-the-line pump or autoloader that would, with luck, be fired at game only once or twice a year in most states. But that's not the only time gunmakers have misjudged their market, before or since.

Harking back to those dimmest days of pre-history known as the 1950s, shotguns with rifle sights were virtually unknown. In the 1955 edition of *The Shoot-er's Bible*, for instance, I can't find a single smoothbore with rifle-type sights. The few workable slug shooters I recall from that distant era were do-it-yourself affairs made in gun shops and garages by soldering on a front-sight ramp in place of the shotgun bead, and drilling and tapping the receiver for a peep sight of some sort. The Ithaca Model 37 pump was a favorite for these conversions. Taking its cue from the field, Ithaca was one of the first, if not *the* first, to offer deer hunters an honest, store-bought shotgun with adjustable rifle-type sights.

By 1965, in addition to Ithaca's Deerslayer, the market offered Browning's five-shot autoloading Buck Special, the Slug Gun by Franchi, High-Standard's Flight King Brush Gun with a choice of a 20-inch or wicked-looking 18-inch tube, Remington's Model 870 Brushmaster, and Winchester's Model 1200 pump and Model 1400 autoloading deer guns. All of which goes to prove that even when gunmakers are slow to come up with a good idea, it doesn't take them long to recognize a good thing when they see it.

Since then, a few makes and models have faded away, but lots more have sprung up to take their places. At the risk of leaving someone out, here's pretty much what today's slug shotgun buyer has to look at.

For seekers of exotic Italian fame, Benelli, Beretta, and Franchi offer autoloaders with rifle sights. Franchi and Beretta give you a choice of 12 or 20-gauge. The only Benelli slug gun I've seen is the Model 121V that, for all I know, may have been replaced by a later model. Benelli's importer, Heckler & Koch, apparently works in secret, so it's hard to guess who's

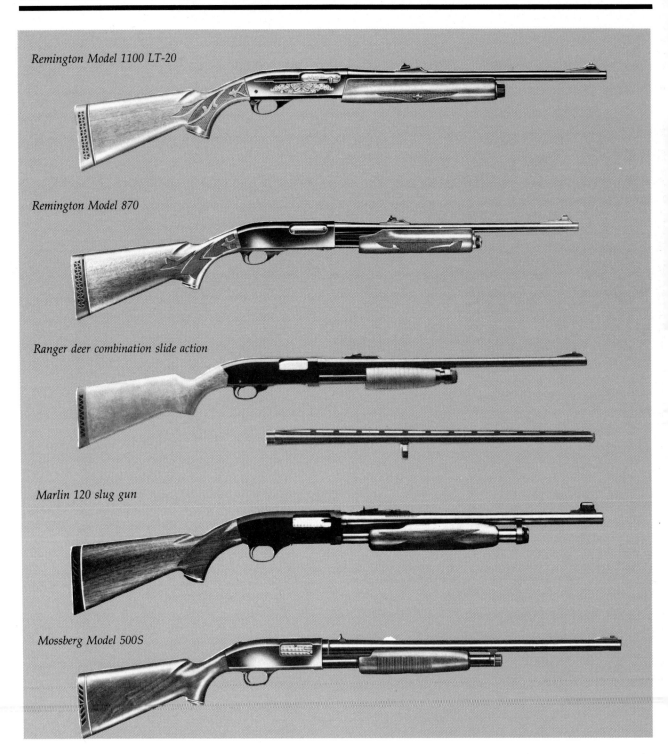

Remington Model 1100 LT-20

Remington Model 870

Ranger deer combination slide action

Marlin 120 slug gun

Mossberg Model 500S

on first. The Franchi Slug Gun is based on the company's well-known, lightweight, autoloading action, which has been familiar to American shooters for more than a generation. The Beretta Model A-301 is a soft-kicking, gas-operated self-loader that has proven its mettle over the past several years, as well. A later version, the A-302, fires three-inch as well as standard-length shells, but I'm not sure if a slug version is available as yet.

Browning, one of the first gunmakers to offer a rifle-sighted shotgun, continues its commitment to

deer hunters with Buck Special barrels in three separate models. The most familiar of these is the unmistakable and dearly loved square-backed, five-shot Autoloader. They offer this gun in Lightweight 12 and 20-gauge versions with standard 2¾ chambers or, if you prefer, the somewhat heavier magnum models in both gauges with three-inch chambers. The offering is duplicated in Browning's latest Autoloader, the B-80. You can have your choice of 12 or 20-gauge with standard or magnum chambers without having to give up lightness, if you go for

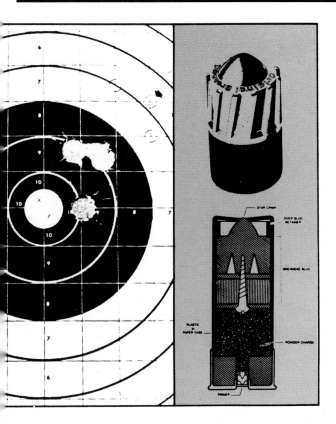

Brenneke slug, right, has attached wad. Three-shot group was fired at 50 yards with peep sights—a typical example of accuracy to be expected from a good gun.

the magnum. This means that the Magnum B-80 in either gauge runs about a pound lighter than its counterpart in the older, recoil-operated, Auto-5 configuration, but don't worry about extra recoil. The B-80 gas-operated system is gentler on the shoulder than the older long-recoil system of the Auto-5.

Browning's third Buck Special is the BPS pump model, which also comes in either 12 or 20 bore. Both come with three-inch chambers, and you can use standard or magnum shells interchangeably.

For the price-conscious, Harrington & Richardson offers its Model 162 break-action single-barrel in either 12 or 20-gauge with three-inch chambers.

The big shot, of course, is Ithaca's Mag-10 Deerslayer. The big Mag-10 autoloader, the gun that breathed new life into the 3½-inch, 10-gauge Magnum concept, has proven itself a reliable performer for almost a decade, so perhaps it was to be expected that, sooner or later, Ithaca would offer it in what has to be the king of the brush busters. The only problem was that no one made 10-gauge slug loads until Federal Cartridge agreed to go along with Ithaca's idea. (We'll talk about performance later.)

Ithaca's first Deerslayer was its Model 37 pump gun with a slug barrel, and the tradition continues with the popular gun still offered in 12 or 20-gauge with rifle sights. The 16-gauge gun has been

dropped. The Model 51, which I still tend to call Ithaca's "new" autoloader, even though it has been around for years, also comes with a 12-gauge Deerslayer barrel.

Marlin's presentation to smoothbore-toting deer hunters is its solid Model 120 pump. With its beautifully machined receiver, hand-checkered walnut stocking, and really good adjustable sights, the M 120 has a lot of that old-time quality gun lovers like to reminisce about. It comes in 12-gauge, and the barrel has a three-inch chamber.

O.F. Mossberg makes its Model 500 pump with Slugster barrels in both 12 and 20-gauge and even offers a special price deal on a Model 500 "Combo Pack," which includes a Slugster barrel plus a wing-shooting barrel with ventilated rib and changeable Accu-chokes. In its economy-priced New Haven line, Mossberg also catalogs the Model 600 pump with Slugster barrel, and the company will make you a special deal on two barrels with this model, as well.

Savage's offering to deer hunters is its Model 24 rifle-and-shotgun combination gun. The only workable deer hunting gauge in which it is offered is 20 bore, but the year-round use it represents makes it worth considering, especially in that the rifle-barrel sights can be adjusted to get a shotgun slug on target. The only M 24 that comes with an open-choke barrel for best slug accuracy is the C, or Camper's Companion model. Before buying one for deer hunting, though, be sure to check your state's game laws to make sure that a .22 Rimfire rifle is legal in the woods during deer season. The Savage works also offers a slug-barrel version of the Model 67 Stevens pump gun. It comes only in 12-gauge, features a three-inch chamber, and has the lowest price tag for a rifle-sighted smoothbore repeater you'll find.

Smith and Wesson, which has now been offering rifles and shotguns long enough so that about everyone is getting used to it, makes its Model 1000 in slug gun configuration in both 12 and 20-gauge. This slick-looking autoloader comes with three-inch chambers as standard in both gauges. The company will also sell you its Model 3000 slide-action with a stubby barrel and rifle sights—but in 12-gauge only. Magnum-length chambers are part of the deal.

Remington makes so many variations of slug-barrel shotguns that the list gets somewhat confusing. If you crave the Model 1100 autoloader, you can have it in either 12 or 20-gauge. The 12-gauge is the standard weight but the current 20-gauge model is in the company's lightweight configuration. Switching to Remington's Model 870 pump, you can have a 12-gauge Brushmaster deer gun or a standard model with rifle sights. Then, to get more confusing, the 870 in 20-gauge comes in either Brushmaster standard or as a lightweight. Regardless of model, the sights on Remington's slug guns are excellent and easily adjustable.

Moving on down the list, alphabetically, we come to Weatherby's Model 82 Autoloader and M 92 pump. The Buckmaster versions of each of these currently come in 12-gauge only, with 2¾-inch

Rifle sights or a scope are essential for slug shooting. This mount is a B-Square on a Remington 870/1100 shotgun.

chambers. The 26-inch barrels have the distinction of being the longest slug-gun barrels available, unless I've overlooked something.

Winchester's line of slug guns is somewhat more streamlined than in past years. Your choice is limited to the Model 1300 XTR pump-action or the Model 1200 Police. Actually, the 1300 is Winchester's serious deer hunter but, for someone who wants something a bit different, the Police 1200 has, in addition to rifle sights, a stainless-steel barrel and a chrome-plated receiver. The Police 1200 isn't a bad idea, if you tend to fall down in water, but it could use a coat of camouflage paint. Both models are 12-gauge with three-inch chambers.

By and large, slug guns offer three fundamental features that make them more effective for deer hunting than ordinary smoothbores. First, the barrels tend to be shorter, making them easier to carry and handle in brush and timber. Except for the Weatherby guns with their 26-inch tubes, most slug barrels range from 18 to 24 inches with the average being about 22 inches. Second, a true slug gun barrel has little or no choke. Rifled slugs tend to shoot measurably better from unchoked barrels. The third and most important, as well as the most evident feature, is rifle-type sights.

Several years ago, I gathered up several boxes of rifled-slug ammo, a dozen or so shotguns in assorted makes and models—all with ordinary shotgun sights—and as many experienced marksmen to shoot them. After lining everyone up before a row of paper targets at 50-yard range, I invited them to shoot to their heart's content. We all quickly discovered that a whitetail deer fired at from that modest range would have had about an even chance of getting away unscathed. At 75 yards, the odds were very much in the deer's favor and, at longer ranges, a hit was a matter of blind luck. In short, there's really not much point in going hunting with rifled slugs and a shotgun without rifle-type sights, unless you intend to get within 25 yards of the quarry or you just want to go for a stroll. It also almost goes without saying that, sights or not, you're better off with a single-barrel gun than a double, especially a side-by-side.

ADD-ON RIFLE SIGHTS

Now this doesn't mean you have to go out and plunk down a wad of greenbacks if you want to go deer hunting with a smoothbore. There are all sorts of ways to beat the system. For example, many of today's pumps and autoloaders feature interchangeable barrels. If you already own, say, a Model 870 or an 1100 Remington, all you need to buy is a slug barrel and you're in business. Then there is the option of fitting rifle-type sights to your existing shotgun barrel. An outfit called Slug-Site makes a simple but expensive little sighting arrangement that sticks onto the receiver of a pump or autoloader. After the deer season, you can peel it off without a trace. Another outfit called Accura 300 makes a more sophisticated sight system that adapts to shotguns with plain or ribbed barrels. The plain-barrel model is held on with screws, requiring drilling and tapping, but the vent-rib model easily clamps right onto the rib with no alterations. And, for lo these many years, most makers of rifle sights—Redfield, Williams, Lyman, Marble, and so on—have been making rifle-style sights for shotguns, as well.

But why just think in terms of open or peep sights for shotguns? Why not scopes? Scopes work fine, and there are some pretty good systems to choose from. Just about everyone who makes scope-mounting systems for rifles offers bases for a few makes of shotguns. Most of these require some drilling and tapping, but one mount by B-Square fits Remington 1100s and 870s without the benefit of gunsmithing.

SLUG LOADS

For decades, U.S. ammo makers muddled along with a seven-eighths-ounce slug in their 12-gauge loads. Then, a couple of years ago, Remington, Winchester, and Federal switched to a one-ounce projectile. That extra eighth of an ounce doesn't sound like much to get excited about but the improvement is considerable. The older seven-eighths-

ounce slug was loaded to 1,600 fps at the muzzle with a remaining speed of about 1,175 fps at 50 yards. This works out to energy levels of 2,175 and 1,175 foot-pounds, respectively. The new one-ounce slugs take off at some 1,570 fps and have slowed down to about 1,200 to 1,300 fps (depending on slug shape) at 50 yards. This means the energy level is quite a bit higher at hunting ranges than it was with the older slug but, more important, for some reason, the new one-ounce slugs tend to be more accurate. Federal offers a 1¼-ounce 12-gauge slug that yields 1,865 foot-pounds of energy at 50 yards, making it the hardest-hitting 12-gauge slug yet.

Twenty-gauge slugs have also taken a weight jump, growing from five-eighths ounce to three-quarters of an ounce, with a corresponding jump in energy. If you've ever been tempted to hunt deer with .410 rifled slugs, my advice is to forget it. They are meant for pest control and, with a 50-yard energy level of only 345 foot-pounds, the little one-fifth-ounce slug has only about half as much knock-down punch as a .30 Carbine round.

Though Federal's 10-gauge magnum slug sounds like it could kill a whale, it really doesn't, at least on paper, seem to live up to its potential. The 1¾-ounce slug starts off at only 1,280 fps for a muzzle energy of 2,785 foot-pounds. At 50 yards, the remaining energy of 1,980 is only 115 pounds more than that of Federal's 1¼-ounce 12-gauge load. Likewise, the trajectory is considerably more curved.

Borrowing from Federal's catalog, here's some ballistic data on the rifled slugs:

The change from seven-eighth-ounce to one-ounce slugs in 12-gauge loads has made a significant difference to hunters. Not only is the energy level higher at hunting ranges than it was with the older slug, accuracy is improved as well.

GAUGE	WEIGHT (OUNCES)	VELOCITY (FPS) MUZZLE	50 YDS
10	1¾	1,280	1,080
12	1¼	1,490	1,240
12	1	1,580	1,310
16	⅘	1,600	1,175
20	¾	1,600	1,270
410	⅕	1,830	1,335

GAUGE	ENERGY IN FT.-LBS. MUZZLE	50 YDS.	DROP IN INCHES 50 YDS.	100 YDS.
10	2,785	1,980	2.9	13.2
12	2,695	1,865	2.3	9.8
12	2,425	1,665	2.0	9.0
16	1,990	1,070	2.1	10.4
20	1,865	1,175	1.9	9.5
410	650	345	1.6	8.2

BUCKSHOT LOADS

A few years back, after participating in a series of deer hunts in areas where only shotguns loaded with buckshot were legal, I got interested in buckshot performance and ran a series of tests. The first thing I found out was that the favorite buckshot deer load, with No. 00 buck, was heir to all sorts of performance problems. Patterns were extremely ragged—sometimes so bad that, even at relatively close ranges, a deer-size target could be missed altogether. What I learned from my tests dovetailed with firsthand reports from deer hunters who were experienced in buckshot deer hunting. On the face of things, the No. 00 buckshot should have had a clear advantage but, in actual use, many experienced hunters were inclined to use smaller buckshot. I was particularly impressed at the number of knowledgeable hunters who preferred No. 4 buck, even though the pellets are considerably smaller (.24 inch as compared to .33). The reasons for their preference tended to boil down to two factors: The No. 4 buck had a lot more pellets in the pattern (41 as compared to 15 No. 00s in three-inch magnum loads); the patterns of the smaller shot tended to be more even, especially when fired from full-choke barrels.

After testing No. 00s in barrels with different chokes, I came to the same conclusions. I was not quite sure of the reason, but No. 00s tended to pattern more evenly in barrels with only moderate choking. There was certainly less tendency for flyers to be three or four feet out of the pattern. My findings led me to make strong recommendation that deer

hunters use No. 4 buck rather than No. 00s, or at least pattern both in their guns and draw their own conclusions.

After that, I laid the test project aside, and it was almost forgotten when I started getting fresh reports from the field. Most reports indicated that buckshot hunters were in a swoon over the then-new No. 000 buckshot loads. These bigger pellets, with a diameter of .36 inch, were loaded eight to the 2¾-inch 12-gauge shell or 10 to the three-inch magnum, and resulted in beautiful patterns and swift kills. This was confusing for a while because I had about decided that the bigger the pellet, the poorer the pattern, but the No. 000s had become all the rage. In some buckshot-only areas, all stocks of No. 000s were completely sold out, and hunters were hoarding them.

About that same time, Winchester-Western was interested in finding out why No. 00 buck patterned so poorly and launched an in-depth investigation. By using high-speed photography, which caught the No. 00 pellets in flight, and recovering fired pellets, they found that the pellets were far more distorted than anyone had imagined. Some were so badly deformed by the time they exited the muzzle that there was little evidence the pellets had ever been round. Some looked like pyramids, others looked like bent coins, and the rest looked like rough gravel. No wonder they wouldn't fly straight. Once they hit the atmosphere, their random aerodynamic shapes caused them to fly off in any direction. Winchester-Western's tests, broken down into statistical data, showed that existing No. 00 buckshot loads fired with a 12-gauge magnum shotgun (12 pellets to the load) would put at least five pellets into a two-foot square (representing a deer's chest cavity) only 50 percent of the time at 40 yards, and only three pellets 50 percent of the time at 50 yards. At 60 yards, the likelihood of getting three pellets on target was only 10 percent. In order to be sure of getting five of the No. 00s into a deer's vital area with a certainty of 90 percent, the range had to be shortened to 35 yards. Clearly, the No. 00s weren't doing their job very well.

These tests were followed by a great deal of developmental work that resulted in improved protective sleeves and, more importantly, granulated plastic fillers that padded the buckshot and the shell and reduced deformation in the barrel. These new Winchester-Western Mark 5 loads proved significantly better than equivalent older loads, increasing the percentage averages by about 20 yards.

With old-style No. 00 buck loads, there was only a two or three-yard difference between the effective range of a Cylinder-bore barrel as compared to a full-choke barrel, as I had earlier discovered myself. But, with the new buffered loads, a full-choke gun did what it was supposed to do. For example, with the new loads in a full-choke barrel, an average of half of the pellets (six) would hit in a 30-inch circle at 70 yards. With the older loads, you had to shorten the distance to 40 yards to get 50 percent in the standard 30-inch circle.

Handgun Hunting: Sport Or Stunt?

By Jim Carmichel

Hunting with handguns isn't new. Even as a boy, I knew hunters who regularly used .22 Rimfire pistols to take squirrels and rabbits. When I was a youngster, my brothers and I used pistols to pot coons and possums treed by our hounds. It never occurred to us that this was unusual. As we saw it, a handgun was the logical gun for close-range shooting in the woods at night. It's difficult to carry a rifle or a shotgun then, and it isn't necessary.

When I moved to the West, I fell in with an assortment of cowhands, packers, guides, and outfitters who routinely used handguns to take all sorts of large and small game, and I began packing a heavy caliber revolver on many of my North American big-game hunts. Over the years, I used a variety of handguns to take whitetail and mule deer, elk, moose, mountain lion, wild boar, and a truckload of assorted javelina, jackrabbits, prairie dogs, foxes, and coyotes. I have not taken any of the big bears

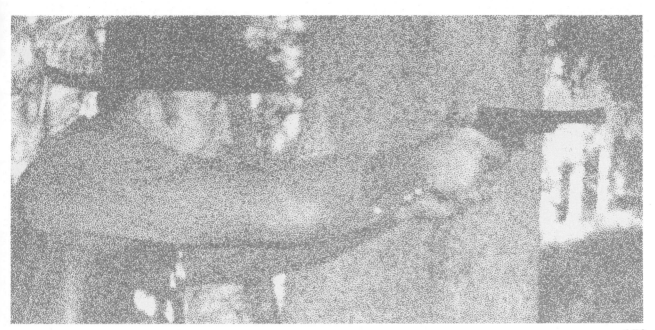

with a handgun, but I know hunters who have.

Even if shooting game with handguns is, in reality, nothing new, we must bear in mind that the majority of handgun hunters are new to the sport. Most of them first hunted with a handgun during the past five years. Though I am only guessing, I have reason to suspect that a good percentage of these new handgun hunters are also new to any form of hunting. Like most target shooters, handgunners tend to be technicians rather than hunters, and only a minority of them cross the line between the target range and hunting. But the fast-growing game of shooting metallic silhouettes with handguns spurred great improvements in handgun performance during the 1970s. Ballistics and marksmanship both improved, and this encouraged many handgunners to go after game. Many of them regarded hunting as the ultimate challenge to their technical skills.

Many riflemen see this new handgun sport as more competition for the game resource, and bitter memories fuel their fears. During the 1950s and 1960s, special-interest hunting groups—archers and blackpowder shooters—were able to influence game management in ways that permitted them to take unfair advantage of special hunts and special seasons in some states. I'll give an example.

During the mid-1960s, I was working for the Tennessee Game and Fish Commission (as it was called at that time). We were approached by an organization of dedicated muzzleloading rifle shooters who petitioned for a special early-season deer hunt for muzzleloading rifles only. It seemed like a good idea, so we scheduled a weekend muzzleloader hunt on one of the state's most productive wildlike management areas. We could hardly have refused because we were already conducting early-season hunts for another special-interest group—bowhunters.

Because I was a blackpowder shooter myself and well known among Tennessee's long-rifle hunters, I was assigned to help manage the hunt. Sadly, it did not turn out to be what I had anticipated. We had hoped that most of the hunters would be skilled and experienced muzzleloading riflemen. In reality, at least half of the hunters who participated had never fired a blackpowder rifle before and they had to be instructed in the most elementary procedures! They didn't even know how to load. They weren't dedicated blackpowder shooters; they were only taking advantage of a special hunt to take an additional deer before the regular rifle hunts opened.

We also dealt with "archers" who could not have cared less about the sport of bowhunting but were willing to give it a try if it meant they could take advantage of a special deer season. I eventually became aware that a whole army of Tennesseeans hunted with bows, muzzleloaders, and centerfire rifles and would have gone afield with spears if it meant another chance to bag a deer. This problem was most acute in states that allowed a deer to be

taken with a bow, another with a muzzleloader, and still another with a modern rifle. Some hunters legally took more than their fair share by hunting with all three.

This unpleasant thought is vivid in the minds of concerned riflemen who see the handgun hunter as yet another special-interest group petitioning for special seasons and concessions.

But is this really a problem, and are the unfair practices of the recent past likely to continue? Probably not. Here's why. In an effort to crack down on these inequitable though technically legal hunting practices, some state game agencies are limiting special seasons with "either/or" regulations. Under them, a hunter who participates in one of the special-interest deer hunts is prohibited from taking part in any other deer hunt that year. In a few of these "either/or" states, however, the bowhunter or muzzleloading hunter is allowed to participate in the general open season.

Here of late, this policy has brought on a lot of weeping and wailing in the archery and blackpowder industries. The manufacturers recognize that, when hunters have an "either/or" choice, a stunningly high percentage of archers and muzzleloading hunters will revert to centerfire rifle hunting simply because it is the surest way to take a deer.

Because of this experience, it's unlikely that handgun hunters will become another big special group with their own exclusive open season. Twenty-five years ago, it could easily have happened, but it's not likely at present. Handgun hunters in most states will be forced to hunt during the regular rifle season, and only skilled, dedicated handgunners will compete with centerfire riflemen.

I don't think many, if any, states will be offering handgun-only deer hunts. For the sake of argument, however, let's say that your state does so for deer and black bear. What would that mean?

Without certain safeguards, I think this would attract many opportunists of the type who have infiltrated the bowhunting and blackpowder seasons. Many men would show up on opening day with a newly bought or borrowed pistol in one hand and a box of cartridges in the other. If this were to happen, the level of marksmanship would be appallingly poor, and wounding shots would be common.

In one sense, this would probably not be important because the American right to hunt is not based on any legal requirement that we hit and kill game. If it were, modern rifle hunters would have been in trouble a long time ago. A high incidence of missed or wounded game does, however, engender criticism, which in this case, would come to bear on legitimate and skilled handgun hunters as well as the inept opportunists.

Certain safeguards would help to assure a high level of proficiency. The surest of these, in my opinion, is a strict "either/or" policy. Under such a policy,

Photo by Irene Vandermolen

most of the handgun hunters would be experienced marksmen, confident of their ability to hit where they aim with heavy calibers.

Another possible safeguard would require handgun hunters to pass a proficiency test. Colorado already has such a regulation. The applicant for a permit to hunt some species of big game with a handgun must put at least four shots out of six in an 11-inch circle at a distance of 50 yards. Any shooting position is allowable, but artificial rests cannot be used. I understand this new system worked well for Colorado during 1979, but such tests bode ill for Americans, very ill indeed. The right to keep and bear arms should not be subjected to any kind of proficiency test. That could only weaken our precious constitutional right under the Second Amendment. If conservation departments could set marksmanship standards for handgun hunters, it would not be long before there would be a push for proficiency standards for riflemen and even shotgunners. And it wouldn't be long after that before anti-hunting and anti-gun groups would try to set these marksmanship standards so high that almost no one would qualify for a license. If they succeeded, gun ownership would decline and, under those circumstances, a massive attack on the Second Amendment might be successful.

I understand that members of a Colorado handgun association were instrumental in the enactment of that state's handgun proficiency regulation, but I do not know firsthand what their motives were. I've been told that the skill test proposal was made as a show of good faith toward policing their own ranks. Similar proposals have been volunteered by other special-interest groups. They were usually made because the special-interest group underestimated its own bargaining position when seeking a special sea-

son. I suspect that some sportsmen's clubs and individuals endorse proficiency tests for hunters in order to cloak themselves in "me in—you out" righteousness. Whatever the reason, trading off one freedom for the supposed advantages of another is never a smart idea.

In any event, legislating good marksmanship is about like legislating morality—accurate shooting depends a great deal on the place and the circumstances. I wholeheartedly endorse giving hunters a solid education in safety and marksmanship, but I will fight to my last wheezing gasp any move to require an American to pass a skill test before being licensed to hunt on American soil.

Most of us tend to base our opinion of pistol marksmanship on service experience with the .45 Auto. Those few days—or hours—with the .45 while in uniform usually amounted to nothing more than a few vague instructions and some target practice with a sloppy, missighted GI .45. The virtually universal conclusion after such an experience is that it is impossible to hit *anything* with a high-powered handgun. This is why so many non-handgunners wonder how anyone could expect to hit a deer with a handgun.

There is no similarity between the performance of today's typical, dedicated handgun hunter and the average GI. Confidence and skill with the handgun is probably what led today's handgunner to take up this form of hunting. Astonishing as it may sound, the average big-game handgun hunter, firing from the standing position and using a two-hand hold from 100 yards, will group his shots *at least* as close as the average rifle hunter! Some of these guys are so good, and their big-bore pistols are so accurate, that they can roll a tin can three shots out of five at

Smith & Wesson model 629

Ruger Redhawk revolver with Leupold scope.

Ruger Redhawk double-action revolver

Ruger Super Blackhawk single-action revolver

100 yards—offhand! You'd better think twice before you bet the farm you can beat them with a rifle at effective handgun ranges.

Any discussion of just how effective handguns are for hunting gets into murky waters. For zapping squirrels out of lofty hickory trees or beaning rabbits in the brier patch, the little .22 Rimfire pistol is clearly adequate. But what works reliably on deer, antelope, bear, elk, caribou, moose?

Right now, the power standard with which all other handgun cartridges are compared is the .44 Remington Magnum. The big .44 is regarded with awe by Dirty Harry fans and it is truly impressive compared with other handgun calibers, but the melancholy truth is that the .44 Mag. is not very impressive (at least on paper) when compared ballistically to ordinary deer rifle performance. The factory-load with a 240-grain bullet develops 1,350 fps at the muzzle. Muzzle and 100-yard energy readings are 971 and 608 foot-pounds. In terms of energy delivered, the .44 Magnum is therefore almost, but not quite, equal to the pip-squeak .30 U.S. carbine cartridge, a prohibited cartridge for big game in many states. That's a terrible thing to have to say about any cartridge when you're talking about deer hunting. Actually, it isn't a fair comparison. Even though the energy figures are almost equal, the .44 slug weighs more than twice as much as the .30 carbine bullet and the additional weight causes more tissue damage. The heavier .44 is also more apt to penetrate deeply.

The ammo I've used for big-game hunting with the .44 Mag. has been loaded with 235-grain, hard-alloy cast bullets, and I load the cartridges to around 1,500 fps. This load gives about one-third more energy at the muzzle than factory ammunition and it stops big game in a very businesslike manner. My longest shots were about 100 yards, with the average distance being about half that. Even with the most potent handloads, though, one has to keep in mind that the .44 Mag. delivers less wallop than, say, the old .30/30 Winchester.

States that list legal handgun calibers for big-game hunting usually provide that the .357 Magnum is the minimum. With a muzzle energy of 535 to 583 foot-pounds, depending on bullet weight, the .357 Mag. has about the killing power of a .22 Hornet. I suppose that is OK for small deer at close range, but that's all. The .357 Mag. is an accurate round, easy to shoot well, and it's one of my favorites for foxes, coyotes, and other varmints.

The .41 Magnum cartridge is something of a compromise. It's more powerful than the .357 but doesn't pack the wallop of the .44. Though it is an excellent hunting cartridge, it has never gained as much popularity as the other two.

Any way we look at the ballistics of the three factory-loaded magnums, they are not very impressive. But this does not mean that all hunting handguns are in the same class. Just as it has produced a whole new race of skilled handgun marksmen, knocking over heavy metal silhouettes has bred new, powerful, long-range pistol cartridges. These, along with some stump-busting rounds developed especially for big game, plus some pistols chambered for *rifle* cartridges, offer the handgun hunter a pretty exotic and effective choice of loads.

Thompson/Center's Contender, for example, is a handsome, break-action single-shot pistol that features interchangeable barrels. These include the .30/30 or even the .35 Remington rifle calibers. With factory loads, these two calibers do not get up to rifle velocities in the 14-inch Contender barrel but, with handloads, it is possible to outperform factory loads fired from a .30/30 or .35 Remington rifle.

I've killed a couple of mule deer with my Contender in the .30 Herrett chambering. This is a do-it-yourself wildcat handload based on sawed-off, puffed-out .30/30 cases. With 125-grain .30-caliber bullets, velocities run over 2,200 fps for a muzzle energy of around 1,365 foot-pounds. This means that the .30 Herrett hits as hard at 100 yards as the .44 Mag. does at the muzzle. An even harder-thumping round, designed specially for big game, is the .357 Herrett, which gets close to .35 Remington rifle ballistics.

Other manufacturers, such as Wichita Engineering, offer compact *bolt-action* pistols chambered for the .308 Winchester, the 7mm Mauser, and an assortment of wildcats based on the .308 case. Hunting handgun calibers and ballistics are so exotic that they are a long story in themselves. The important thing right now is that pistols are available that do indeed deliver the necessary stopping power to kill American big game cleanly. I've seen enough big game taken with handguns to be convinced that it is a workable proposition, provided the hunter can really shoot.

Almost every hunting handgun can be fitted with a scope and this improves marksmanship a great deal, though it does *not* increase the effective killing range of hunting loads. With a two-hand hold and a scope, a good handgunner is very deadly indeed.

I like the idea of hunting with handguns. Though I deplore "stunt" shots at game and special-privilege seasons, there are many hunting situations where handguns are sensible, logical, and effective alternatives to rifles. One of the main reasons I favor handgun hunting and look forward to increasing numbers of handgun hunters is because it proves beyond all doubt that pistols do have a legitimate sporting purpose. This is important to handgunners, who must continually respond to the charge that handguns have no legitimate sporting use. By accepting handgunners in the ranks of legitimate sport hunters, all hunters gain allies who will prove invaluable in the battle against anti-hunters. Pistol shooters in general have been fighting in the anti-gun wars longer than any other group of firearms owners. Handgunners are well organized, outspoken, and politically tough—just the sort of guys we need on our side.

PART 5

BOWS AND HUNTING

The Compound Factor

By Jim Craig

The big doe showed no sign of alarm at the release but, as the arrow came closer she either heard it or saw it, and tried to run. The compound bow proved too fast. The arrow disappeared high in her chest.

The broadhead, shot from a 70-pound Bear compound, dropped less than 10 inches in its flight of 50 yards. The hold, as I confirmed later, was on the center of the deer's neck as she faced us. From my position behind the bowman, I was able to watch the action almost as if I were taking the shot myself. The incident occurred during the Pennsylvania bow season. The clean bowkill proved once again how the faster, flatter-shooting compound bow has increased the effective range of the bowhunter.

The compound is also helping the new archer to develop good shooting skills from the beginning. And, it's holding the interest of shooters who might easily be discouraged by the heavier hold weight of the recurve. Overall, the compound is helping to make good archers of beginners and better archers out of experienced bowmen.

The transition from recurve to compound took place at a far greater pace than did the transition from straight bow to recurve. When the recurve was first introduced, it offered little advantage over the straight bow. The design was dynamically new but the bow material was not. It wasn't until the fiberglass-and-wood lamination process was developed that the recurve's potential was recognized. Unlike the recurve, the compound has had the advantage of the finest bow materials available.

The major opponents of the compound were the serious bowhunters who believed that the new me-

The compound bow offers what serious-minded bowhunters have always tried to achieve with the recurve—superior speed, flat trajectory, and good penetration. It requires less physical effort than the recurve, allowing a bowhunter to enjoy the sport well into his later years.

chanical bows would take the simplicity and glamor from bowhunting. Today, these serious-minded bowhunters are promoting the compound. It offers what they were always trying to achieve with the recurve—superior speed, flat trajectory, and good penetration.

Some bowhunters recognized the advantages of the bow from its initial development. Cliff Wiseman—one of the nation's top bowhunters and a member of the Pope and Young Club, the bowhunter's counterpart of the Boone and Crockett Club, believes the faster arrow from the compound makes it a superior hunting weapon to the recurve. He also cites the compound's reduced hold weight as a definite advantage. Most important, the bowhunter who couldn't handle a heavyweight recurve can now shoot a heavy bow with less physical effort. The compound will also allow a bowhunter to enjoy his sport into his later years.

Most questions about the compound seem to come from newcomers to the sport. First, the prospective compound owner must realize that the compound bow is not a cure-all for his archery problems. The bow, with all its mechanical advantages, does not add to a bowhunter's skill. The man behind the bow is still the final deciding factor. The compound simply makes it easier to achieve a good degree of shooting ability.

The question most frequently asked is: How difficult is it to set up a compound and keep it in tune? During its evolutionary period, the bow's basic design encountered many tuning problems. The bow was difficult to set up because of complicated mechanical parts, and constant adjustments were needed.

The standard compound, with its pulley and cables, should come from the factory with a standard tune or should be set up that way by your dealer. This means the bow should be set up to your specifications for draw length, weight requirements, nocking point, arrow rest, and proper tiller adjustment. (The tiller is the distance between the bowstring and where the limbs meet the riser or handle section.)

The shooter should have to make few or no additional adjustments to a tuned compound. Your bow will be adequately set up for practice and hunting. Only after the shooter becomes proficient with his equipment should any fine-tuning be necessary.

Most compound manufacturers now offer economy models. These bows are less complex than the standard compounds. The nocking point and arrow-rest adjustments are the same as those required of a recurve, but a tiller adjustment is necessary on a few models.

Len Cardinale is one of the top archery coaches in the country, a member of the Pope and Young Club, a member of the Ben Pearson professional advisory staff, and a nationally known bowhunter. From his archery shop and range—Butts and Bows, in Belleville, New Jersey—Len sells and services compound bows. He says that non-adjustable economy models are proving to be almost trouble free. Len indicated that the major problems have been with the adjustable models, and that the problems were not necessarily with the bows themselves but, rather, the result of adjustments the shooter made.

As simple as the bows are to adjust, Len feels that adjustments can be properly checked only with the aid of a compound scale—an expensive piece of equipment. He suggested that the new compound-bow owner work closely with his dealer in making all major adjustments.

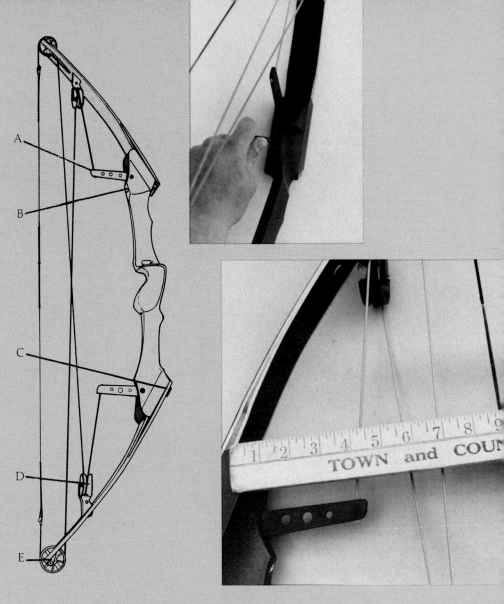

Compound Bow Adjustments. With an Allen wrench and a ruler, a compound is adjusted and checked for draw weight (above), draw length (far right, top), and tiller (far right, bottom). The sketch shows mechanical components of a modern compound: A) cable or speed bracket; B) draw-length adjustment; C) draw-weight and tiller adjustment; D) idler pulley; and E) eccentric cam.

Overall, Len views the compound as superior to the recurve, and as a definite advantage to the bowhunter. He also sees the compound as a great advantage for young bowhunters and for women.

The economy compounds offer as much as 50 percent reduction in peak draw weight after break-over, which occurs somewhere between half and three-quarters of the way through the draw. Although this reduction permits the shooter to aim and hold with less physical effort, it adds to one of the archer's major problems—a good, clean release.

For this reason, many archers have switched from the shooting glove to the finger tab or to a mechanical release. The mechanical release has proven most effective, but it is not legal for hunting in many states. The release problem is not so critical in the standard compounds with 20 to 35 percent reduction as it is in the economy models, but it is still present. This problem seems to be less evident when the hold weight is in the 35-pound range and heavier.

Probably the compound's greatest advantage is that it can shoot an arrow faster and with a flatter trajectory than can a conventional recurve of equal peak weight. Several manufacturers claim their top-of-the-line bows are as much as 50 percent faster than an equivalent recurve bow.

There are two reasons a compound can shoot an arrow faster and with flatter trajectory. First, the compound stores more energy than a recurve for a given draw weight. The compound delivers an arrow completely by mechanical means, while the cast of an arrow from a recurve is accomplished by the forward movement of the upper and lower limbs. When the string of a recurve is released, the forward movement of the limbs immediately begins to slow down. From the time the string is released until the arrow is cast, much power is lost. Therefore, the arrow is cast with far less force than the bow's actual draw weight.

The mechanical action of the compound works in reverse of the limb action of a recurve. When the string is released, the forward movement of the arrow is accelerated until the arrow has moved approximately one-third of the draw length, at which time, peak bow weight is reached. When the arrow is cast, it is propelled at peak bow weight.

This mechanical action also permits the use of lighter arrows than you can use with a recurve of equal draw weight. With peak draw weight occurring after the arrow has moved forward about one-third the draw length, the length of the column of the arrow between the string and pressure point (at the arrow rest) is shortened. This, in effect, creates a shorter, stiffer shaft at the time of application of peak draw force. That's why you can shoot a lighter arrow from a compound than you can from an equivalent recurve.

The advantages to hunters of the compound have probably been recognized more in the West than in any other area of the country. Steve Richards, a Colorado bowhunter, hunts in six Western states each year. He thinks that, in areas where long shots are common, the compound is the only choice.

Interestingly, Steve didn't think the compound had greatly increased the range at which the Western archer would take game. The most important fact, he explained, is that the Western bowhunter can now be a better shot at the longer distances he must shoot.

To illustrate his point, Steve described his first hunt with the compound bow. Hunting the high country around Roan Creek, near his home in Colorado, he stalked within 70 yards of a feeding mule deer buck. Although he had put in many hours of practice at this distance and felt confident with his new equipment, this would be the real test.

Steve pulled the 53-pound Jennings compound to full draw and held the tip of the arrow on the tip of the deer's ear. Maintaining that elevation, he moved the arrow to a point directly over the deer's shoulder. This hold put the arrow about two feet above the deer's back and about three feet above the vital area. Steve released the ultralight 1913 aluminum shaft and watched in amazement as the arrow flew about a foot over the buck's back.

The arrow spooked the deer, but the big buck, not knowing what had disturbed him, resumed feeding. Given that rare second shot, Steve held about eight to 10 inches over the buck's back.

The buck never knew what hit him as the arrow cut into the vitals. The arrow had dropped about two feet at 70 yards. Steve believes that, if he had been shooting his 62-pound-pull recurve and used the same hold, the arrow would have buried itself in the dirt 10 feet in front of the buck.

Another plus for the compound is that many of the models are adjustable in draw weight. This feature lets the archer increase the draw weight of his bow as he works into his equipment. With a recurve, you must buy either a new bow or, with the take-down models, additional sets of limbs.

At a bowhunting seminar sponsored by the United Bowhunters of New Jersey, I talked to a number of bowhunters about the compound. Of the 36 I spoke

with, 28 were shooting compounds. Five of the eight non compound shooters expressed a desire to buy a compound but were undecided about make and model. The three archers who had no interest in the compound nevertheless respected the weapon.

One of these three, Bruce Leger, expressed the thoughts of most bowhunters who do not care to shoot a compound: "As long as I can accurately shoot a recurve and consistently take game with it, I'm going to stay with the recurve."

All of the compound shooters indicated they'd had few or no problems with their bows—except for adjusting bow weight without the aid of a scale. Even by following the instruction manual, most shooters were unable to get their bows to shoot right and had to have the dealer readjust them.

Most shooters are solving this problem by marking a line on the side of the limbs along the side plate as the dealer tunes the bow for different desired weight. That way, the archer can change the weight cf his bow and be reasonably sure that the bow will be in tune.

The modern compound weighs about 3½ to four pounds—considerably lighter than the older models, which went around six pounds, but still on the heavy side. Add a bow quiver and a hunting stabilizer, and you're back in the six-pound range again. Recurves weigh 2½ to three pounds, which makes them easy to handle and carry.

If you're a sight shooter and can handle recurve equipment with some skill, you'll probably find that, under normal conditions, the compound will add very little to your shooting ability. Where the sight-equipped compound will be a definite advantage is under severe wind conditions. The faster arrow from a compound will be less affected by wind than the slower arrow from a recurve.

The new shooter using sights may find a definite advantage in a compound. If he finds he is unable to hold the sight pin steady on the target, the steadiness gained by the reduced hold weight of the compound could be the answer.

John Lupi, the New Jersey State Field Archery Association champion in the bowhunter division, has won the title for several years. He says it was the compound that made the big difference in his shooting.

John sees the compound as a definite advantage to the competitive field archer, especially in the bowhunter division, where the heavier bows are required. John feels that the lighter hold weight of the compound lets the archer hold steadier and longer on the target, allowing more time for concentration. He also says that, with the faster, flatter arrow from the compound, the competitive archer and the bowhunter have an advantage over a recurve shooter because there are smaller degrees of adjustment to be made with the bow when shooting at longer ranges.

One of the mechanical bows could be just the kind of equipment you need.

When You Take Up Bowhunting

By Rich LaRocco

A few weeks ago, I was talking with a construction worker who was complaining about his lack of deer hunting success. He'd taken time off from his job to spend the last week of the rifle season in one of the best deer ranges of the West.

"I must have covered 10 miles a day," he said, "and all I saw was one little two-point. And it got into the timber before I could get off a shot. You seem to fill your deer tags most of the time. How about some advice?"

"Take up bowhunting," I replied.

"What?" my friend said in surprise. "If I can't even get a deer with a rifle, how could I expect to get one with a bow?"

Good question. And it's one I've been asked dozens of times. Most rifle hunters know that bowhunting success rates are low and they're not interested in taking on what seems to be an insurmountable challenge. What they don't realize is that good hunters regularly score during archery season. I know one fellow who has filled more than 50 buck tags during bow seasons. Only once did he fail to fill an archery deer tag—and that's because he'd already taken an elk and had to stop hunting to care for the meat.

Bowhunting certainly has its disadvantages and I'm only too well acquainted with many of them. But it has its advantages, too, and that's why I tell unsuccessful rifle hunters to take up the sport. I maintain that most hunters would learn more about deer hunting in one archery season than they would in five gun seasons. In short, taking up bowhunting is a shortcut to becoming a better big-game hunter.

I wasn't too successful in my first four rifle seasons. During that time, I saw only five bucks. Then, I took up bowhunting. I saw more bucks in the first day than I'd seen in my previous hunting career. Hunting only on three weekends, I saw about 40 bucks, several of them record-class animals, and I even managed to get a few shots. Though I didn't tag a buck that year, I learned a great deal about how deer behave, what kinds of food and cover they prefer, and how to spot and approach the animals.

The next bow season, I ambushed a herd of small mule deer bucks as they left an alfalfa field early one morning, and I shot a forkhorn through the lungs. Despite the small size of his antlers, I have them prominently displayed in my home. That buck deserves the honor because he represented my passing from the ranks of hunters who hope luck passes their way to the kind of hunters who make their own luck. As one of my most successful bowhunting friends says: A good hunter puts himself in a position to be lucky.

So is that all there is to it? Just buy a bow and hunt for two or three years until you learn the ropes? To an extent, yes. But a gun hunter can make the transition to being a successful bowhunter more easily if he knows what he's up against and what common mistakes to avoid.

The greatest difference between gun hunters and bowhunters is that the latter must get very close to their quarry before they can even hope to score. The average distance at which bowhunters kill deer is probably less than 25 yards. Even the best bowhunt-

Two bowhunters seeking blacktail deer in northern California discuss strategy.

ers rarely shoot farther than 50 yards because the chances of missing are great at that distance. By contrast, I know several rifle hunters who have never shot a deer at less than 200 yards, and 400-yard kills are fairly common in the Rockies.

Getting close to a deer is a challenge for many reasons. All deer, whether they're whitetails, blacktails, or muleys, possess fantastically sharp senses of hearing, smell, and sight. Bowhunters must learn to overcome all three to become consistently successful.

HEARING

Rifle hunters can make a great deal of noise and still take deer. Many hunters wear vinyl, fluorescent orange vests that make unnatural crackling and ripping noises as they hunt, but they still manage to fill their deer tags. You *can't* make this kind of noise and expect to saunter within bow range of a buck. The most successful bowhunters wear flannel, chamois, or soft wool clothing—materials that are almost noiseless. One acquaintance of mine wore a ripstop-nylon camouflage vest during his first three archery hunts. He couldn't even draw his bow without making noise, and it wasn't until he left the vest home that he got his first shot.

Expert bowhunters take great pains to be silent. One of the best whitetail hunters in New Jersey showed me how to put soft, adhesive-backed moleskin on my sight window and arrow rest to ensure silence. Now, I even have a strip of moleskin over the plastic arrow-rest button so that my aluminum arrow shaft makes absolutely no noise as I draw it back.

Many bowhunters carry daypacks or beltpacks containing canteens, snacks, survival kits, and the like. I've made small sacks out of scrap cloth to cover each individual item in my beltpack. I can even run while wearing it and not make noise. My canteen is made of collapsible plastic. I can squeeze all the air out of it so that the water makes no sloshing noises when I move. Would a rifle hunter concern himself with such details?

A bowhunter who stalks or stillhunts must be especially quiet. Dwight Schuh, an expert stalker from Oregon, taught me during a blacktail hunt in California to remove my boots and stalk the last few hundred yards to a deer in my stocking feet. The tactic worked wonderfully. During my first bootless stalk, I got within 10 yards of two fine blacktail bucks. Later, during the same hunt, I sneaked within 10 *feet* of a bedded record-class buck! Unfortunately, I didn't get a shot at that animal because he detected me at the last moment and jumped out of sight over a bluff before I could even draw my bow. (Sometimes you can simply get too close.) Now I carry an extra pair of heavy woolen "stalking socks" that I slip on before making my final approach. You can actually sneak noiselessly—even down a steep, shale rock rockslide, which I've done—if you take enough time.

Incidentally, now I never try to sneak within 10 yards of a bedded animal. Instead, I carry a few small pebbles in my pocket. Once I'm within excellent bow range, I flip a pebble to the other side of the animal and immediately draw my bow. Usually, the animal stands to investigate the slight noise and all I have to do is aim and release the arrow.

I had a perfect opportunity to employ this tactic last year. One afternoon, I watched a heavy-beamed three-point mule deer bed down behind a patch of three-foot-high sagebrush. After slipping on my wool socks and dropping a few pebbles in a hip pocket, I slowly stalked within 20 yards of the buck, flipped a pebble to the other side of him, and quickly drew my bow. Nothing happened, so I tossed another pebble and drew my bow again. The pebble rattled a dry bush and the deer jumped to its feet. My arrow flashed in the sun as it smacked into the buck's shoulder. The animal bounded twice and crumpled.

SMELL

Overcoming a deer's sophisticated sense of smell is a challenge to which many hunters have devoted their lifetimes. Research has shown that deer detect odors so well that it is practically impossible to mask human scent. Some bowhunters use skunk scent, either genuine or artificial. I've tried both with little success. I believe the best way to keep a deer from smelling you is to stay downwind of the animal. Because that's not always possible, I try to keep my body as clean as possible and bathe every day, if I can. A little baking powder rubbed on your body can eliminate an amazing amount of scent. One of the best bowhunters I know, Dave Snyder of Las Vegas, takes five complete camouflage suits with him. He wears a fresh, clean suit every day. Of course, he doesn't wash these suits in scented detergent—just plain water.

It might pay to experiment with various scents, however. Some hunters wear bobcat or fox urine, available from trapping supply houses. During the rut, scent derived from deer glands or the urine of a doe in heat can actually attract a buck within bow range. I know several whitetail hunters who swear by this stuff, but I've never seen a muley or a blacktail attracted to a so-called sex lure.

A good way to deal with a deer's fantastic nose is to hunt from a tree stand—which is also an excellent way to keep from being seen, as deer rarely look up except in places where tree stand hunting is common. I've watched many whitetail and mule deer walk directly downwind of my stand without giving any indication of scenting me. Even if they do smell me, they usually act as though I'm farther away than I really am, probably because air currents dissipate my scent well before it reaches ground level. Even when an animal appears to have detected me, it often continues to walk within bow range. That has happened to me several times.

Don't fall for the line that tree stand hunting might be effective for whitetails but not for mule deer. In Utah, one fall, I had as many as eight bucks a day come within bow range of my tree stand.

SIGHT

Never underestimate the ability of a deer to see movement. The closer you get to game, the more you must concern yourself with this problem. If a deer is looking directly at you from, say, 15 yards away, you can't even blink or move a little finger without being detected. Try not to draw your bow if a deer at close range is looking at you. Move only when the deer's eyes are hidden or if it's looking in another direction.

Deer, however usually don't see slow movement past 30 yards or so. Cal Coziah of Soda Springs, Idaho, has killed several record-class mule deer on snow-covered ground just by stalking very, very slowly. He doesn't even wear snow camouflage or white clothing.

In my opinion, though, camouflage is a great aid because deer usually can't see a hunter who "blends" into the environment, as long as he doesn't move. I believe in full camouflage, right down to wearing face paint or a head net. Be sure to camouflage your hands and bow. You must move them in order to shoot and, if they're light-colored or shiny, a deer could easily see them move.

Judd Cooney, a successful bowhunting guide in Colorado, wears so much face camouflage that he looks like an African warrior. He says most bowhunters don't darken their faces enough.

When camouflaging yourself, pay attention to any jewelry you might wear. One of my friends once hunted pronghorn antelope from a pit blind in Colorado and bucks kept shying away from his blind until he removed his wedding ring. The new breed of digital watches often have flat crystals that reflect sunlight like little mirrors. I cover my crystal with a short length of dull-finish cellophane tape.

Getting within bow range of an animal does you little good unless you're capable of putting an arrow where it counts. I believe bowhunters often miss for four main reasons: a poor choice of equipment, lack of shooting practice, poor range judgment, and buck fever.

What kind of bow and arrow you have isn't really that important. But it's vital that they match each other. In other words, your arrows must be neither too stiff nor too flexible for your particular bow, or they'll fly erratically. Unless you know how to select the proper arrow shaft, I would suggest you buy arrows from a competent archery pro shop. I use Easton XX75 shafts, which have a hard-anodized orange finish. They're made of an extremely tough aluminum alloy and can withstand a great deal of abuse without bending. The color does not alarm deer but the orange finish makes an arrow much easier to find after you've shot it.

There are three main types of bows: longbows, recurves, and compounds. I've taken game with each type but I recommend that new bowhunters buy compounds. My choice is a two-wheel model because it has few moving parts and is, therefore, less likely to break down in the field. Select a model that has the eccentric wheels mounted in splits in the bow limbs rather than on metal hangers.

Do not attempt to hunt deer with a bow that has a draw weight of less than 40 pounds. A more reasonable minimum weight would be 50 pounds. I recommend a bow with adjustable draw weights—mine goes from 50 to about 70 pounds. A good rule of thumb is to use the heaviest bow you can shoot *accurately* under hunting conditions. My bow is set at 66 pounds, which gives plenty of penetration. It has twice sent broadheads all the way through bull elk.

One piece of equipment that you should give special consideration to is the broadhead. Most models on the market are adequate. There are two main styles—heads that feature replaceable, razor-sharp blades, and the traditional fixed-blade heads such as the Bear Razorhead or Zwickey Black Diamond. I prefer the traditional heads because they have a knifelike leading edge and penetrate extremely well. They must be hand-sharpened, however. If you can't put a literally shaving-sharp edge on a blade, select a head with replaceable blades. Avoid very narrow broadheads and make sure the blades are positively locked in place. My favorite model features extra-heavy-gauge blades.

I strongly suggest using a bowsight. In my opinion, the chief advantage of a compound bow is that it lends itself well to bowsight shooting. A compound's advantage in slightly greater arrow speed is not as important as many hunters think.

You'll want to buy a few other gadgets, too, such as an armguard to protect your bow arm from your bowstring, and a shooting glove or tab to protect your fingers. Some hunters use mechanical release aids but I don't like them because getting off a second shot is often difficult.

Once you obtain the necessary gear, have an expert archer teach you to shoot. Then practice, practice, practice. Do not make your practice sessions too long until your shooting muscles build up. You can progress rapidly even if you shoot just half an hour every other day.

The best shooting practice is the type that simulates hunting. Every year, I make a life-size deer target of foam or cardboard and practice shooting at various unmarked distances. Take just one shot from one range, then move to another place for the next shot. If you plan to hunt from a tree stand, practice shooting from an elevated position. Practice shooting at twilight because objects at dawn and dusk usually appear to be farther away than they are.

No matter how hard and long you practice, however, you'll still misjudge range occasionally—and that could cost you a winter's supply of venison. A good solution is to use an optical rangefinder, such as those made by Ranging Inc. The larger models are remarkably accurate if protected from jolts.

Even if you do everything else right, you still might succumb to a case of buck fever. I define buck fever as intense excitement that adversely affects your hunting or shooting ability.

"I don't get too excited when I'm gun hunting," one friend of mine said. "But when I get 20 or 30 yards from a big buck, and all I have is a puny bow in my hands, I get so cranked up I can't even think straight. I forget all about aiming and releasing the arrow smoothly and all that. I'd hate to say it's buck fever but it couldn't be anything else."

If you have similar experiences, don't fret. One of the attractions of bowhunting is that it provides great thrills, and hunting wouldn't be fun if it weren't exciting. But you can learn to control this excitment. The best bowhunters seldom get buck fever simply because they've accumulated years of hunting experience. An excellent remedy is to simulate hunting experiences. Practice stalking or tree stand hunting for several weeks before archery season opens. When you get close to a deer, or if it gets close to you, raise your arms and pretend that you're shooting an arrow at it. This might sound ridiculous but it can help tremendously.

If you've never tried bowhunting, you're in for a thrill the first time you get within pea-shooting distance of a deer. Your knees will tremble, your breath will come in ragged gasps, your pulse will actually pound in your ears, and you'll wonder whatever possessed you to take part in this craziness. That's bowhunting!

The First Bowhunt

By G. Howard Gillelan

The bowman on his first deer hunt is usually one of three types: A newcomer to both archery and hunting; an experienced archer who has never hunted before; or a rifleman or shotgunner who is trying the bow and arrow on game for the first time. For each, the approach to bowhunting success is somewhat different, yet the same general principles apply to all.

It's hard to say which of the three requires the most education in the strange ways of bowhunting.

The newcomer to both archery and hunting has to contend with two things that are new to him.

The target archer is knowledgeable about and perhaps skilled in one branch of bowbending, but he's a greenhorn when it comes to using his archery tools on live targets, let alone getting close enough to a clever, unfamiliar game animal.

The novice bowhunter in the third category, the man who has hunted with firearms, must learn to handle a weapon that is believed to have originated some 25,000 years before even the most rudimentary firearms were used. Though he may have shot a deer each season for the last two decades, he must make a drastic change in his deer-hunting technique when he hunts with a bow.

Whether you're entirely new to archery, a target archer, or a powder-burner turned bowhunter, bear in mind that you're now dealing with short-range shooting—not that a broadhead arrow can't be lethal at a couple of hundred yards. It's capable of killing at its maximum range, which may be nearly one-eighth of a mile, depending on the potency of the armament. Yet, no archer ever born can be sure of hitting a deer at such long range, much less pinpoint his hit in the vital area. Remember, it's not enough to merely arrow the deer—you must hit the animal in a vital spot.

It's often tough for the seasoned rifleman and the experienced target archer to make the transition to the comparatively short distances involved in bowhunting. A good target archer can loop his arrows at a 60-yard bull's-eye and, once his sight is adjusted, hit it dead center consistently. A rifleman who knows his onions can flatten chucks at unbelievable distances, thanks to a high-powered scope and hot loads. But 60-yard target archery and long-range rifle shooting do not accustom a hunter to realistic bowhunting ranges.

Yet, a goodly number of deer are nailed at 50 and 60 yards—in most cases by better-than-average archers hunting in rather open country. At the other extreme, plenty of deer—mostly whitetails in brushy areas—are arrowed from amazingly close distances. While a shot from 15 yards or less may seem like a sure thing, "it ain't necessarily so." A surprising number of very close shots are missed. The reason is that few bowhunters do any practice shooting at distances of less than 20 yards. When they're faced with a deer that's only feet from them, they often miss by shooting high.

I was on a group hunt once, in the Catskill Mountains, and a fellow I knew slightly was the first archer to haul a deer into camp. After inspecting his buck and the place where the broadhead had gone in close to the heart, I asked the inevitable question: "How far was he when you shot?"

165

"Fifteen feet, broadside," the successful bowhunter answered with a laugh.

I asked him if he'd ever done any practicing from such a short distance.

"Yes," he replied. "Believe it or not, I do a lot of practicing at targets under 20 yards."

He told me he'd once missed a perfect shot at a good buck that was standing only 12 yards away. Ever since, he had devoted at least half of his practicing to extremely close shots—10 feet to 20 yards. It's a good idea.

The problem of getting to within 35 yards of a wary animal is the essence of bowhunting, and the need to perform that feat sets the sport apart from hunting with firearms. It calls for careful attention to details, which is why most bowhunters wear camouflage clothing and use quite a number of gadgets.

Wind direction is one of the important things a bowhunter must consider at all times, and to a much greater extent than the rifleman. A friend of mine, a career Army officer, hunts deer with bow, rifle, and shotgun. As a result of his bowhunting experience, he knows you can't get close to a keen-nosed critter if the wind is from the wrong quarter. Like all savvy bowmen, he checks the wind direction at regular intervals, regardless of which weapon he happens to be using. He once told me he's astonished that so many riflemen and shotgunners pay no attention to wind direction while hunting deer. On one shotgun hunt on an Army post, the other members of the colonel's party thought he had gone around the bend when he insisted on using wind direction as a criterion in selecting his stand.

Just as in hunting with firearms, the bowhunter follows one of three hunting methods: driving, stillhunting or stalking, and hunting from a fixed stand or blind.

Driving with hounds or by humans produces a substantial number of deer for hunters with firearms but is generally considered unsuitable for bowhunters. When a driven deer is sighted, it's tearing full-tilt away from the drivers and offers an almost impossible shot for the bowman who wants to be fairly sure of centering his arrow in a vital area. Some bowmen do take deer on drives, and there are places where it's the only way to get the animals to show themselves. But driving is neither the most desirable nor the most productive hunting method for archers.

Stalking and stillhunting are just about synonymous to most hunters, though some think of stalking as approaching an animal silently and unseen after it has already been sighted from a distance. Stillhunting to them means moving through the hunting ground slowly and quietly while looking for the quarry.

One of the sportiest challenges in bowhunting is to spot a deer that is not aware of you and then try to stalk into bow range. In fairly open country, a good rifleman only needs to close the distance to a few hundred yards. The bowman tries for 40 paces or less. Depending on the terrain, this is less difficult in certain parts of the country. It's most challenging in the heavy brush in the mountains of some Eastern states, where whitetails rely on the thickest cover for their safety. When the underbrush is dry and every footstep sounds like an air-raid siren to woods dwellers, a successful stalk is next to impossible, even for an expert bowhunter.

The wind can muck things up when it shifts about. Sometimes, instead of a discernible wind, there are only subtle air currents, which are difficult to detect. If the currents are not too gentle, you can keep tabs on them by tying a wispy thread to the upper tip of your bow.

My most satisfying stalk was made possible by a very strong wind. While stillhunting, I spotted a buck some 300 yards away. Thanks to the roar of the wind and the racket it made in the treetops, I didn't have to worry too much about stepping on dry leaves and twigs. By taking advantage of the cover provided by tree trunks, I was able to surprise the buck at 18 yards.

Stillhunting has an element of luck, but it nevertheless requires skill and experience. Look for a section of woods where there are tracks and droppings; then move into the wind with a minimum of noise. Stop at frequent intervals and remain still for several minutes each time. During these pauses, be on the alert for moving deer. Double-check every bush and every mound of leaves. One of them may harbor a bedded deer. If you come across a particularly likely

This young hunter's small mule deer, taken in Utah, is a satisfying reward for a hunt well planned. Photo by Rich LaRocco.

A razor-sharp broadhead in your bow is necessary to turn a hit into a kill. This successful hunter packs out the meat and antlers from a mule deer. Photo by Rich LaRocco.

looking area where deer sign is abundant, stop for a longer period. Sometimes, you'll find a spot with several piles of fresh droppings or a place where game trails intersect. Then it may be smart to settle down and stay for several hours or even for the rest of the day.

There's a difference of opinion among archers about whether or not you should carry an arrow on your bow while stalking and stillhunting. In the interest of safety, some experts advise against it. If you slip or stumble, there's a chance of driving the broadhead into your leg or foot. My own thinking is that, when you're negotiating a slippery surface such as mud or ice, the arrow should not be kept on the bow. It should be carried in the quiver. And, on the rare occasions when it's necessary to run, you're taking a big risk if you carry an arrow on your bow.

In most situations, however, the arrow should be in place on the bow. When you round a bend suddenly and find a deer staring at you or come upon one unexpectedly in some other way, you don't have

time to yank an arrow out of your quiver and place it on the bow. When stalking a deer or stillhunting, you're supposed to be moving slowly and carefully anyway. There's not much danger of tripping or slipping as long as each step is taken quietly and deliberately.

Hunting from a blind or concealed stand, because it's a method that lacks activity, is not as satisfying as stillhunting, but it is the method that accounts for most arrowed deer. You may go slightly mad while waiting hours for something to appear but, if your location is good and you're properly concealed, you can figure on some shooting eventually.

Whichever of the three hunting methods you use, it's wise to have one or two arrows for warm-up shots in the field. Use arrows with blunt tips or dull broadheads deliberately reserved for practice shots. When there's a lull in the hunting and you figure the activity is not likely to spook any game, shoot your two practice arrows at a clod of dirt. This will loosen up stiff muscles and keep your eye sharp. When you take your lunch break, you can do some more shooting to take the kinks out.

Some of your practice shots in the field should be snap shots—draw, aim, and release, all in one fast motion. It's not a habit to cultivate, but it's good insurance against the time when you may have only a second or two to get your arrow away.

Far too many beginners hunt with dull heads. For a broadhead to penetrate and cut a deer's tough blood vessels, the blades must be razor-sharp. With a good mill file, the edges can be brought to a fine edge. After a rough day in the field, your blades will probably need to be resharpened, even though they were not used. Get in the habit of checking them each evening and use your file to keep them keen.

In the excitement of getting off a shot at a deer, you may have a tendency to shoot at the whole animal. This technique usually results in a miss or a wounding hit. You're so anxious to let that arrow go before your venison disappears that you shoot at the entire deer instead of deliberately selecting a spot on its chest as your aiming point. Even veteran bowhunters—some of them with walls full of trophies—worry about this problem. The best way to lick it is to talk to yourself silently when you first see the deer. As you get ready for the shot, repeat over and over, "Pick a spot; pick a spot." It's just a reminder, but it seems to work.

A few years ago, the Pennsylvania Game Commission made a study that produced some interesting figures on bowhunting. Because Pennsylvania's deer herd annually attracts more archers than deer in any other state, the figures are significant. If you're an average bowhunter, according to the study, you'll spend 36 hours in the hunting field during the season. If your hunting skill is better than average, you'll get a shot at a deer. The figures show that 60 out of every 100 bowhunters get shots, but only two of the 60 bag a deer.

Whether or not you score, you'll get a tremendous kick out of your first bowhunt for deer.

Prepare Early
For Deer Hunting

By G. Howard Gillelan

The spring or summer seems like an odd time for a bowhunter to start preparing for the fall deer season. Fishing, boating, and beating the heat seem more appropriate. But, for hunters who know what it takes to arrow a deer, midsummer is none too early to start getting in shape.

There was a time when bowhunting for deer was strictly a fall sport. But now, the trend is toward earlier and longer archery seasons. In some Western states, including Utah, bowhunting for deer opens in August. Quite a few Eastern states get their bowhunters off to an early start by opening in September. So, regardless of where you hunt, you won't be rushing the season if you start to train early.

To be sure, some deer will be taken this year by hunters who get their bows out of storage a short time before opening day. Their success, in most cases, will be due more to luck than to ability. Some deer will also be taken by bowmen who are such sharp shots or such skilled hunters that they require little or no warm-up. But most deer will be arrowed by average bowhunters who made an above-average effort to prepare for a successful hunt. If you want to be among the successful ones, here are a few things you should do.

First, start planning your hunt early. If you haven't yet decided on a hunting location, get going. Bowmen who hunt fairly close to home are fortunate because, without much trouble, they can go to the hunting area, check for deer sign, and decide tentatively where their stands should be. But, they should realize that the foliage and fields may be somewhat altered come hunting season, and they should plan accordingly.

If you have any landowner contacts, renew them now and make definite arrangements for hunting rights. Ask the state game department and local conservation officers where deer crop damage has been running high this year. Your state game agency and its local men are in business to help you, and you should be able to count on their cooperation in directing you to an advantageous area.

You may have found in the past that your best bowhunting is in a neighboring state or another part of your own state. In this case, it would probably pay you to devote a summer weekend to deer reconnaissance and hunt planning. Remember, though, that deer shift their habitat with changes in the food supply. A certain woodlot bordering a cornfield may have been a hotspot last season but, this year, it may be devoid of deer because of crop rotation, an unusually heavy kill by gunners, or a severe winter.

If you're one of the growing number of bowhunters going to a distant state to hunt with an outfitter or to a commercial hunting camp, your plans are probably set well before fall. But make sure all the details are in order—things like proper licenses and special game permits, transportation, and shipment of meat back to your home. Be sure the outfitter knows you're a bowhunter and that he's equipped for the special requirements of archers.

Once you've chosen the best possible place for your hunt, there are three other elements that will

affect your success. These are hunting ability, equipment, and marksmanship.

Your hunting ability depends more on experience than on practicing. But, if you're a greenhorn or even a veteran of several bowhunting seasons, you'll do well to learn as much as possible about the nature and habits of the deer you plan to hunt, as well as the country you'll be hunting in. Study contour maps of the area until you know it well—its ravines, streams, and ridges. Read everything available about the deer in the area. There's no substitute for on-the-spot experience, of course, but reading will give you a head start.

Get out into the wilds of the hunting country and attune your senses to the sights and sounds vital to hunters. The more you do this, the better you'll be able to distinguish between woods noises—the rustling of squirrels, the regular cadence of human footfalls, a puff of wind rattling through the treetops and, most important, the sound of an unalarmed deer advancing toward you. Get in the habit of noting the wind's direction and positioning yourself accordingly. Note whether a train or a plane goes by your stand at a certain time of day so you'll be able to take good advantage of the covering sound.

Bowhunting for woodchucks is the ideal way to hone your senses to the fine edge needed for deer hunting. Chuck hunts help condition your hunting muscles and also get you in the habit of holding steady when drawing on game.

Don't wait until a week before opening day to see if your hunting gear is in order. Go over every article now, from mosquito dope to handwarmers. Was there anything that would have been helpful last year, but which you didn't have—an extra compass, a folding pocket saw, a length of rope, a plastic bag for the deer's heart and liver? Midsummer is the time to tie up loose ends.

Get some up-to-date catalogues from archery manufacturers and visit your dealer to see if any new, practical bowhunting gadgets have been introduced this year. There are some fine new bows out, as well as some interesting broadheads. There are also some new accessories.

If you shop for gear early, you'll find a better selection of supplies and you'll also have time to get accustomed to any new components in your equipment. This is especially helpful with gear that requires some breaking in, such as boots, clothing, bows, arrows, and quivers.

Suppose you usually use a shoulder quiver or a hip quiver for practicing and field shooting, and a bow quiver for hunting deer. This is a good idea but, when deer season approaches, you should start shooting with your hunting equipment. The bow quiver adds weight to your bow and this addition,

For realistic bowhunting practice, your clothing, tackle, and target should simulate hunting conditions. Note that archer is taking an angled shot, instead of taking all his practice shots at a broadside target.

though small, could throw off your aim. One of the purposes of a bow quiver is to afford quick reloading of the bow. Here again, it takes practice to develop the smooth motions of quickly and silently pulling an arrow from the bow quiver and placing it in shooting position.

The best kind of shooting practice for bowhunters is the most realistic. In other words, your equipment, clothing, and target should approximate hunting conditions. If you're using a lighter bow for plinking and field archery, you should now start shooting with your hunting bow. You can't expect the heavier weapon to do its job unless your muscles are sufficiently hardened to handle it with ease.

If the weather isn't too warm, start wearing hunting duds and boots during shooting practice. Be sure you do some shooting in the dim light of early morning and dusk, and also try some shots during a rain, unless you prefer not to hunt on rainy days. Practice in terrain similar to that of your hunting area. Many of the good deer areas are in rolling country, which means you should learn how to shoot up or down on a hillside, and across ravines and streams. Archers who hunt from tree stands should do their final practicing from elevated positions.

You never know how you'll be situated when you get a chance to shoot at a deer, so some of your practicing should be from unusual and awkward positions. Train yourself to change positions quickly and to get off a quick snap shot. Last year, I was hunting with an archer who missed getting a shot at a magnificent whitetail buck from the unbelievable distance of four yards. Because the hunter was wearing camouflage clothes, the buck couldn't see him, but it got a whiff of his scent and slipped away through the dense cover. The archer was sitting on the ground after a grueling morning hunt. He saw the buck coming but, for fear of alarming it, didn't raise himself to shooting position. Because he'd had no practice in jumping up and getting off his shot quickly, he passed up the opportunity of a lifetime.

National statistics indicate that the average archer-killed deer is shot from a range of less than 35 yards. The target distances of your practice shooting, therefore, should be between 20 and 40 yards. But learn how to hold for shots closer than 20 yards because you never know what the range will be when you get your big chance. Without some practice from what may seem like ridiculously short distances—five to 15 yards—you'll have a tendency to shoot high at deer that are so close you can't believe it.

Don't shoot too many arrows from one position. Start at about 35 yards and take a couple of shots, then move up to 25 yards for two or three more. Go back to the 40-yard mark for one or two shots, and complete the group by letting your last arrow go from 15 yards. Follow a different sequence for the next batch of shots. At the same time, train yourself to estimate the yardages.

Take some long shots, too, at 50 to 60 yards from your target. But, unless you're an exceptional archer, you'll get such large groups on the long shots that

Using simulated deer targets will help the bowhunter become accustomed to shooting at the chest cavity.

you'll understand why you should confine your shots at game to less than 40 yards. It's desirable for a practicing bowhunter to shoot several times a week, and it's ideal if he can shoot every day, even if only for short periods.

For early, pre-season practice, bowhunters should not use a bull's-eye target. Instead, shoot at lifesize paper or cardboard targets, or at a deer-shaped target made of synthetic foam material that will stand up to broadheads. Most bowhunters, after a steady diet of shooting at ringed targets, run into trouble when shooting at the real thing. With no bull's-eye to aim for, they often shoot for the whole animal. But, after a month or two of arrowing simulated deer, the bowhunters develops the knack of automatically aiming for the chest cavity.

Because broadhead arrows generally fly differently from field arrows, the wise bowhunter will start shooting with broadheads now. As a result, he'll be accustomed to them and won't have to make an abrupt transition when the season starts. One difficulty in practice shooting broadheads arises from the target backstop. Because straw backstops take a beating when broadheads are pulled out of them, some archers prefer to mount their targets in sandpiles or mounds of sod. You can also shoot at a target on the side of a steep hill or on a deeply cut stream bank, if it's free of rocks. Regardless of where your target is placed, be sure no one can wander into the line of fire.

Getting a head start won't give you an iron-clad guarantee of bringing home a deer. But, if your hunting ground is carefully selected, if your gear is right, and if you know how to use it, you'll have the closest possible thing to a guarantee of a successful deer hunt.

PART 6

AFTER YOUR DEER IS DOWN

How To Skin And Cape Your Trophy

By Michael Lapinski

One of my most bittersweet sporting memories concerns a huge mule deer buck I dropped on a foggy, late-November morning in northern Idaho. My goal that fall was to shoot a trophy muley and, if it were an exceptional animal, I intended to have it mounted.

My buck was a gray-muzzled, big-nosed deer with five points that spread upward from each heavy main beam.

I dropped off the cape and antlers at a taxidermy shop that evening, my spirits high as I anticipated having that old buck join me in my den in a few months. But the next day a call from the taxidermist left me sadder and wiser. I had not caped out the buck correctly. The cape was too short and the taxidermist had no choice but to discard it. He told me not to worry, though, because he had a few extra muley capes that he'd bought from other hunters, and one of those capes would fit my antlers nicely.

The thought of displaying those trophy antlers with someone else's head turned me off, and I sadly decided against having the mount made. Those antlers now gather dust in a corner on my reloading table.

I made a vow that I'd learn how to cape and skin game properly so that any future trophies would not be ruined. From talking with other hunters, I've learned that many find disappointment at the taxidermist's shop when they are told that they have caped their trophies incorrectly. There is really no reason for it because the caping and skinning of an animal is a simple and logical process.

Many hunters get the wrong idea that a mounted

Dotted lines show the cuts made to start caping of any antlered animal for head and shoulders mount. Leave a generous amount of hide for the taxidermist to work with.

The Y-shaped cut on the top of the head ends in circles around the antler bases.

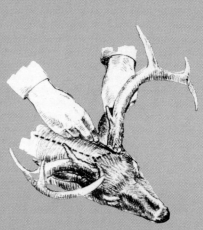

Skin around the bases is tough and thick and hard to cut. Some hunters therefore use a dull screwdriver instead of a knife and pry the hide away from the antlers.

After all cuts are made, skin out from rear just as though you were doing any other skinning job. Be very careful with the ears. Leave complete ears on the skin by cutting them off inside the hide. Do the same with the eyelids. Later, your taxidermist will "turn" or "split" them.

Work your way toward the nose. Be sure to leave the upper and lower lips on the hide by cutting them off inside the hide just as you did previously with the ears. Again, cut the nose off so that it remains part of the cape. Dealing with the nose is another job for the taxidermist.

Finish the job by removing the antlers from the skinned head. Do that by making a wedge-shaped cut into the skull. Use a hunter's meat saw or an ordinary hacksaw.

Illustrations by Wayne Trimm

trophy consists of the head and neck only. However, a buck mount almost always runs right down to the brisket under the shoulders. And this is where most sportsmen make their big mistake: They begin caping in front of the shoulders instead of behind them.

When caping an animal, you should make your first cut behind the front shoulders, and this incision should circle the chest. Next, cut along the back of the neck to the base of the skull. Then cut around the front legs about a foot from the chest and make a connecting cut along the inside of the leg to the chest incision. Now, all you need to do is slowly peel the hide until you reach the base of the skull.

Few sportsmen have the skill to skin out the head, so it is best to cut off the head, leaving the cape attached, and give it to the taxidermist that way. Most taxidermists prefer to receive future mounts this way, and many will skin out heads at no extra cost.

However, if you happen to take a trophy animal during an early-season hunt when temperatures rise into the 80s at midday, you might need to skin out the head yourself. If you don't, the head might begin to rot and hair might slip.

The first step in this chore is to continue the cut along the back of the neck until it is between the antlers. Make another cut to form a T between the antlers, and carefully skin the hide away. The flesh around the base of the antlers is stiff and resembles cartilage. Mistakes are easy to make, so go slowly.

After the hide is free from the antlers, peel the hide over the head until you get to the ears. Sever the ear close to the skull and continue to peel the hide over the face until you get to the eye sockets. This is a critical area because the cape must have the eyelids intact if a taxidermist is to create a lifelike mount.

Feel under the hide first for the exact location of the eyes and then make your cut close to the skull. Next work on the lips and nose. Leave a good portion of cartilage so that the taxidermist can securely attach the lips and nose to a plastic skull mold.

Finish the job by removing the antlers from the skinned head. Do that by making a wedge-shaped cut into the skull. Use a hunter's meat saw or an ordinary hacksaw. Remember, both antlers must be attached to the sawed-off skull plate.

Almost every horned or antlered big-game animal should be caped this way.

The Big Rip-Off Or How To Skin Your Deer With A Rope

By George H. Haas

This method of skinning a deer has several advantages. The skinned carcass has no hair on it and you avoid the work of picking it off. The hide has no knife cuts in it and the tanner will be delighted. It's also easy to gut out a deer that has already been skinned. This assumes, however, that you can get your deer to a place where you can skin it before spoilage starts. Don't risk souring the meat by leaving the internal organs inside the animal too long. If, however, a bullet has pierced the paunch, intestines or an abdominal organ, field-dress the deer where it falls and take the hide off later. Abdominal fluids can ruin the flavor of the meat. The rip-off method works well with a field-dressed deer. If the spine has been broken by a bullet, it doesn't work at all. Pulling on the rope would tear the deer in two. Don't take the hide off this way if the head is to be mounted; the preliminary cuts ruin the cape. The rip-off works well on many big-game animals, including elk and bears.

Illustrations by Ken Laager

1. *Cut leg off at joints. Slit skin around head in front of ears.*

2. *Slit hide from previous cut at bottom of throat to end of breastbone. Do not open the body cavity.*

3. *Turn deer over. Skin out top of head and neck. Cut ears off inside skin.*

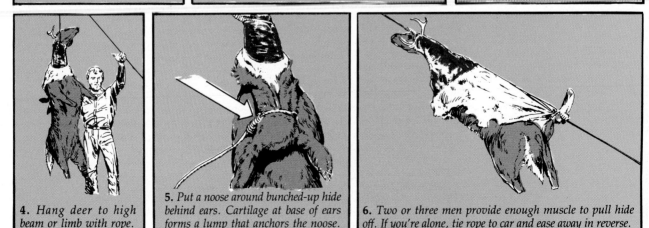

4. *Hang deer to high beam or limb with rope.*

5. *Put a noose around bunched-up hide behind ears. Cartilage at base of ears forms a lump that anchors the noose.*

6. *Two or three men provide enough muscle to pull hide off. If you're alone, tie rope to car and ease away in reverse.*

7. *Hide usually pulls off easily but, if it sticks or tears at a bullet hole, stop and do some knife work to free it or get beyond bullet hole.*

8. *The hide peels off loins and hindquarters with internal organs still inside deer. They are held in place by thin but strong tissue just under skin.*

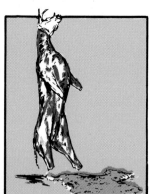

9. *Hide comes off completely. The tail turns inside out.*

10. *Slit tissue over abdomen to anus. Pass to one side of skinned-out penis and testicles. Do not pierce any organs.*

11. *Intestines, liver and most organs fall right out. Cut out any that remain in deer. Retrieve liver and cool it immediately. The bladder and rectum remain.*

12. *Cut out organs still in chest: the diaphragm, lungs and the heart.*

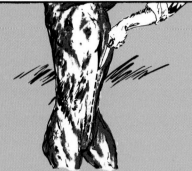

13. *Reach up inside chest and grasp windpipe and gullet. Pull down and cut them off inside chest with knife in other hand.*

14. *Cut out bladder; sever its neck so as not to spill urine. Then cut around rectum to free it from hams.*

15. *Pull end of intestine and rectum out from inside. Cut out testicles and penis and sever tail. Clean empty cavity with dry cloth, and cut off head.*

16. *Hang deer neck down with legs spread by running rope or hooks behind tendons in the rear legs.*

17. *Use saber saw or carpenter's crosscut to saw deer in half lengthwise through backbone. Start where you cut tail off, continue through neck.*

18. *Cut out bloodshot meat around bullet holes. Then divide sides into quarters by cutting sides just behind last rib. Age quarters at about 40° for a week and then cut into portions for freezing.*

Venison Fit For A King

By Edna Wagner Piersol

Nothing riles me more than a raised eyebrow from a friend when I mention that I am preparing venison for my family's dinner. I immediately make a mental note to invite that uppity friend to dinner very soon. I won't tell—until after I've been begged for the recipe: "What exotic spices did you add to that beef to give it that fabulous taste?"—that we've been eating venison with no exotic spices at all.

Maybe some folks have a "thing" about venison because of the way it is killed. Well, given one visit to a stockyard slaughterhouse, these same people would never eat another filet mignon. A deer, on the other hand, is usually shot out in the fresh air while it is roaming free. We'd all be vegetarians if we worried about how all our meat is killed.

A friend of mine is a veteran hunter who has brought us several deer that were shot with bow and arrow, not to mention many he has felled with a rifle.

Venison was accepted table fare in my home in Economy Township in western Pennsylvania when I was a little girl, but no one in our family developed any very special recipes. They just adapted beef recipes to venison. After my hunter friend started giving us venison, I did the same thing. It's still a good plan, but I soon discovered that many of our friends didn't enjoy the meat as much as we did. Some of them wouldn't even cook the meat.

"If deer meat was good enough for kings," I thought, "surely I can make it good enough for my friends."

So I began experimenting with gourmet venison dinners—with the following results. There are three simple rules for preparing venison so that it becomes a gourmet treat:

1. Always serve it piping hot onto heated plates, and keep the seconds hot while they're waiting to be eaten. This rule is the most important. If venison becomes even slightly cooled, the fat turns hard the way lamb tallow does and some of the taste of the meat is lost.

2. Keep it moist. Venison always becomes a little dry while roasting. Some of this dryness can be avoided by adding butter or margarine in place of most of the fat, which should be trimmed off. In the case of steaks and chops, *never overcook!* Serve them rare, if possible. If you must have them well-done, stop cooking the second the juices stop flowing. Always spoon a little gravy over the meat on the serving platter, or pour on the pan juices.

3. Always cook venison in something tart, such as wine, lemon juice, or sour cream. This doesn't make the meat sour. It just enhances the flavor and also preserves the juices and tenderizes the meat.

176

Pot roast is the queen of recipes for the meat of kings.

Use a sheet of aluminum foil large enough to wrap the roast completely. If you must use two sheets, make sure the bottom one comes well up around the roast so that it catches all the juices. Place a three or four-pound roast on the foil, sprinkle on top of it a package of dry onion-soup mix, and dot it with butter. Sprinkle one-quarter cup wine over all.

Place the foil-wrapped roast in a pan, and cover the pan. Bake for three hours at 300°. By the way, if you want to be out all afternoon and still have dinner ready on time, you can roast at 200° for six hours.

Forty-five minutes before dinner, start boiling a large kettle of water. Cook noodles as directed on the package. Just before dinner, drain them and stir two or three tablespoons of butter into them.

When the roasting time is up, the meat will be tender and falling apart and very brown. Place it on a hot platter. Pour juices from the foil into the pan. Rinse foil with one-quarter cup wine so that all juices from the foil are caught, and pour into pan. Place foil over meat to keep it warm.

Add 1½ cups of water, and one small can of mushrooms, plus their juice, to the juices in the pan. Now, in a small bowl, mix three tablespoons cornstarch with a little cold water. Heat juices to a boil, and stir in cornstarch mixture. Keep stirring and boiling until gravy becomes thickened and shiny and smooth.

At this point, slice the roast. Strangely, venison rarely is pretty enough to serve as a whole roast. It looks really good only when carved. Then, the fine, close texture of the meat shows up and the surprising quantity in a small roast becomes evident.

After arranging the slices on the hot platter, spoon a little gravy over the meat (remember, never let venison get dry or cool). Put the rest of the gravy into a hot dish, to be served on the hot buttered noodles, into which you have also stirred one tablespoon of poppy seeds. Serve your favorite vegetable or salad.

Venison steaks have terrific possibilities. They can be dotted with butter and sprinkled with garlic powder, then broiled till done, and placed on a hot platter. The juices from the pan are then rinsed with one-quarter to one-half cup of Cherry Kijafa or Burgundy wine, and all liquid is poured over steaks on platter. Serve with baked potatoes, tossed salad, and more red Burgundy.

If you really want to get fancy with steaks, try Venison Stroganoff.

For Stroganoff for four people, start by cutting about two pounds of steak into one-inch cubes. Brown the cubes in two tablespoons butter. Stir in a package of dry onion-soup mix. Add four cups water, two tablespoons chopped parsley, one-quarter teaspoon garlic powder, dash of pepper, and one-quarter teaspoon oregano. Bring to a boil, turn heat very low, and cook gently about 1½ hours. When meat is tender, add one-half cup sour cream (dairy type). Do this by first taking

For some reason, venison roast looks really good only when carved. Then, the fine, close texture of the meat shows up and the surprising quantity in a small roast becomes evident. Photos by John Weiss.

a little hot sauce from the meat and stirring it into the sour cream, then stirring all back into the meat mixture. Blend one-quarter cup cornstarch into a little cold water till smooth, and stir into meat mixture. Stir and cook until sauce thickens. Serve over cooked rice or noodles along with a salad and vegetable. Fortunately, there is enough here for second helpings.

For Stroganoff for four, start by cutting about two pounds of steak into one-inch cubes. Brown the cubes in butter.

After the deer is butchered, there will be a few packages of chops. They look like small pork chops but are a dark, rich red. Fry them in butter over a fairly hot fire until barely done—rare, preferably. Either rinse the skillet with one-half cup wine and pour over chops, or make gravy using one-half cup wine (Burgundy or Cherry Kijafa) and 1½ cups water in drippings, thickening the gravy with flour mixed into cold water.

The heart and liver will have been removed in the woods when the hunter dressed the deer.

Wash liver in cold water, and cut into three-eighths-inch-thick slices. Remove as much gristle and skin as possible. Refrigerate or freeze it for a few hours until ready to cook.

Meanwhile, soak heart in salt water overnight or all day. Drain heart for a few minutes and rub the inside with salt. Stuff heart, using mixture of bread cubes, chopped celery, chopped onion, and ground sage moistened with a little warm milk and some melted butter. (Amounts of these ingredients depend on size of heart.) Close up with skewers as tightly as possible. Put heart in roasting pan, and pour over it one-half cup water and three tablespoons brandy. Bake in covered pan at 350° for 1½ to two hours, or until tender. Add more water if necessary, and baste now and then. Bake potatoes in the oven at the same time. Prepare your favorite salad and vegetables for the dinner.

About 45 minutes before dinnertime, melt one-quarter cup butter in a skillet. Dip slices of liver into juice of one-half lemon. If deer is an older one, sprinkle meat tenderizer on liver. Slice two large onions into skillet and saute for about 10 minutes, or until tender but not brown. Put onion slices into a warmed dish

and quickly saute liver slices until barely done. Serve rare, if possible. When liver is done, heap onions on top and carry all to table. Serve hot from the skillet.

Remove heart from oven, and slice onto heated platter. Pour juices over it.

This liver-and-heart dinner really does justice to the occasion. Try toasting your success in the hunt with a good dry sherry just before dinner.

Now for the ground meat, of which there is always a lot. When your deer is being cut up, tell the butcher to put everything that he feels will not be tender into ground meat. There is no use trying to tenderize a lesser cut when there are so many delectable things to do with ground venison.

Last year, our deer was a fat young buck—just the kind for the pot. When cut up, the buck turned into: six roasts (three pounds each), four packages of chops (eight per package), 14 large steaks (wrapped two to a package for our family of three), two packages of stew meat, and 11 packages (1½ pounds each) of ground venison, in addition to the liver and heart.

Do not let the butcher add ground pork to your ground deer meat. Many people suggest this, to add fat and tenderize the meat, but I think that pork only adds to the problems. If I want sausage, I want plain sausage. If I want venison, I want unadulterated venison.

Everything that pork is supposed to do for venison can be done by adding lemon juice for tenderizing and flavor, and butter or margarine for fat, which is also what makes meat tender.

The crowning glory of ground deer meat is Meat Loaf. The following recipe serves four to six people.

Mix into 1½ pounds ground deer meat the juice of one-half lemon, two tablespoons soft margarine, one

The hunter will have removed the liver in the woods. Once at home, slice and refrigerate it until ready to cook.

Meat loaf is an easy dish to prepare. Add lemon juice to tenderize the ground venison, and butter or margarine for fat. After that, onion, celery, egg, cracker crumbs, spices, and tomato sauce are all you need to complete the recipe.

cup cracker crumbs, one teaspoon salt, one-quarter teaspoon pepper, one small finely chopped onion, one beaten egg, one-quarter cup milk, one small celery stick, and a few tender celery leaves (very finely chopped or ground). If you have a blender, put everything from the salt to the celery into it, and puree. When using a blender, you don't need to beat the egg first, and you just cut the onion into quarters and the celery into two-inch sections.

When all ingredients are mixed together well, shape them into a loaf. Place loaf in a buttered pan. Pour one-half cup water into pan. Pour an eight-ounce can of tomato sauce or a can of undiluted tomato soup over loaf. Bake, uncovered, for 1½ hours in a 325° oven, adding water from time to time if meat begins getting dry. Don't pour the water over the loaf, for that will spoil the tomato coating. Just add water to the pan, about one-half cup at a time, and only if needed. Slip some baking potatoes into the oven just ahead of the meat loaf and, at serving time, pour the pan juices either over the meat-loaf slices or onto the potatoes.

If you go on experimenting with ground venison, I'm willing to bet that, before long, you will come up with a specialty that will make you famous in your circle. Just be sure to add the lemon juice to your meat—if the recipe calls for it—before you add any other ingredient, and mix well. And don't forget to add two tablespoons of butter or margarine for each 1½ pounds of ground meat.

Last, but by no means least among my recipes is Venison Stew. Daniel Boone himself could not have thought up a better stew, I'm sure. And you won't have so much trouble cooking it as he would have had.

In the bottom of a six-quart pressure cooker brown 1½ pounds stew meat or cubed roast in two tablespoons margarine. Add one cup chopped onion, one-quarter teaspoon garlic powder, one teaspoon salt, one-quarter teaspoon pepper, one tablespoon sugar, one tablespoon vinegar, one-eighth teaspoon nutmeg, one-half cup water, four potatoes (peeled and quartered), four carrots (cut into pieces).

At this point, it is best to follow the directions for your own pressure cooker; those for mine say to cook stew for 20 minutes at 15 pounds pressure and then to cool the cooker at once by placing it in cold water.

If you don't have a pressure cooker, you can use a heavy, covered saucepan or covered skillet, but then you must cook the stew for about two hours after the vegetables are added. A pressure cooker assures more tender meat.

How about it? Have you been missing out on the fun of eating what our pilgrim ancestors considered the food of kings way back before beef became a respectable meat? If so, cook up one of these delectable meals. Let the aroma waft to your family. And then watch out for the stampede!

Index